HAKIM ISLER

Foreword by Stephen K. Hayes

NINJA
WILDERNESS
SURVIVAL GUIDE

Surviving Extreme Outdoor Situations

EARTH　　WATER　　FIRE　　WIND　　VOID

TUTTLE Publishing

Tokyo | Rutland, Vermont | Singapore

CONTENTS

FOREWORD

Years ago, Hakim came to me as a young man from New Jersey. He was seeking the methods of self-protection and empowerment through the unique training of Japan's legendary ninja shadow warriors. I accepted him as a student. It became clear that he was motivated to learn the methods that I had traveled to Japan to learn decades earlier. He became my personal student. I spent hours teaching him ninja physical skills at my school and survival in the wilderness behind my home.

Many may not realize the connection between the ninja and the wilderness. The natural landscape was their home. It was a guide for how to live as they sought harmony with the scheme of totality.

It was my own quest to study the esoteric survival skills of the ninja and bring that knowledge back to America. People came

from everywhere to learn how to protect themselves, how to better relate to nature, and how to overcome obstacles they faced. However, as technology became more dominant and personal gadgets became more available, interests in such nature skills seemed to fade. Many came to rely on technology to replace natural skills.

I was delighted to hear from Hakim that such knowledge was once again in demand, after television shows featured survival and off grid living. I am so happy to learn that these skills have had a resurgence. The wisdom of the ninja once again is becoming valued and studied as a means to empower modern people as it once did ancient ninja clans. I am pleased to know that Hakim Isler carries this knowledge to future generations. I salute his commitment to the 900-year-old legacy of the art of ninjutsu, the once-secret way of Japan's ninja.

Enjoy this book. Read it cover to cover or skip around the contents as you are motivated. This will become one of your core go-to references for survival, transforming a hostile world into your own personal storehouse of resourcefulness.

Stephen Kinryu-Jien Hayes
Founder, To-Shin Do Ninja Martial Arts
Member, Black Belt Hall of Fame

PREFACE

NINJA ARE REAL

I was only 9 when I first professed that I wanted to be a Ninja. My mother and aunt were in the living room talking when I entered. They stopped, and randomly, my mother asked me what I wanted to be when I grew up. I smiled and said without hesitation, "a Ninja"! She said they laughed but were not sure how to tell me there was no such thing, and if it was, there was no way to ever make a living doing it. I was already in karate at the time, and as far as she knew that was what I meant by being a Ninja.

Fast forward 10 years to late 1997 and my best friend was just arrested for murder. I was horrified and afraid for him. He was like my brother and I felt we were the same person. "How could he have done such a thing?" I thought, and as I felt that we were so similar, this made me question my own identity. He was not a horrible person. He was just in a bad place faced with horrible choices and, unfortunately, he chose a path that sent him to prison. Although in my mind I was different, I felt I was susceptible to this same outcome. If I learned anything, his circumstances showed me that living your life was important and following your dreams was paramount. I wanted to get away and start a new life to do exactly that. I searched for what I was good at to see if that could give me guidance.

My major activities at the time were music and martial arts. Music was something I felt I could do anywhere, but at this point, I had been a practitioner of martial arts for 11 years training in multiple arts such as kung fu, karate, boxing and kickboxing. Although I loved the arts, I had never settled on anything as a core. I trained in so many systems because I felt versatility and adaptability were paramount in combat. By this point in my life, I had been involved in over 30 street fights, so I was no stranger to hand to hand combat, even at such a young age. However, I felt so connected with the combat arts, that I felt it would be a good way to stay out of trouble, as well as gain the healing I needed from the pain I was feeling.

I began researching different arts searching for the one that had the best sense of flexibility that I was looking for. I soon found Bruce Lee's basic training books and his combat style of Jeet Kune Do. It seemed like just the thing for me and, living in North Brunswick, New Jersey, there was training available. A month after discovering Jeet Kune Do, and deciding I would begin studying it, I ended up bumping into a friend who I had not seen for a while. This friend was an older guy in his late twenties, and he had heard about our mutual friend's arrest. He knew of our relationship and asked to see how I was. I told him that I

was not doing well. I also told him that I wanted to get away or, at a minimum, find a positive and righteous warrior's path. I explained that I had settled on Jeet Kune Do.

He smiled and said, "That sounds more like a Ninja to me."

I paused for a second trying to determine if what he was saying was a joke. He was not laughing so I figured I would smile to signal that I got his dry humor.

My smile was short lived as he immediately followed up with, "I'm serious. Have you ever thought about studying the art of Ninjutsu?"

Taken aback by his statement I replied with, "no, I did not realize it was a real system." He went on to talk about the first American who had gone to Japan to study the art of Ninjutsu under the 34th Grandmaster and who now resided in Ohio.

"Stephen K. Hayes was the name of this Ninja master," he stated. We talked for another hour as he told me what he knew about Ninjutsu. I left the conversation invigorated and hungry for more information about this guy in Ohio. The next day I went to the library and checked out several books about the Ninja, all of which were written by Stephen K. Hayes. Over the next few weeks, I had read all of the books and spent hours on my slow one gigabit computer with dial-up internet capability. Everything about the Ninja spoke to me, and I felt Ninjutsu was the art for me. I was surprised to find that there were teachers living right here in New Jersey. However, after careful consideration, I knew that if I was serious about dedicating my life to this, I would have to be bold and train with Hayes himself instead rather than any student of his. Once I had made the decision to at least visit Hayes, with the goal of determining if the art truly was for me, I discussed it with my mother.

I approached her in the living room and sat down near her on the couch. "Mom, I need to tell you something." She knew I had been going through a rough time due to the imprisonment of my friend so I could see the concern on her face. Before she could ask what, I began to tell her my plan of saving up and going to Ohio for two weeks to meet and train with this Ninja master. A look of total shock came over her. I could only imagine how crazy it was to know your son was going through a life-changing crisis, and then suddenly he says he wants to go meet a Ninja with the idea of determining if he will move there to train.

She looked at me and exclaimed, "You knew! You knew!"

I asked, "What did I know?"

She replied, "you told me you were going to be a Ninja when you grew up, but I did not believe you." I had forgotten those statements that I had made as a boy, but now at 19, I felt even more compelled to pursue the trip. She and I talked about my plans and although she worried that I had no family or friends in

Ohio, she saw a level of commitment that she had not seen in me before, and thus she gave me her blessing. A few months later, I found myself in my car sitting in the parking lot of Stephen K. Hayes's school, The Quest Center. There was no more dreaming, no more speculation; the time for discovery was a few steps away.

THE QUEST

After meeting and training with the legendary Ninja master Stephen K. Hayes, I was sure of what I wanted to do. After so many years of training in martial arts, the two weeks of Ninjutsu training in Ohio was beyond anything I had experienced. This was the art for me, the one I had wanted to dedicate my life to. The movies made Ninja out to be these over the top, acrobatic, eccentric and flamboyant mercenaries. However, what I was learning proved to be otherwise. The training I received

showed that the main focus of the Ninja was to become a fully actualized human. They strived to understand the world through a deeper understanding of themselves. Through this knowledge they were able to become empowered, and through that empowerment, they were able to enrich their communities. All this aside, yes they fought and yes, they spied, however, this was due to the need of trying to ensure the survival of their community. In the modern day, I learned that the focus was still the same. Mr. Hayes was teaching these principles in a way that was applicable to western life. Understanding how I work helps me discern the world's influence over me, whilst understanding how others work, helps me to recognize how I can influence them. This basic knowledge helps in understanding my interactions with the world and how best to succeed in all endeavors. Ninja call the responsive and reactive flow of two forces "Nagare," and this Nagare was not only physical, but also mental and emotional. Therefore, if our emotions and mentality influence our activities in the world, it is not overreaching to think that one's method of defensive or offensive combat would match the state of their internal makeup. It was amazing to think that I got all of this from a few books and two weeks of training. Until that point, most of my martial arts training was about being faster, stronger, having quick reflexes and being clever. I did meditate so I could achieve better results in training, but I thought nothing of exploring who I was or even why I responded in certain ways. I was being taught that what made Ninja such a formidable opponent was their command over self and acceptance of their connection to their world, even down to the adversary opposing them in battle.

I returned home trying to explain this to my family and friends as the reason why I wanted to move to Ohio and train in this art. As you can imagine, the idea was not as welcomed as I would have wanted. Many scoffed at the

thought, not out of jealousy or absurdity, but because they cared for me and was uncertain how this would play out for my future. Reminiscent of the thoughts of my mom and aunt when I told them I wanted to be a Ninja at nine years of age, the questions I got the most were "what can you do with that knowledge; how can you make a living with that; and are you joking?" Looking back on it now I can see how absurd it must have sounded to hear me as a young 20-year-old saying that I was going to move to Ohio to train with a Ninja master with the goal of becoming a Ninja. It would be another year before I could save up enough money and move to Ohio to train.

THE SERVICE

It was Tuesday morning, September 11th, 2001. I woke up, walked into my living room in my tiny apartment in Dayton, Ohio and greeted my friend that stayed the night on my couch. We turned on the television and saw the news showing a plane crashing into the World Trade Center. It was unbelievable to see, and as I watched it, I felt that I would be a part of what was to come in some way.

By 2001, I had been training in To-Shin Do Ninjutsu for 2 years. I was a college student

by day, a Ninjutsu practitioner in the evening and a DJ at a popular nightclub by night. Life was good for me as I was living my dream. I had come a long way from the city boy training in different arts with no real commitment to any and no outdoor experiences other than playtime at the local park. I was now training as a personal student of a Ninja master. A few years later after earning my black belt, I found myself invited to Stephen Hayes's house for closed-door training sessions with him and a few of my seniors learning about Ninja

Mind Science, outdoor skills and traditional Ninja hand to hand combat. The magnitude of knowledge was everything I wanted as a kid and now as a young adult searching for my place in the world. The training was comprehensive, extensive and utterly empowering. I was becoming more than a warrior; I was becoming a protector.

One day I found myself in bodyguard training with Stephen K. Hayes. This was not my first such training with him, and as one of the dignitary protectors for the Dali Lama, his knowledge was vast and unique. People from all around came to join in this training. Whilst there, I met a soldier serving in the reserves who was from Colorado. He flew out just to attend the seminar. We hit it off right away and over lunch, I told him I thought about becoming a soldier as a way to put my skills as a Ninja to good use in serving my country. He explained that this was his exact reasoning for going into the Army and for why he chose his military occupation specialty (MOS).

I asked what that was, and he snickered replying, "My job. I am a Psychological Operations Specialist. Basically, a fancy name for someone that specializes in Psychological Warfare."

As he went into more detail, I could sense the same feeling that led me to Ohio guiding me towards serving my country. He explained that sometimes he hosted weekend-long wilderness classes and military preparation courses. He invited me to come to one if I was ever serious about joining the Army. A few months later, I was trekking through the snow-covered mountains of Colorado getting a feel for military-style training. I came back with a strong conviction to join the Army. The war was still going on and I had a strong set of skills that I felt, along with what I would learn through military training, would make me a strong asset for my country. A few months after arriving home I joined the delayed entry program. Several months later, after receiving my 2nd-degree black belt, I was in basic training at Fort Benning. This was the beginning of a new journey towards becoming a Psyop Warrior.

THE TEST

My mouth got dry just looking at him talk as he grabbed random plants along the path and started eating them. Plant particles were shooting everywhere as he talked about plant identification and what to eat and what not to eat. Retired Sergeant Major Smith (a.k.a "Smitty") was his name and he was one of the senior instructors at the Army S.E.R.E school (survival, evasion, resistance and escape).

I was done with my language school training and was now here on assignment to learn how to survive if I ever found myself lost or taken hostage in hostile territory. Although by this point, I had spent considerable time in the woods during land navigation and tactical field exercises, in addition to the time I spent learning with my Ninjutsu instructor, Stephen Hayes, and my friend in Colorado, I had not had much tactical survival training. This was different than lost in the woods survival training. The intent of this training was about surviving in the wilderness and urban environment whilst being hunted and with the overall focus of escape or rescue. The training was top notch, but it culminated in a final exercise that was absolute hell. After learning each skill, students were tested and had to perform to a given standard. The conditions were miserable as it was cold and rainy. Even

still, we had to find our own food during evasion, where I learned nothing tasted better than a road-kill opossum. We also had to collect kindling and start a fire during a continuous rainstorm. At night, our hide site (concealed shelter) was wet and cramped because we did not ensure its size and waterproofing beforehand. Life was tough during those three weeks, but I learned so much more about survival and, even though it was a miserable time, I fell in love with learning survival skills.

Soon after I was out of S.E.R.E school, I was off to put my skills to use in both Iraqi Freedom and Enduring Freedom. My desire to serve my country was no longer something I was considering—I was living it. My time on the war-torn streets of Ramadi would be the first real test of my Ninja and military skills and would teach me more about survival physically, mentally and emotionally than I could ever imagine.

THE CHALLENGE

I had been out of the army for 4 years when a friend of mine made mention of a new show where 2 people who have never met each other go out into the wilderness and survive for three weeks with no food, water, shelter, or clothing. It sounded like a great challenge but not something I was completely interested in. It was not until a Special Forces friend made the statement "I would like to see if you could do that show" that I felt I had to accept the challenge. My goal was to go online and apply, but I was certain I would not be picked. At least I could say I tried, and satisfy the challenge from my friend. Several weeks went by with no word, and I had forgotten about applying for the challenge altogether, when suddenly I received a call from the casting staff for the show. It was not too long after that I was on a plane to India to participate in another adventure that would change my life forever. Like many of my major life courses, this one was very dangerous and most of my family cautioned me against it. The show was very

new, and the idea that I would be alone with a
stranger, in a foreign land, and with no resources
but what I could find on the land was risky and
obviously scary. This was not like my previous
military or personal survival training. At least in
those challenges, I had clothing, shoes and a
real knowledge of my location as a bare minimum. This challenge was void of all of these
basic necessities which made it extremely
more difficult.

It was November 2013 when I arrived in India.
Oddly enough, I would end up in the Himalayan
mountains which was the home of some of the
Ninja esoteric mind and spirit training roots. It
was here that I would find out things about myself
that I did not know were there. I had survived the
streets of Newark and New Brunswick, N.J., trained with
a Ninja master, fought in a war, started a business during the
height of a recession, and now here I was on the side of a mountain, naked with a person whom I had never met before.

Over the course of the next few weeks, I found myself changing. Within the first several days I
noticed all my senses sharpening. I felt stronger for the most part, after my body had purged
itself of all impurities and adjusted to operating on a no food regime. However, this did not last
long as I eventually got worn down. My partner and I had a tenuous relationship to start, food
was extremely sparse, and it was extremely cold with a low in the high 30s during the night and
a high of 62 degrees during the day. Without clothes and shoes, mobility was extremely difficult.
We spent day after day struggling to improve our shelter, collecting firewood and finding drinking water. We did not spend a lot of time searching for food or eating, as our priority was to survive the cold. I learned so much about survival in the most extreme of circumstances and in the
most extreme of places. I was given a new perspective on my Ninja tradition of survival, as for
the first time, I understood what it was to be so immersed in nature that you lose yourself in it.

THE PASSION

"It is a futile exercise to attempt to control your surroundings without first learning to control your own perceptions of and reactions to the surrounding. Power begins in the center of our beings and awakening to that reality is a natural development of training in Ninjutsu."

Stephen K. Hayes

After the challenge, I came home a new man. I had not only lost 40 pounds, but I also lost a sense of self and a redefining of my spirit. Nature taught me about a true connection to the wild, the truth of who I was, and the power of living in harmony with nature. I now understood my Ninja roots in a more internal way. However, during my transition to this natural awakening, I came upon an aspect of my psyche that had been hidden deep in the recesses of my mind. Being so far removed from modern living, as well as any and everything that gave me a sense of identity, my mind could no longer distract itself from deep reflection. As both a Ninja practitioner and a Psyop Warrior, I was confident that I understood how the mind worked. I had countless hours of meditation, self-reflection, academic study and real-world application under my belt. When I returned home from the war I had believed that I was in total control of my thoughts and emotions. Although I had witness atrocities, explosions, ran through the war-torn street, been shot at and lost friends, I came home and jumped right back into my life feeling in control. I believed that I did not have any issues because I understood the mind so well, along with actively meditating on a consistent basis.

It took a divorce and 5 years to finally confront my innermost demons related to the war, and as do many harsh awakenings, it came at the most inappropriate time, at my lowest

moment. My mind chose my time in the pine forest on the Himalayan mountains while I sat naked and depleted to introduce me to my pain and sorrow from the war. I was alone in the morning, cold and hungry, staring up at the sun trying to absorb its rays for warmth. The camera crew had not arrived yet, and my partner was somewhere else doing the same thing I was doing. It was in these moments that I realized that I had not been seeking out and trying to dissect and resolve my time at war during my meditations, but instead I had tricked myself into believing it had not existed as I buried it under the mountain of identity that comes with reintroduction and reintegration to normal society from war society. The plethora of emotions that came with being reunited with my family, home and work in an environment that was not an active danger to my life allowed my war demons to hide. Now, here I was deep in the bosom of the wild facing them for the first time in 5 years. At first, I started to panic, but it quickly turned into great sorrow. I had done so much during

my 300 plus missions in Iraq, but I had also lost so much of myself without realizing it. As I continued to get emotional like a zap of lightning, I instantly became calm and, as if I was not even in control, I began to smile and feel a sense of peace. Mindful of what just took place, I immediately searched for how I went from feeling like I was going to have a breakdown to smiling. Was I going crazy due to the combination of sleep-depravation, starvation and the extreme cold? I did not search for long as I looked down from the cliff I was sitting on, recognizing the peace and beauty of the natural landscape. I felt it was nature helping me to relinquish these feelings. Although it was fair to say that my body was suffering, nature at that moment was healing my heart and mind. I saw this as a potential lesson in my personal training. Is this what the Ninja mountain warriors of the past knew?

Is this why there are so many accounts of them exploring internal refinement immersed in nature?

This moment stuck with me when I returned and made me decide to dive heavy into teaching outdoor skills. I even went a step further and decided to purchase 60 acres of land and start a not for profit organization aiming at providing wilderness retreats and therapy for the military, civil servants and all the youth that struggled with emotional challenges. Our goal is to get people off the grid so that nature may have a chance to help them relax, heal and relinquish any inner struggles. The name of the organization is The SOIL Foundation, and it is located in North Carolina. It is on this land that I continue to honor my awakening by sharing my outdoor skills and passion with my community.

MY NINJA WAY

I understand that this preface may be long, but it is important in understanding who I am and why I do what I do. From the age of 9 until now I have always wanted to be a Ninja. Each of my stories above shows that life itself is about a form of survival. It seemed as though it was always my destiny to serve my community and use my skills to improve my family, friends, community and country. My bond with nature has become one way that I have found to do this. Even greater than just wilderness survival skills, the Ninja were survivalist in every facet of the word. They understood that survival was not about just how to live off the land, but it was about how to live a healthy and happy life as well as helping others do the same. Danger can come in many forms; threatening your mental health, emotional health, physical health, or the health of your family and community. Therefore, the true Ninja seeks to understand himself as a way to determine the best way to survive all that would harm him. Then, he seeks to help others so they may do the same. This book is part of that philosophy, but all about survival. It is designed to give the reader a framework of how to enhance their lives through knowledge that I gained studying the multifaceted and dynamic lessons of the Ninja tradition.

ENJOY!

CHAPTER

NINJA SURVIVAL
FUNDAMENTALS

NINJA NO
IKINOKORI KIHON

IN THE NAME OF PERSEVERANCE

In the Lessons of Nature, there is wisdom for the Ninja. He becomes the whisper of the leaves, the smell of the earth and the taste of the sea. In order to accomplish what must be done and live to celebrate yet another day."

Stephen K. Hayes

Life is a constant struggle for survival.

The word Ninja is actually 2 words; Nin, meaning perseverance or endurance and Ja, meaning a person. As a student, I was always reminded that Ninjutsu was the art of life. Life itself is about endurance and perseverance, and at each stage we are faced with different challenges that we must overcome. If you truly look at life at a base level, every living being's primary mission is to not die. Life is a constant struggle for survival. Every human has to fulfill daily basic needs in order to survive another day. When we can fulfill this with a sense of certainty, we then seek to enhance it through internal survival in the form of inner fulfillment. This comes in the form of knowledge, work, friends, etc. No one is without the struggles of basic life, though there are obviously people who have such an abundance they may not have to work as hard to fulfill their core needs as others. The Ninja was born out of a need for a group of people to survive the oppression of personal and spiritual freedom. They were wilderness people adept at survival skills and an internal understanding as they lived opposite of the mainstream culture of Japan. For this, they became enemies of the state and found themselves in danger of losing their communities. This new threat to their survival birthed a name that symbolized their will and reflected their desire to live. They became known as Ninja, masters of enduring hardship and overcoming obstacles.

In the modern world, there is no shortage of need for the ways of the Ninja. Life in most communities of America is not operating on the same level as a small Ninja village hundreds of years ago. Today, we enjoy running water, grocery stores, toilets and climate-controlled homes. For most people in our modern society, our need to endure has shifted to be more internal than external. People lose jobs and go on rampages hurting others, kids take their own lives over words said on the internet and people miss a sense of identity and join controlling cults. The empowerment of self-understanding is one aspect of Ninja training that can be helpful in the modern day. However, in addition to our gain of the commonly placed amenities such as easily accessible water, food, and shelter, modern society has also lost the ability to persevere if these things are disrupted. In the event that we lose these necessities during a natural disaster, we see so many suffer, having to be rescued because they do not have the basic skills to survive and endure. For all our steps forward, sometimes it seems that we are going backwards in other aspects. In all of these examples, there is a basic concept that survival is the very core of our existence. A universal truth that perseverance is as much a part of life as life itself.

THE 3 SECRETS OF POWER

"The Ninja of old used his mind to observe, visualize and affect his surroundings by harmonizing the vibrations of his thought with the varying wavelengths of the environmental aspects he wished to alter."

Stephen K. Hayes

In the base sense of the word, we are all in a way, Ninja. However, we are not truly Ninja without the lessons inherent in the time-tested methods of Survival that the Ninja lived as common practice. After all, perseverance is in the name.

It was not the Ninja way to believe that they were just helpless observers of the world around them. They did not believe that they had no control over the happening of their environment. Instead, the Ninja believed wholeheartedly that they could alter their physical reality with the power of unified intention of their thinking, speaking and acting. The idea of think it, speak it and live it, was the core of their power. They worked

diligently to master the skill of projecting their intention into the world with this process called **Sanmitsu**.

Through controlling his thoughts, the Ninja was able to connect with the power of aligning his mind towards a single purpose. Through the articulation of those thoughts, the Ninja was able to project real power into the world. Through physical action consistent with the intentional alignment of his thoughts, with his words, the Ninja was able to unify all of himself towards affecting his environment in a way consistent with his needs.

By speaking words with the power of clear intent, the Ninja was able to send sound vibrations through the air, which on a scientific level, vibrate at a certain sound frequency that affects air pressure in a way that is interpreted as a language.

THE 3 SECRETS OF POWER

SANMITSU

THOUGHTS (I-MITSU)
INTENTION

WORDS (K-MITSU)
THE INTELLECT

DEEDS (SHIN-MITSU)
PHYSICAL ACTION

The Ninja believed wholeheartedly that they could alter their physical reality with the power of unified intention of their thinking, speaking and acting.

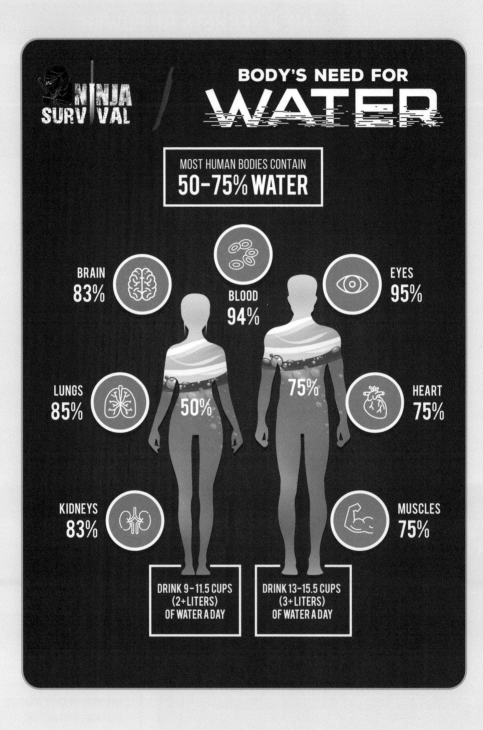

The Ninja believed this effect went deeper. These vibrations held a power that could influence his environment towards the manifestation of his desire.

In recent years, this ancient Ninja knowledge has grown more accepted, as science has performed many experiments that have helped prove the theory that mental intention, projected in a word can influence the physical world. On a rudimentary level, sound vibrations can break glass. In recent years, the growth of YouTube videos that have been released, show how sound vibration can alter the shape of water, levitate small objects, and manifest frequency shapes in small sand particle and Styrofoam beads. On a more personal less scientific method, if you have ever stood in front of a speaker, you can feel the base vibrate in your body. In addition, you can feel the air currents produced by the vibration of the diaphragm.

If we take the proven and visible effects of sound waves on water as a base of understanding, then we can comprehend the Ninja belief in even more depth of how certain sounds can influence humans and the environment. Depending on their age and size, humans are 50-75% water. The human brain is made up of 73% water and even at a micro level, our cells contain water. When it comes to our environment, every living thing on the planet contains water. So, if we were to accept that certain sound vibrations can indeed affect water, then it is not hard to assume that sound

can have an effect on all living things too. In 1839, a Prussian physicist named Heinrich Wilhelm Dove was the first to discover a phenomenon called binaural beats. However, this knowledge did not become fully mainstream until a biophysicist by the name of Doctor Gerald Oster published a paper called "Auditory Beats in the Brain" (Scientific America, 1973). The binaural means "having or relating to two ears." The science behind binaural beats states that by sending a different sound frequency to the brain at different times, it then will perceive a new frequency, much like adding different ingredients to make a cake. These frequencies would produce different mental states which then result in physical responses. The 5 main frequencies and states are:

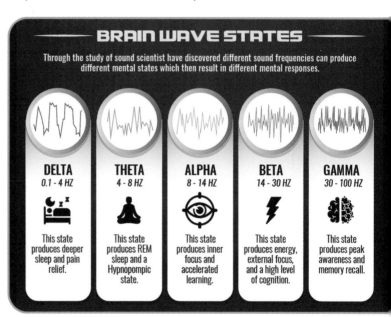

BRAIN WAVE STATES

Through the study of sound scientist have discovered different sound frequencies can produce different mental states which then result in different mental responses.

DELTA	THETA	ALPHA	BETA	GAMMA
0.1 - 4 HZ	4 - 8 HZ	8 - 14 HZ	14 - 30 HZ	30 - 100 HZ
This state produces deeper sleep and pain relief.	This state produces REM sleep and a Hypnopompic state.	This state produces inner focus and accelerated learning.	This state produces energy, external focus, and a high level of cognition.	This state produces peak awareness and memory recall.

The perception of sound in the form of words can also have an effect on the human mind. In several different experiments, people were given oral placebos that they were told would have a specific result. Because these people believed what they were told, even though the medicine was not real, they still experienced the intended result. There has been plenty of data that shows if people are talked to negatively it will likely result in them having a negative mood.

This knowledge does not venture to say that if I want the universe to give me food in a sur- vival situation, then all I need to do is speak it and it will fall into my lap. But it does highlight how the power of thoughts, when given life through the articulation of words, can impact our world and vice versa.

THE SURVIVAL SPHERES OF ACTIVE INFLUENCE

In my personal growth as a Ninjutsu practitioner, I began to understand that there were themes and common threads as to how people operated in the world. Because humans are humans, no matter what the circumstance, these common threads naturally extended into the realm of survival as well. As I delved deeper into learning about the survival techniques of the Ninja, I was able to narrow the knowledge down to 3 primary aspects of direct influence governing the actions and reaction of understanding how to plan and act in a way that will increase your chances of surviving any survival situation. These 3 aspects deal with the 3 primary aspects of human nature, which are physiological, psychological and interactive. These 3 aspects are what I have termed the Survival Sphere of Active Influence:

- **The law of Human Needs** – Physiological.
- **The Understanding of Personal Needs** – Psychological.
- **The A.D.A.P.T. Principle** – Interactive.

Each of the spheres deals directly with how a person experiences, perceives and acts when dealing with a survival encoun- ter. In the same manner, as all things within existence, the spheres operate on a "cause and effect" dynamic. When your body feels low on energy it signals to your mind that you are hungry, tired or getting sick. You perceive this feeling and filter it through the knowledge and experiences of your life and your current situation. After the analysis phase, you determine what it is that you need and move to fulfill it through interaction with the world by eating, going to sleep, or taking medication.

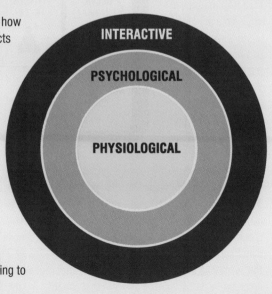

THE LAWS OF HUMAN NEEDS

The first ring in the Sphere of Survival Influence is that of physiological needs. This deals directly with what your body requires to function to a standard that will allow you to actively work towards survival.

The Survival Rule of 3s, sometimes called the Law of 3s, is a relatively new phrase, but the concept behind it has been around as a part of survival understanding for centuries. The rules are a guideline on how to understand and prioritize your physiological needs and act on what is important based on the functional requirements of your body. This is similar to the ABC's (Airway, Bleeding, and Circulation) concept in the medical field which was created as a means to aid those attempting to help injured individuals or groups in critical conditions by prioritizing and treating the most important issues first. The Survival Rule of 3s state that, in general, the danger zones for human beings emerge when they go:

- **3 seconds or more without responding to a critical event.**
- **3 minutes without air.**
- **3 hours without proper thermoregulation.**
- **3 days without water.**
- **3 weeks without food.**

It is within the range of these timelines that a person's survival capabilities are severely diminished. This, of course, is only a framework to give an individual parameters by which to determine the best survival strategy for themselves in the situation that they are in. It is important to understand that these are just generalities and not hard laws. There are varying factors that go into a person's ability to survive. If a person was drinking coffee and soda most of the day before finding themselves in a survival situation, then they most likely will not have 3 days before dehydrating. If a person has a high content of fat stores, they may be able to live longer than 3 weeks without food. There have been several survival cases where people have lived longer than a month without food. However, even taking into account that all people are different and therefore may be able to last a little longer or less within each category, there is a clearly defined hierarchy of importance that still exists. Even if a person can survive a day of exposure, they will most likely need to find shelter before water. In the same vein, even if a person could survive five days without water, they will undoubtedly need it before they need food. Much like the ABCs, the framework of the Rule of 3s provides a good foundation on how to plan and take action on a survival strategy.

Breaking down each of the rules further helps in gaining a strong foundation of human physiology. There is a lot of tactical research that identifies the first 2-3 seconds of an encounter are very critical. In that timeline, your mind has to go through an accelerated process of decision making that may cause you to zig instead of zag which can save your life. In survival, your first decisions are very important. This is often a time phase when a person decides to fight, flight or freeze. Your instinctive response to put your hand behind you to break your fall could instead break your wrist; turning your head at just the right time could keep you from getting a stick in the eye; or choosing to pause and assess yourself after a fall before hopping back up to your feet could keep you from further injuring a damaged knee or ankle. Your initial reaction to a survival situation is, in many cases, as important as the steps you take later.

The second rule is the 3 minutes without air. In my opinion, this rule seems a little out of place when it comes to individual survival. There are few situations that I could imagine

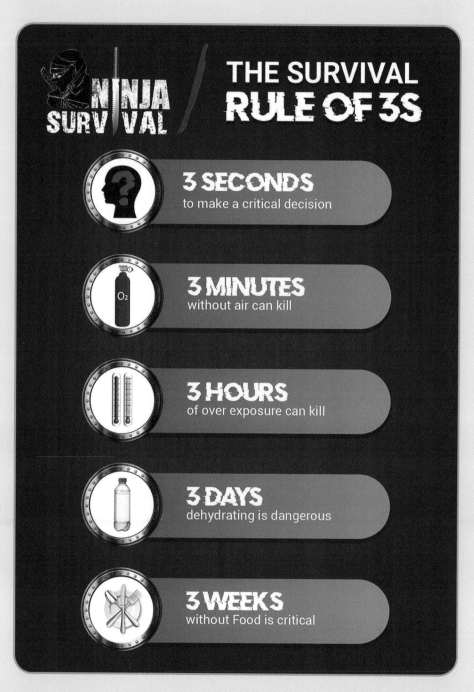

THE SURVIVAL RULE OF 3S

3 SECONDS
to make a critical decision

3 MINUTES
without air can kill

3 HOURS
of over exposure can kill

3 DAYS
dehydrating is dangerous

3 WEEKS
without Food is critical

where I would be consciously aware that I would be without air for 3 minutes. The 3-minute rule is normally referenced when speaking about drowning. However, if a person is drowning, I cannot imagine that they would consciously be thinking about the time they have been drowning. This concept applies individually for a person suffocating from smoke or a person starting to faint due to altitude. I do recognize the importance of this rule in instances pertaining to helping someone in these situations. If you are trying to help another individual who is unconscious and not breathing, or their heart has stopped, it is important to know that the brain can go up to 3 minutes without air before permanent brain damage. If the brain is without blood and oxygen for 6 minutes or more, it will die. On the contrary, the rules that pertain to exposure, water and food are normally within the capabilities of the survivor. The survivor normally has the option to construct something that can protect them from the harshness of the sun, the dampness of the rain or the chill of the wind. The same goes for water and food. It is directly within their power to decide

to try and accomplish these tasks as a means to keep themselves alive whereas providing air and circulation to oneself is not a possibility with the exception of air flow in which moving from a smoky area, or getting to a lower altitude are some examples.

In addition to the 5 rules listed above, there is one less commonly known rule that falls less under the physiological sphere and more under the psychological sphere. It is the rule that states that after 3 months without social interaction, humans become at risk of severe depression and a general loss of hope, which diminishes a will to act and a desire to survive. As social creatures, humans, for the most part, seek companionship. Of course, there are exceptions to the rule as there are hermits that live alone in the wild, but for the majority, each human seeks out and needs social interaction. There is more to be said about this aspect of the Rule of 3s. However, since it is a psychological need and not a physiological, we will explore more during the second stage of the Survival Sphere of Active Influence.

THE NINJA GUIDE OF NATURE AS OUR NATURE

"The warrior tradition of Ninjutsu was developed from the training methods of Japan's Shugenja (warrior ascetic) and Yamabushi (warrior priest) mountain mystics. These wild men of the mountains lived on the very edge of danger cultivating their strength and wisdom from nature and the wilderness."

Stephen K. Hayes

Dealing with nature is much simpler when one understands that it as not something separate from us, but instead something that is a part of us. This acceptance was an aspect that

made the Ninja seem almost magical in their ability to exist in the natural realm. There were several different aspects and levels of their training to understand and harness the powers of nature. However, the most fundamental was the 5 natural elemental manifestations called the Go-Dai. As depicted in a more sensationalized and imaginative concept in popular fantasy movies and cartoons, the Go-Dai gave characters the ability to strike people with water spears, call forth fire dragons and rock monsters to destroy their enemies. To the contrary, this knowledge was never depicted as something real or obtainable outside of the land of make-believe. The truth is these sensationalized concepts had a more practical and pragmatic use for effective survival in the wilderness. The five elements are:

- Chi – Earth.
- Sui – Water.
- Ka – Fire.
- Fu – Wind.
- Ku – Void.

Each of these elements manifests on multiple levels when it comes to internal human potential (the physical makeup of the body and the human condition), as well as interactive

potential (how humans interact with the world around them). One such potential is the relation of the physical dimensional state of each to that of the physical state of man. It is easy to relate Earth to the concept of solid mass; Water to the concept of liquid matter; Fire to the visible process of combustion; Wind/air to the breathable mixture of particles and gases in our atmosphere; and Void to the ether in which subatomic atoms and energy operate to create and destroy. It is far more difficult to recognize these aspects of the human body and in human interactions. The Ninja recognized the connection of these elements, working within them, which aided in their true appreciation for the power of fitting in and using them as an extension of themselves. On a more socially interactive level, Earth can represent confident leadership and a desire for things to be stable. Water represents responsive and analytical responsiveness and a desire to see solutions for solving problems. Fire represents a passionate connection and a desire to take control and get things

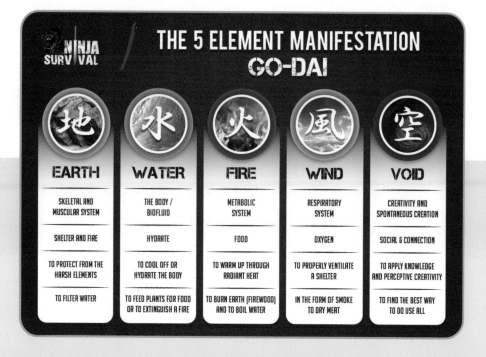

EARTH	WATER	FIRE	WIND	VOID
SKELETAL AND MUSCULAR SYSTEM	THE BODY / BIOFLUID	METABOLIC SYSTEM	RESPIRATORY SYSTEM	CREATIVITY AND SPONTANEOUS CREATION
SHELTER AND FIRE	HYDRATE	FOOD	OXYGEN	SOCIAL & CONNECTION
TO PROTECT FROM THE HARSH ELEMENTS	TO COOL OFF OR HYDRATE THE BODY	TO WARM UP THROUGH RADIANT HEAT	TO PROPERLY VENTILATE A SHELTER	TO APPLY KNOWLEDGE AND PERCEPTIVE CREATIVITY
TO FILTER WATER	TO FEED PLANTS FOR FOOD OR TO EXTINGUISH A FIRE	TO BURN EARTH (FIREWOOD) AND TO BOIL WATER	IN THE FORM OF SMOKE TO DRY MEAT	TO FIND THE BEST WAY TO DO USE ALL

NINJA SURVIVAL

THE 5 ELEMENT MANIFESTATION GO-DAI

REPRESENTED IN THE
HUMAN BODY

EARTH

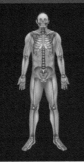

Representing the skeletal and muscular system.

WATER

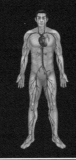

Representing the body/biofluids.

FIRE

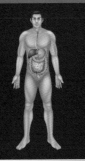

Representing the metabolic system.

WIND

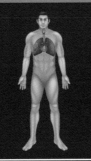

Representing the respiratory system.

VOID

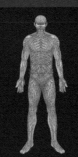

Representing creativity and spontaneous creation.

Because the Ninja did not perceive himself as a spectator in the world but rather a part in it and of it, he was able to find survival solutions in the most dangerous of environments.

The connection of each element and how it can enhance or detract from another made for a simple formula in planning, reaction and action while surviving in nature.

done. Wind represents freedom and a desire to use knowledge to help others. Void represents creative and adaptive instincts; this state of interaction is depicted by the capability to embody what is needed when it is needed. This depth of perception allowed the Ninja to understand any given situation on a very deep level. It also provided for a strong framework for analyzing and overcoming a plethora of obstacles and challenges. This natural approach to understanding nature and acceptance of its connection to their own is what provided a special apprehension and approach when it came to survival. Because the Ninja did not perceive himself as a spectator in the world but rather a part in it and of it, he was able to find survival solutions in the most dangerous of environments— Environments where others without such knowledge would be unlikely to go.

It became somewhat elementary to a Ninja how to survive in the wild after his indoctrination in the understanding of the Go-Dai. The connection of each element and how it can enhance or detract from another made for a simple formula in planning, reaction and action while surviving in nature. Earth can be eroded or solidified by water in the example of molten lava being transformed into solid matter through the cooling of the sea. Water is absorbed by the earth to keep the land fertile and by feeding the trees and grass whose roots help hold the earth together. It can also nullify the chemical reaction that forms fire. Fire causes water to boil and evaporate turning it to a gas state. Water vapor moves to clouds, cools, and condenses causing it to change to precipitation and fall back to the earth. All the elements spontaneously working in unison can create an island through a sea born volcanic eruption. Just as they are in our bodies, each element is separate and yet a part of the other.

On a base level, this knowledge of the symbiotic relationship of the elements gives the fundamental formula for survival. A holder of such knowledge sees it as rudimentary that one can use:

- Earth – To protect from the harsh elements. Using the trees, leaves, dirt, grass, and vines of the earth as a means to build a shelter.

- Water – To cool off when overheating or hydrate the body when it begins to dry out and not function properly.

- Fire – To warm up through radiant heat or by boiling a cup of warm tea.

- Wind – To properly ventilate a shelter allowing old air out and new air in to enhance air quality. Air is also used to support fire in its creation and growth.

- Void – To apply knowledge and perceptive creativity in the aiding of strategizing and constructing methods of survival from the raw canvas of the landscape.

Or in another model one could:

- Use **Earth** to filter water.

- Use **Water** to feed plants for food or to extinguish a fire.

- Use **Fire** to burn earth (firewood) and to boil water.

- Use **Wind** in the form of smoke to dry meat and also to produce movement by blowing in the sailing of a raft.

- Use **Void** to find the best way to do use all these methods in an environment, and how to change the state of elements. For instance, understanding how to create an ember by rubbing two solid sticks together.

From the influence of void, a student of the Go-Dai can discover a deeper understanding. Through inventive reasoning, it is possible to see that one element has an expanded capability that goes beyond the influence of just one or two of the other elements. One element is capable of harnessing or nullify all the others. Earth, for instance, can be used to direct water in a trough or block it in a dam. It can be used to hold and reflect the radiant heat of the fire in a fire pit with a reflective wall, or dirt can be used to put the fire out. Earth can also be utilized to harness wind by building a windmill with wood or block it by building a wall.

The principal knowledge behind the Go-Dai is so connected to the human condition that it remains timeless. Revisiting the concept of the Rule of 3s, the ancient concept of the Go-Dai also connects to the make-up of this newer principle for survival:

- **Earth** is symbolized by shelter and fire.

- **Water** is symbolized by the need to hydrate.

- **Fire** is symbolized by the need for food as it is broken down in your metabolic system.

- **Wind** is symbolized by the need for oxygen.

- **Void** is symbolized by the creative means of how to fulfill these needs in the environment. It can also relate to man's desire to be social and connect with others.

With the basic understanding of the 5 elements, the Ninja was able to find ways to reason and solve a multitude of challenges posed by his environment. In some ways, knowledge of the dynamics inherent in the Go-Dai gave him what others thought of as other-worldly abilities to exist in the bosom of nature and will the power in it.

THE UNDERSTANDING OF PERSONAL NEEDS

"The best procedure is to openly and honestly examine those things we think we wish to avoid... In knowing himself, the ninja can come to an honest appraisal of his weaknesses and those areas where he is vulnerable."

Masaaki Hatsumi, *Ninja and Their Secret Fighting Art*

"The first step toward personal control and the exercise of power in one's world is to merely be aware of one's body and the effects of its surroundings."

Stephen K. Hayes

> There is so much depth to what goes into a person's ability to overcome hardship; some of it is preparation; some is strength of spirit/will, and some is the skill. The aspect I want to discuss is in a sense of preparation. Preparation is not just about what items you have, or how you are built, but it is also about your personal psychology.

Many people overlook the importance of the psychological aspects of an individual's needs to survive. In many survival manuals, the psychological aspects are summed up in a single phrase, "The Will to Survive."

As we discussed earlier in this book, the will to survive is important, but it is just one aspect of what a person needs psychologically to survive. The hardships of survival are not cookie cutter. The ability to mentally overcome the hardships is not as easy as saying you just need the strength of spirit. This is much like saying a person with little or just basic swimming skills just needs the will to swim twenty miles in a cold, choppy ocean. There is so much depth to what goes into a person's ability to overcome hardship; some of it is preparation; some is strength of spirit/will, and some is the skill. The aspect I want to discuss is in a sense of preparation. Preparation is not just about what items you have, or how you are built, but it is also about your personal psychology. There are things in each person's psychology that causes them to seek that which is comfortable. However, what is comfortable for each person psychologically is relative to that person. Because people come from different backgrounds and have different experiences they will undoubtedly interpret hardship differently. For one person who loves food and has never missed a meal, they may become psychologically distraught after missing a day of eating even though they know they can live without food for weeks. Fear of bugs crawling on a person at night could give them so much anxiety that they have a nervous breakdown, or the thought of making the wrong choice and wasting valuable resources could be so overwhelming that a person could become debilitated and instead of acting they do nothing to improve their situation. You may even be reading this thinking that none of these examples sound bad to you and you would agree with what I am trying to explain. This is what makes group dynamics and relationships so challenging. Each person in a group experiences the world from a different psychological standpoint. One person does not mentally or physically feel uncomfortable sleeping on the ground, while another person in the group does. One person loves sitting in the dark staring up at the stars, whilst another person fears the dark immensely. This does not mean that two people cannot have the same psychological comfort with the same experience. It just highlights that our experiences shape our psyche which then influences our actions. The things that cause a person's fear or concern will dictate the actions they take. Going back to the example of a person not being comfortable in the dark, means that this person may well then strive to make a fire regardless if the weather really requires a need for it. This can waste valuable time and resources, and can cause that person to, at first, feel comfort but could be detrimental if it begins to rain and the fire goes out. Now that person has to try to survive in the dark and through the possibility of hypothermia. The Ninja approaches survival from the perspective of acknowledging the importance of an understanding of his own mind and heart. The process of "I have" thoughts, and those thoughts cause me to take action; that action causes an effect in the world and that effect, will have an impact on my psychology. Any effect on my psychology will affect my physiology. This is why it is important to understand yourself from a psychological perspective as your psychological needs will also affect your physical need since the two are synergic.

The synergistic relationship between the rings in the Survival Sphere of Active Influence is why the diagram is designed as a sphere and not a bar graph or directional chart. There is no real boundary between each aspect of influence. The Ninja understood that their psychological state influenced their physical state just as much as their choices affected their physical being, and the outcome of

those choices could impact their morale. Even in the thought of doing nothing and then physically not taking action is still at its fundamental core a way of action. Therefore, the power of understanding personal needs cannot be underestimated when trying to survive.

It may sound confusing, but the Ninja had a simple way of determining and understanding their psychological needs as well. This goes back to the Go-Dai. The Ninja believe that each person operates under the influence of one of the elements.

What are your needs? Are you afraid of the dark? Do you fear the idea of making the wrong decision? Do you feel disgusted by the thought of eating snails or worms? Each one of these can make your task of surviving harder or easier. If you are okay with the dark, you can make a shelter to sleep cozy at night in instead of spending the day burning calories finding firewood only to burn more by staying up all night and keeping the fire burning, not to mention being extremely tired the next day. Fear of making the wrong decision can lead to inaction, which could lead to suffering due to lack of survival resources and a loss of moral. Snails and worms require little energy to acquire and can provide a way to nourish the body and replenish energy. Understanding how you operate and what you need psychologically allows you to operate and plan more effectively under the extreme stress of survival.

> **The Ninja approaches survival from the perspective of acknowledging the importance of an understanding of his own mind and heart. The process of "I have" thoughts, and those thoughts cause me to take action; that action causes an effect in the world and that effect, will have an impact on my psychology.**

A.D.A.P.T. AND OVERCOME

"It is a futile exercise to attempt to control one's surroundings without first learning to control one's own perceptions and reactions to their surroundings."

Stephen K. Hayes

The Ninja believed that they had to be mindful of how the multidimensional aspects of experience, perception, action, and reaction worked in accordance with their life.

As we discussed earlier, a Ninja's greatest skill was his ability to adapt and overcome hardship and challenges. He understood that success meant that sometimes he had to be patient and observe, while other times he had to plan and then there were times he had to act. Ninja believed that they were part of a tapestry they called the scheme of totality. They did not happen to the world and the world did not happen to them but instead, they were a part of its working. Here again, the Ninja believed that to understand themselves on a deeper level they had to refine how they perceived and interacted with the world. This meant they had to be mindful of how the multidimensional aspects of experience, perception, action, and reaction worked in accordance with their life.

As I grew in my survival training, I sought to find an easier way to explain this concept to my students. Class after class, I would struggle to teach these multifaceted Ninja survival guidelines in a way that was easy to remember and use. After a few years, I created

A – Acclimate.
D – Decide.
A – Act.
P – Pace.
T – Trim.

the **A.D.A.P.T**. acronym as the answer:

There are many studies done on how to retain usable information. One answer is to place the knowledge in an easy to remember and easy to apply acronym. One phrase I coined from the culmination of my many years teaching self-defense and operating under extreme stress during my military time is, "when under stress, less is best." Having a compacted guideline really gives you a higher possibility of using the information to succeed. This is why having the A.D.A.P.T. acronym is so important. At the time of its inception, I did not realize that I had subconsciously connected it to my Ninja Training. In a later review, I found that the acronym fitted within the guidelines of the Go-Dai model.

Acclimate – is akin to the Earth elemental manifestation of confidence.

In a survival situation, there will be a sense of loss of control, and the mind will often want to wonder and avoid the problem at hand. Denial may want to keep you from seeing the situation for what it really is. At this moment, grounded perception is of the utmost importance. The goal is to get things back to a stable state where you feel safe and confident. To do this, you must calmly and clearly take the full scope of what is happening regardless of how scary it is. One way to regain this calmness and clarity is to consciously breathe. The brain controls the body and requires about 20% of the oxygen it brings in through the automatic function of breathing. As you become stressed or anxious, your breaths become shorter. Shorter breaths mean less oxygen in the body and thus less oxygen for essential functions. The brain always allocates oxygen resources to the mandatory functions first, whilst the non-essential or secondary actions such as rational thought,

A.D.A.P.T. & OVERCOME

ACCLIMATE
Earth elemental manifestation of confidence.

DECIDE
Water elemental manifestation of intelligent action.

ACT
Fire elemental manifestation of connection and dynamic action.

PACE
Wind elemental manifestation of freedom through acceptance and mindful attentiveness.

TRIM
Void elemental manifestation of transition and flux.

focus, etc. are last. Therefore, the shorter breaths that come with stress inhibit the brain's ability to focus and concentrate. Having the awareness to pause and breathe deeply is more than a clique statement. It is a physiological must that is very important to survival. The Ninja trained to focus on the breath as a meditative practice that eventually allowed them the ability to control mind and body functions in the most stressful of scenarios.

Decide – *this is akin to the Water elemental manifestation of intelligent action.*

Once you have had a chance to relinquish your shock and process the details of your situation, you have to make a decision on which survival steps you will take. Going back to the physiological and psychological aspects of the Survival Sphere, this is where you decide what is immediately important to your physical and mental well-being in relation to the environmental factors.

Act – *this is akin to the Fire elemental manifestation of connection and dynamic action*

After truthfully assessing your situation and determining what you have to do, you take action and assert direct control over the environment with the intention of improving your situation. In this phase, you begin acting out your informed decision to building a shelter, collecting firewood, applying first aid, etc.

One of my Ninjutsu training buddies and survival instructors had a saying, "Whatever you're doing, that's what you're doing." I would often easily get distracted when performing a task. I would start building a shelter and while retrieving

> Studies have shown that attempting to multi-task can increase cortisol levels causing additional emotional and mental stress and strain.

wood for my shelter, I would somehow end up creating bundles of firewood. In a situation during class, once I returned with the material to start building my shelter, I found most people were halfway done. I thought, well I will have more firewood than those guys, but I was wrong. Not only did they complete their shelter before me, but they were also able to collect more wood than I was. I had this happen to me more than once before my friend enlightened me with his wisdom. "Whatever you're doing, that's what you're doing." It means to focus.

Focusing on one task at a time conserves energy and also makes you more efficient. Even though there have been several studies done on the notion of multi-tasking, many

> F – Follow.
> O – One.
> C – Course.
> U – Until.
> S – Success.

people still believe that this is not only possible, but it is an effective and efficient way to work. On the contrary, the studies show that the official term for Multi-Tasking is actually called Task-Switching. Task Switching is the rapid switching between one task to another without the completion of either. Since tasks often require different actions and cognitive processes to fulfill, different parts of the mind are activated. As the mind determines what needs to be done and how to best accomplish it, there is time lost. Often because we are living the experience, we do not register the lag or loss of time. It has been reported that it can take up to 5 minutes to get back to the level of productivity and functionality you were at when switching back to a task after an interruption or task switch. In a survival situation where time is paramount, this is a major issue. Studies have also shown that attempting to multi-task can increase cortisol levels causing additional emotional and mental stress and strain. This is not good in a survival setting and will only serve to add to the depletion of your neurological resources.

These reasons serve to support the concept of my friend's statements. It is important to focus on a set task to completion. An acronym I once heard that puts this well is **F.O.C.U.S**.

I am not sure who created this acronym, but it is brilliant. I think anyone in a survival situation can benefit from its use. If you are collecting wood, you are collecting wood; if you are building a shelter then build a shelter. With all that said, it is important to acknowledge that nothing in survival is perfect. There are times that switching tasks may be required, or there will be times where you will have to pay attention to more than one thing at once, but you have to understand the cost of doing this. You may see some good wood while gathering materials to build your shelter, but instead of stopping the shelter building process completely, you may want to mark the area or pile the wood so you can come back to it later.

Pace *– this is akin to the Wind elemental manifestation of freedom through acceptance and mindful attentiveness.*

Once you have begun to take action, it is important to stay aware of your body and resources. When overwhelmed with the challenges of a survival situation, it is easy to get lost in the urgency of actions taken to preserve your life. However, it is this urgency, brought forth by the fire element, which can also cause your own destruction. Pushing yourself too hard in the heat can cause heat injury; reaching for a log or stick without checking it first could cause you to be bitten or stung; expending too many calories collecting firewood could cause you to crash and miss a prime opportunity to improve your situation. Although the situation may be desperate, it is important to not inadvertently overextend yourself. Acknowledge the freedom that comes with a plan but be mindful of your energy and resources at all time.

Trim *– this is akin to the Void elemental manifestation of transition and flux.*

Stay flexible and open to changes in your situation. Sometimes you may succeed and sometimes you may fail. Sometimes, something was possible or available, and then it was not. These dichotomies are a part of fluctuations in life and should not be taken personally. This is why it is important to be capable of liability. You should constantly evaluate your past and present actions with the open mind of deciding if any of these actions are needed and, if not, remove them. Accept that your ability to survive will always be changing and therefore, so should your approach.

This goes back to the ending of the Act section of A.D.A.P.T. In this section, I stated that task switch could be detrimental, but the concept of keeping an open mind while simultaneously focusing on a task is important. Just as a switch back and forth can harm your survivability, so too can being so focused on a task that you lose sight of the bigger picture or you put yourself in a worse position. I remember watching a friend struggling with the bow drill during a class in the hot North Carolina sun. He was drenched in sweat and before long the sweat stopped, which was a bad sign, as it showed that he had become dehydrated. He refused to quit, and it put him at risk of a head injury. In this instance, his focus was too strong and because he did not re-evaluate a possible switch in the task, he made his situation worse. It is good to re-evaluate and be able to switch tasks even if your last one is not complete.

For the modern person facing a survival situation, the A.D.A.P.T. acronym is an easy way to remember important life-saving strategies based on the ancient principle of the Ninja.

CHAPTER
2

NINE INITIAL
SURVIVAL PROCEDURES
OF THE NINJA

KEY PRINCIPLES OF SURVIVAL

Ninja were constantly aware of the potential of life-threatening situations that could occur in nature as well as in society. To them, life was about survival, and survival had a cycle and an order. To others that do not focus on the inherent principles and presence of universal order, it would seem that everything is just happening outside of human control and understanding. But for the Ninja, this was not completely true. Through a deep understanding of nature, one can tell when storm season is coming; through the understanding of animal behavior a hunter could predict the actions of animals; through the understanding of the human body a person could gauge how long he could sustain the pace of a certain activity. Of course, there are things that can and will happen outside of our control. However, the acknowledgment of this caused the Ninja to plan for a multitude of situations. The Ninja did not fight this reality, they embraced it with a proverbial phrase Ban-Pen Fu-Kyo 万変不驚 (there are no surprises or 10,000 changes but no surprises). In our modern day, one aspect similar to this acceptance that things out of our control will happen, is insurance. Most adults in American society have insurance on a multitude of things. There is insurance for health, home, car, travel, teeth, business, etc. Regardless of what they have it on, insurance is based around the acceptance that things can and will happen that are out of our control. Unfortunately, the difference

is that the Ninja had direct participation in ensuring their survival, whereas in our modern society, it is easy to pay a fee and pass the responsibility to a company to do for us. This type of system removes the personal responsibility and, therefore, the connection of self-preservation practice. It weakens a person's understanding, resolve and survivability when it comes to dealing with the unexpected. It is a common occurrence to read or hear stories of people who had an accident, were struck by natural disaster, or had a major health issue that was not planned and that was not covered by insurance. It is common to hear people say "I did not plan or I never would have guessed this would happen." However, often times the truth was that due to a false sense of security they never gave survival in any of these situations any real thought beyond paying the insurance bill every month. Nothing was a surprise for the Ninja, as even the unexpected was expected since it is part of the total scheme of reality. The Ninja had 9 initial survival areas and procedures they focused on when it came to surviving an incident or for just survival in a wilderness environment. The 9 areas were:

1. Safe surroundings – Anzen Dai Ichi.
2. Medical care – Chiryo.
3. Awareness – Jikaku.
4. Usable aids on hand – Yukobutsu.
5. Shelter – Hinan.
6. Fire – Hi.
7. Water – Mizu.
6. Food – Shokuryo.
9. Navigation – Hogaku.

> The Ninja did not fight this reality, they embraced it with a proverbial phrase Ban-Pen Fu-Kyo 万変不驚 (there are no surprises or 10,000 changes but no surprises).

Ninja were masters of preparation, however, accepting that missions can be unpredictable and chaotic they prepared their minds to find and create solutions. Preparation may be the kingdom but wisdom is king. Without good wisdom, gear can only get you so far…

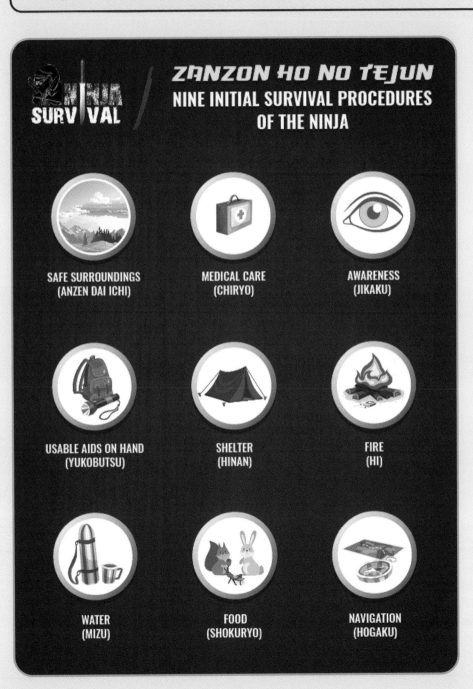

ZANZON HO NO TEJUN
NINE INITIAL SURVIVAL PROCEDURES OF THE NINJA

SAFE SURROUNDINGS
(ANZEN DAI ICHI)

MEDICAL CARE
(CHIRYO)

AWARENESS
(JIKAKU)

USABLE AIDS ON HAND
(YUKOBUTSU)

SHELTER
(HINAN)

FIRE
(HI)

WATER
(MIZU)

FOOD
(SHOKURYO)

NAVIGATION
(HOGAKU)

Step 1: *Discern and act based on the status of your surroundings and situation – Safe surroundings – Anzen dai Ichi*

The first step of the 9 initial procedures of survival is to determine whether you are in a safe place and to follow through with what comes next. This is the point where the Ninja uses the A.D.A. portions of the A.D.A.P.T. principle discussed earlier. In any survival situation, the first step should be to Acclimate yourself. What is happening? Are you in a safe place where you are not at risk of injury? What is the best course of action to take? One of the major causes of a survival situation in the wilderness is not an animal attack, but instead, injury or medical issues. Some of the primary issues are:

- Falls (causing concussions or mechanical injuries).
- Health issues such as heart problems.
- Hypothermia.
- Heat injuries (heat exhaustion, heat cramps, heat stroke).
- Drowning.

Although not as high on the list as one may think, animal attacks do happen, but they are not that common. Either way, the chances are that if you are in a survival situation, you may be hurt or injured. It is important at this point to immediately assess your situation and

determine the severity of your condition. Are you bleeding so bad that you have to address the bleeding first? Is your leg broken, and you are stuck in a ditch filling with water so trying to climb out takes priority over splinting the leg? Did you pull yourself out of icy water, but you are in the middle of a frozen lake, therefore, making it to the stable ground takes priority over trying to immediately get warm? Be honest with yourself and focus on resisting the desire of going into denial, anger, or depression, which are often results of psychological shock. Often your mind will not want to accept the gravity of a situation. Sometimes it will try to wander and not allow you to focus on the true issue. You have to be mindful of this and be willing to be truthful in your perception of the situation. Additionally, this response can sometimes cause a lack of a will to live which leads to inaction, then possible death unless rescued.

After your initial physical assessment, it is important to assess your surroundings and whether it poses an immediate danger to you. Are you in an area where rocks or dead tree limbs could fall on you? Are you in an area known for flash floods? Are you in an unstable location that could give way and drop you? Will your animal attacker return to finish the job?

Acclimatizing yourself by reviewing all the factors of your situation is imperative in deciding the best course of action to take. Psychological stress can cause a distortion

Often your mind will not want to accept the gravity of a situation. Sometimes it will try to wander and not allow you to focus on the true issue. You have to be mindful of this and be willing to be truthful in your perception of the situation.

Acclimatizing yourself by reviewing all the factors of your situation is imperative in deciding the best course of action to take. Psychological stress can cause a distortion of perception and reasoning.

of perception and reasoning. This impairing of cognitive processing can cause failure in logic-based decisions, which could lead to further injury, immediate, or intermediate death. When you perceive immediate danger, it manifests two responses that have a multitude of effects on the human body. These effects are physiological (physical) in nature and serve as a primary way for helping you survive an immediate emergency. The first effect is the response of the autonomic nervous system. The autonomic nervous system deals with the automatic functions of the body such as the respiratory system, heart function and digestion. The autonomic nervous system is responsible for activating the bodies "fight or flight" response based on the perception of environmental stimuli. The second effect is the response of the Hypothalamic Pituitary System (HPS). Once the fight or flight response is activated, the Hypothalamic Pituitary System (HPS) releases adrenalin and cortisol, which aids in the body's ability to combat or flee the threatening situation. This can be important in dealing with any immediate physical danger. However, there are two additional effects that these systems can have which are not favorable in a survival situation. The stress-induced release of adrenalin and cortisol have been linked to a decrease in working memory and other cognitive functions. In addition, physically the activation of the fight or flight response causes increased stress on the body. This requires plenty of calories and additional resources that can leave a person feeling fatigued, further degrading their physical abilities for continued survival after an incident has occurred.

Regardless of the situation, you have to acclimate and then decide what to do. It is important to note that this is easier said than done. The fact still remains that you may be injured, lost, facing an immediate continued threat, or a combination of all 3. This means that you

> **The idea is to talk through the problem and manifest the state you need to survive the immediate issue through the evoking of your physical objective through verbalization.**

may be in shock, disoriented, scared, or all of the above. This can impede your ability to think rationally and your ability to focus on the details of your situation. The Ninja would deal with this challenge using the concept of Sanmitsu, which is discussed on page 21. He would first focus on the thought of being calm, and then he would speak that desire into existence by saying his intent out loud. This helps unify his will towards affecting his actions. The idea is to talk through the problem and manifest the state you need to survive the immediate issue through the evoking of your physical objective through verbalization. On a basic level, many people understand this principle, which is why you may know of someone whom you've heard talking out loud about a situation without realizing they are doing it. They are in essence using an unconscious method of Sanmitsu.

After talking through your options and making a decision on what needs to immediately happen to ensure your safety, you have to act on it. Staying proactive is one of the main ways to survive. The will to live is not enough alone, you have to fight to live. The battle to survive has three major aspects that are mental, emotional and physical. The Ninja understood this as a part of life in the wilderness. Nature has a natural order that is beyond the desires of man—it is not malicious, it is not working

> **Staying proactive is one of the main ways to survive. The will to live is not enough alone, you have to fight to live.**

against you, it is just operating based on its natural cycle. This mindset helped give the Ninja perspective. It also helped with morale, because to the Ninja, no matter how bad the situation, the feeling that nature was their enemy was not an added stress. Learning to act in accordance with nature should be the focus of anyone wanting to survive in the wild. For the Ninja, this went back to the limitless wisdom found in the Go-Dai. Understanding and acting in accordance with the working of one's own nature, and the nature of the natural world, proved to be a better recipe for success to the Ninja. However, the overall key factor was to ACT! Carefully planned actions, based on honest situational assessment, and deciding with a sound mind will give you the highest potential of survival.

Step 2: Provide or get medical care – Medical care – Chiryo

After ensuring his safety from continued danger, if the Ninja was injured, he would then administer any medical care needed. As with many wilderness cultures, Ninja were masters of medical care. Their knowledge of the functions of the human body made them masters of healing and harming it. There were no Google searches, convenience stores, or care clinics in the mountains of Japan hundreds of years ago. People had to understand how to care for themselves or they would not survive. On a mission, Ninja could be in the wild for an undetermined amount of time observing an enemy and gathering intelligence, much like a modern sniper but without the modern aids that come in the standard first aid kit.

In the modern day, having a foundation of medical knowledge is not as high on the list of priorities as how to operate a cell phone. People are quick to call 911 for the slightest of injuries. The average person lacks basic medical skills that are important for survival

> In the modern day, having a foundation of medical knowledge is not as high on the list of priorities as how to operate a cell phone. People are quick to call 911 for the slightest of injuries. The average person lacks basic medical skills that are important for survival in their own homes, so survival in the wilderness is not even on the radar for most.

in their own homes, so survival in the wilderness is not even on the radar for most. It is important to note that not every survival situation will require someone needing medical care. Whether or not you ever have to use it, everyone should have basic medical knowledge, especially those wanting to venture into the wilderness.

Step 3: Maintain active awareness – Awareness – Jikaku

After providing the needed medical care, next the Ninja sought to stay clear and focused on all aspects of his situation. Maintaining active awareness is very difficult in a survival situation. As mentioned earlier, you may be hurt, lost or stranded. There will be several physical, psychological, and physiological factors that will influence your ability to look past what is happening with you directly and stay mindful of the environment around you. Your mind may want to drift and retreat to a place of denial instead of accepting your situation. Additional feelings that may arise during a survival situation are despair, anger and fear. Even if you are able to escape these psychological traps at first, the longer your situation continues the more likely they will surface again. Throughout your survival situation, things will constantly be in a state of flux. If you are injured, the injury may get better or worse; if you are cool you may get extremely warm;

Additional feelings that may arise during a survival situation are despair, anger and fear. Even if you are able to escape these psychological traps at first, the longer your situation continues the more likely they will surface again. Throughout your survival situation, things will constantly be in a state of flux.

or the area may become unsafe because of a lurking predator. Without maintaining active awareness many of these things can go unnoticed or could be handled poorly. It is important to always re-evaluate your situation and stay mindful as you live out the constantly changing reality of a survival situation.

Step 4: *See the potential of your environment – Usable aids on hand – Yukobutsu*

It is common to hear the word glamping, a luxurious form of camping where one has a lot of expensive equipment, among campers today. People have backpacks and RV's full of the latest and greatest outdoor gear. With the camping and outdoor industry booming, the concept of going into the woods with few amenities and the intention of really exploring and enjoying the outdoors in a very low-tech way is slowly becoming a thing of the past. There are gadgets for everything, and these gadgets have blinded modern Americans to the potentials that exist all around them. We spend more time looking in our bags or searching the RV than exploring the potentials of the landscape.

The Ninja did feel that it was important to be aware and know how to use new technology. The Ninja also acknowledged that he could not always have the tools he needed to aid in surviving any situation. Therefore, he honed

his skills of perception and adaptability. The Ninja were masters of ingenuity by necessity. They lived as a monetarily poor wilderness people, and thus, did not have means of purchasing or paying to have things made for them. They often had to create and build the things they needed themselves. Of course, having the tools to perform a certain task was better, but this was not always possible, so learning how to make or acquire the tools was of even greater concern to the Ninja. This was also important to a tactical level Ninja that commonly operated as a one-person operation. It was impossible to carry all of the items needed to complete a mission. It was common practice to learn how to turn or use items in his or her operational environment to aid in the purpose of accomplishing a specific task.

The Ninja also acknowledged that he could not always have the tools he needed to aid in surviving any situation. Therefore, he honed his skills of perception and adaptability. The Ninja were masters of ingenuity by necessity.

In a more general sense, humans have existed all over the world for centuries. Although each environment is different, mankind has found ways to survive in virtually every environment on the planet. There is always potential in an environment that could aid in one's survival. If the person understands the needs of the body, is knowledgeable enough and creative enough to recognize how to use his current environment, he can find a solution for many issues.

Although each environment is different, mankind has found ways to survive in virtually every environment on the planet. There is always potential in an environment that could aid in one's survival.

Knowing how to spot edible plans or medicinal herbs are a more direct example of this skill, while a more abstract level is being able to find naturally made shelters, or a natural tree cradle/stand that you can sleep on, and identifying animal trails that may lead to water are all concepts of recognizing the potential of one's environment.

More important than having an over-abundance of gear is the ability to see how to get or create what you need in your environment. Having modern means of performing tasks are important but they cannot replace wisdom. It is easy to lose or damage gear that is valuable to life; however, it is more difficult to lose the knowledge on how to see the potential of your environment to provide these things for you.

Step 5: Seek elemental protection – Shelter – Hinan

Based on the Rule of 3s, the human body can die from exposure to the elements in a few hours. Overexposure to heat or cold is commonly protected against by shelter more so than fire. A shelter provides many benefits and comes in different forms. One of the first forms of shelter is clothing. Clothing not only serves as a protective barrier, but its main purpose is that of all shelter, which is to help the body regulate its core temperature **(Shinbu taion)**. Unlike a shelter, a fire cannot protect you from rain, snow, or heavy winds as these natural weather conditions can extinguish or burn it out. In addition, fire expels radiant heat which easily warms the surface of your body but takes longer to warm your core. These are a few of the reasons why, if you find yourself in a survival situation, having shelter is so important.

The Ninja focused on working in the environment by working with it, not against it. To exist in the wild, they knew that there were things they would need to survive. One of their primary focuses was to protect against the elemental and primal dangers that existed in the wilderness. Knowing the importance of the need to regulate body temperature, stay hidden, and serve as a barrier of protection from predators, a shelter was very important for the Ninja. Their shelters were either made from things in their immediate environment or were natural parts of the landscape such as a turned over tree, a cave, or a rock cliff.

When faced with a survival situation where you may be outdoors for an extended period of time, decide whether you need or have enough time to build a shelter. If you determine it is important then, like the Ninja, use your perceptiveness to see the potential in the environment. You should scan your area to find things that you can use to build a shelter. Rely on what you know about your body and what you know about the challenges of the environment as a foundation on how to design your shelter, and then begin.

Step 6: Establish comfort and increase capabilities – Fire – Hi

Aiding his survival on several different levels, the Ninja would know several ways to make a fire to help fortify his survivability. Fire would provide warmth, it would allow him to boil water and cook food. If concealment was of great importance, the Ninja would use below ground fires to reduce smoke and visibility. Beyond just being pretty to look at, the Ninja believed there was a certain power that existed within a fire. The process of solids combusting and transforming into gas and light had empowering energy that could boost the mood and morale of the Ninja. In addition to its power to transform the state of raw food matter to a safe edible substance through the process of cooking, a fire was also looked upon with great reverence. Modern campers often feel this energy as it is common to hear people comment on the hypnotizing and energizing effects of fire as it inspires a myriad of active states like congregation, conversation, and meditation.

The debate on whether you should build a fire or a shelter first is situationally dependent. Understanding your situation, your body, and the environment is paramount in making the proper decision. If you decide to build a fire first instead of shelter, then it is important that you are able to create that fire in the easiest way possible. Having a lighter or matches would be better options than trying to find proper materials to make a primitive fire. Also, knowing how to properly light a fire in a moist environment is important as well. Sometimes making a fire can be a challenge, even in good conditions, so adding in uncertainty such as a flood of emotions and a possible injury creates a major challenge.

Step 7: *Hydrate and lubricate – Water – Mizu*

The Ninja understood the importance of water to the human body even without the proof of the WHY that came with later physiological science. Although young Ninja had guidance from elders on how to survive, the young Ninja also learned from life experience. From childhood, a Ninja played and worked toward the eventual goal of supporting the village. Through this constant play, work and then training, they became very acquainted with the needs of the body to survive and perform at optimal levels. As they trained for their eventual use in the field, learning how to find, purify, and carry water was among the most common and important skills they had to possess.

Most people know and understand the importance of drinking water. Depending on age,

> **Although young Ninja had guidance from elders on how to survive, they also learned from life experience.**

most people's body contains 50 – 75%. All of the major organs contain a high content of water as well as the cells in the body. Without water, the body will slowly start to lose its functionality until it ceases to function. For these reasons, water is one of the first things, you would need to acquire for surviving more than a day or two in a survival situation. The Rule of 3s states that on average a person can go 3 days without water, but the truth is that many Americans are in a constant state of dehydration. We spend more time drinking coffee and soft drinks than water. Even when hiking, it is common to see people drink coffee in the morning. Often, people are not aware of the amount of water they need to stay hydrated, which is evident by the number of people in regular society who suffer from heat injuries (heat exhaustion, cramps, and stroke) after a few hours mowing the lawn or walking on the boardwalk at the beach. The stress of a survival situation, shock from injury, and weather conditions can contribute to a major loss of water in the body. Mix this

> **Many Americans are in a constant state of dehydration. We spend more time drinking coffee and soft drinks than water. Even when hiking, it is common to see people drink coffee in the morning. Often, people are not aware of the amount of water they need to stay hydrated, which is evident by the number of people in regular society who suffer from heat injuries (heat exhaustion, cramps, and stroke) after a few hours mowing the lawn or walking on the boardwalk at the beach.**

with the fact that the person was doing an activity before being lost or injured, and now 3 days seems like a ridiculous number. It would not be fair to leave out that there have been people who have survived without water for weeks. However, these people are more of an anomaly than the norm. The truth is that the number of days you can survive without water is debatable, but it is not negotiable that you need water. No matter how severe the situation, it is better to have water sooner rather than later.

Step 8: Refuel and Energize – Food – Shokuryo

The Ninja understood the importance of food and its role in survival. They knew that having small compact nutrient-rich meals would provide them with long-term stamina for achieving certain missions. Ninja often carried small compact food sources similar to the modern-day protein/snack bar. One such food pill, called the Hyourougan, is a blend of several ingredients such as glutinous rice, yams, cinnamon, ginseng, lotus seeds, and more, all aimed at providing a Ninja with the carbohydrates, protein, fat, and other nutrients needed to sustain during missions that required mental and physical endurance. In addition to what he would carry, the Ninja would additionally be skilled in identifying edible and medicinal plants. The combination of personal rations, along with the quick resources found in nature, gave him a variety of ways to stay energized and healthy while performing the demanding tasks of a mission.

If you are in a survival situation that lasts more than a few days, it will be important to find sources and methods for obtaining food. Food is more important in the long term than the short term. Although it would not be pleasant, the average person can go 3 to 8 weeks without food. Food is fuel for the body

and without it, the body will burn through carbohydrates, fat stores and then the muscles. At first, you may even feel a heightened energy level as your body becomes more efficient and moves to a Ketogenic state as it transitions over to burning fat stores. However, if you do not find a consistent food source, naturally your energy will drop.

It should also be noted that you should ensure that you have a good supply of water as eating, especially protein, will require water to aid in the metabolic process. Having food without water will help solve one issue while jeopardizing your survivability through dehydration. In addition to dehydration, food will also cause body temperature to fluctuate, which will also have an effect on your ability to thermoregulate. For example, many fitness savvy individuals are aware that eating smaller meals throughout the day helps to increase

> Having food without water will help solve one issue while jeopardizing your survivability through dehydration. In addition to dehydration, food will also cause body temperature to fluctuate, which will also have an effect on your ability to thermoregulate.

the body's metabolism. This increase in metabolism will burn more calories and produce more heat which will aid in increasing warmth. Food is an important part of long-term survival and understanding what the body needs to perform and how to get it is very important.

Step 9: Seek and find rescue – Navigation – Hogaku

Ancient Ninja were a wilderness people and thus understanding how to navigate and identify terrain features in their surroundings was a part of their natural living and not so much a special skill. Without clocks and weather meters to rely on, each Ninja from childhood, became so in tune with their environment that they were able to understand time through the position of the sun and stars. In addition, through changes in air pressure, moisture, clouds, and sky color they could determine weather patterns.

In our modern day with the advent of GPS (global positioning systems) that can be placed on smartphones and in vehicles, understanding how to navigate and find our way around without these electronic gadgets has become increasingly difficult. In addition, knowing how to determine time and weather is also something that is hard to understand for the average civilian. For anyone lost, injured, or stranded in a wilderness environment, being able to determine this information is paramount. These skills can mean the difference between life and death on so many levels. There have been several stories of people getting lost during hiking and dying because they could not navigate their way to safety. Having a basic understanding of time, navigation and weather, can help on many levels when surviving. Knowing how long you have before the sun goes down can help you prioritize what type of shelter to build or how much firewood you can collect. Understanding terrain can help you find areas likely to have water. Knowing how to find north can assist in determining where you need to travel to find help. These are just a few examples of how this knowledge can assist in survival.

Understanding terrain, weather, and geography not only helped with survival in the wild, but also in various aspects of survival during potentially dangerous encounters on a mission. In addition to the Go-Dai mentioned in Chapter 1, which assisted in understanding how aspects of nature were manifested, relate to one another, and can be used as a model to understand how this process is reflected in man's actions and makeup. The Ninja used another model based on nature's natural order as a means to retain, recall, and apply appropriate methods of energy change and interaction in the world. This was called the **Go-Gyo**, 5-elemental transformations.

The Go-Gyo, which came to Japan primarily through Chinese refugees, categorized the elements as:

- **Water – Sui**.
- **Wood – Moku**.
- **Fire – Ka**.
- **Earth – Do**.
- **Metal – Kin**.

The Go-Gyo focused on the balance of how one's energy can enhance, change, or inhibit another. It was more about the process of transformation and not the process of manifestation. Through the understanding of the Go-Gyo, the Ninja developed strategies and concepts for using the environment to their advantage as a means to operate in a symbolically invisible manner by impeding or distorting perception. They called this concept the **Goton-Po**, 5-element escape method. Through the Goton-Po the Ninja was able to understanding what his enemy would look for in an environment in order to find him, as well as the environmental hardships his enemy was willing to face in search of him, and the natural constantly changing aspects of his environment. This gave the Ninja a framework on how to move freely and disappear in his environment at will. The concept of the Goton-Po was far more in-depth than just putting on some camouflage and hiding. It could be seen more as an escape from the experiential realities that place names to previously experi-

5 ELEMENTAL TRANSFORMATION
GO-GYO

WOOD
MOKUTONJUTSU
*Use of vegetation
for escape or evasion.*

WATER
SUITONJUTSU
*Use of water for
escape or evasion.*

● GENERATE
● OVERCOME

FIRE
KATONJUTSU
*Use of fire for
escape or evasion.*

METAL
KINTONJUTSU
*Use of metal objects
for escape and evasion.*

EARTH
DOTONJUTSU
*Use of earth element
for escape or evasion.*

enced forms and images in the mind. The quickly recalled experiences that help us identify what we perceive, also known as recognition. Understanding in essence, not how to hide but how to become a part of the landscape, would be one aspect of explanation. The Goton-Po had five methods of using the concepts of the Go-Gyo roots to aid the Ninja. The 5 methods are:

The Use Of
GOTON-PO

DOTONJUTSU *Use of earth element for escape or evasion.*

In the Past	In the Present
A Ninja would use the terrain and an understanding of geography to deter his enemy. He may purposely build a hidden shelter.	Could aid in helping you find higher ground where you can be seen. This can also help in finding waterways that could be followed to civilization.

SUITONJUTSU *Use of water for escape or evasion.*

In the Past	In the Present
A Ninja could navigate on water or use the rain to obstruct visibility and evade an enemy.	Could aid in moving across bodies of water when navigating to a rescue location or floating on a current to an area where you may find others that can help.

KATONJUTSU *Use of fire for escape or evasion.*

In the Past	In the Present
A Ninja use fire and smoke as a means to confuse or distract enemies and cover his escape.	Could aid in helping you to deter animals and alert rescuers to your location.

MOKUTONJUTSU *Use of vegetation for escape or evasion.*

In the Past	In the Present
A Ninja would use areas of dense vegetation to conceal his position or deter investigation into a particular area.	Could aid in helping you build shelters or visible signs and signals that can be seen from the sky or by rescuers on foot.

KINTONJUTSU *Use of metal object for escape or evasion.*

In the Past	In the Present
A Ninja would use metal objects like a shuriken (throwing blades) to deter an enemy or gain access to a castle.	Could aid in helping you making a signal by reflecting sunlight, cooking food, or as a cutting tool.

Using Dotonjutsu, a Ninja would use the terrain and an understanding of geography to deter his enemy. He may purposely build a hidden shelter in a place that was tough to navigate, or use strategic movement to make it a challenge to determine his route. Using Suitonjutsu, a Ninja could navigate on water or use the rain to obstruct visibility and evade an enemy. Using Katonjutsu, a Ninja could use fire and smoke as a means to confuse or distract enemies and cover his escape. Using Mokutonjutsu, a Ninja could use areas of dense vegetation to conceal his position or deter investigation into a particular area. Using Kitonjutsu, a Ninja could use metal objects like a shuriken (throwing blades) to deter an enemy or gain access to a castle.

Although it may seem that on the surface this information would not be valuable in our modern day to anyone other than a military survival, escape, and evasion expert, the reality is that this knowledge is very useful to anyone trying to survive an outdoor emergency. Ninja believed that all knowledge had a dualistic nature. Any knowledge used to hurt, could be used to heal, and knowledge used to build, can be used to destroy. Using this understanding and applying it to modern day rescue, knowing signs and signals rescuers would be looking for during a search is as important as knowing how to find your own way to safety. Applying a working knowledge of terrain and geography (*Dotonjutsu*) could aid in helping you find higher ground where you can be seen. This can also help in finding waterways that could be followed to civilization. Using an understanding of how to navigate on water, swim, and build flotation devices (*Suitonjutsu*), could aid in moving across bodies of water when navigating to a rescue location or floating on a current to an area where you may find others that can help. The use of smoke and fire for distraction (*Katonjutsu*) can instead serve as a means to deter animals and alert rescuers to your location. The use of wood or vegetation to hide or conceal (*Mokutonjutsu*) can be utilized to build shelters or visible signs and signals that can be seen from the sky or by rescuers on foot. Lastly, the use of metal to defeat locks or climb (*Kintonjutsu*) can be used in our modern day to signal by reflecting sunlight, cooking food, or as a cutting tool. This Ninja skill can also be used to help in the identification of medicinal plants to aid with injury and edible plants to stave off starvation.

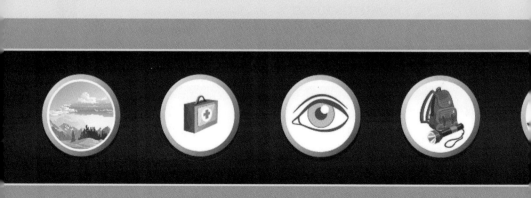

HOW NINE EQUALS TEN

These 9 initial survival steps of the Ninja had one focus, and that was to ensure the life of the Ninja using them. In many ways, it can be considered that these 9 aspects equal to a 10th which is life itself. Without the 9 survival steps, one would either die or would arguably live a life that was unfulfilled, difficult and demoralizing. As discussed earlier, the Ninja believed that the base primary goal of all life is survival. First, every day is a struggle, and beyond that is the level at which one survives based on their personal needs and desires. Therefore, survival is not based on one thing alone, but instead a conglomerate of things. This, of course, sounds like more of a philosophy, but the truth is that it is also a framework on how to live if lost in the woods

> The Ninja believed that the base primary goal of all life is survival. First, every day is a struggle, and beyond that is the level at which one survives based on their personal needs and desires. Therefore, survival is not based on one thing alone, but instead a conglomerate of things.

as is described in the previous description of the 9 initial steps. If we are to take one overall lesson from the 9 steps that would be to acknowledge and remember every day is survival, and you are not a survivor until you have survived!

CHAPTER
3

MEDICAL CARE

CHIRYO

There were no hospitals or urgent care clinics. People were primarily responsible for their own care. The pharmacy was nature, and therefore, every Ninja was aware of basic healing practices. In addition to what he had access to in and around his village, a Ninja in the field would need to have a strong understanding of how to heal himself while on a mission.

The Ninja grew up living a challenging life in the mountains of Japan. There were no hospitals or urgent care clinics. People were primarily responsible for their own care. The pharmacy was nature, and therefore, every Ninja was aware of basic healing practices. In addition to what he had access to in and around his village, a Ninja in the field would need to have a strong understanding of how to heal himself while on a mission. Different from the standard first aid that we know of today, the Ninja field agents first aid was more like that of the combat lifesaver or tactical first aid of the modern military sniper. The difference was in the quality of materials. Today, we have an industry dedicated to creating medical aids for individual use. There is an abundance of first aid kits and equipment to choose from and with the affordability of such aids, there is virtually no barrier to getting what you need. In our modern society chances are if you do not have basic first aid equipment then someone in your immediate vicinity does, or you are just a convenience store trip away from having what you need. On the contrary, there were no Band-Aids, EpiPen (Epinephrine Auto-Injector), or ibuprofen in ancient Japan. The things Ninja had were the things they created or what they could find in the wild. In addition, there was a limit to what they could carry in order to move long distances in a fast and tactical way. Therefore, understanding the common threats to one's health and how to overcome those threats was a major part of their training and preparation.

FIRST-AID VERSUS SELF-AID

For the average person, going on a mission behind enemy lines like the Ninja or a modern sniper is not the norm, thus tactical first aid is not a focus. However, there are still important lessons to be gleaned from the Ninja when it comes to medical aid in general. Besides, the rare case of a disaster thrusting our society into chaos and forcing people to run to the hills, there are 3 primarily common reasons the average person will be in a survival situation while in a wilderness setting. These 3 primary causes are:

1. Getting lost.
2. Getting stranded.
3. Getting injured.

> The dynamics inherent in aid for another can change things as in most cases you are physically healthy enough to aid someone else, and therefore, the knowledge and resources available to you give you a greater capacity to provide help. On the contrary, my second perspective is Self-Aid, which is arguable one of the most important parts of survival. If you are not able to improve your condition then chances are you will not be able to do anything else.

Although listed separate, there could be a scenario that encompasses any combination of these 3. This knowledge alone is valuable, and thus, can aid in one's planning for survival. The first 2 can lead to a need for medical aid and we will explore them in later chapters, however, this chapter is dedicated to medical aid due to injury. In addition, there should be a further breakdown of medical aid as it relates to self. Personally, I teach medical aid from 2 perspectives. The first is First-Aid, which in my opinion is the first medical help you can provide for someone in your vicinity who is injured. The dynamics inherent in aid for another can change things as in most cases you are physically healthy enough to aid someone else, and therefore, the knowledge and resources available to you give you a greater capacity to provide help. On the contrary, my second perspective is Self-Aid, which is arguable one of the most important parts of survival. If you are not able to improve your condition then chances are you will not be able to do anything else. Self-Aid is when you are personally injured and have to help yourself. In my opinion, this is drastically different from First-Aid because even if the resources are available to you, you may not physically be able to get to them or it may be a challenge based on your injuries. You may mentally have challenges providing Self-Aid as you may be dizzy, in shock, or not completely coherent due to a head injury. A person could also have sustained mechanical injuries to joint and limbs that could impede movement. Mentality also plays a huge role in Self-Aid as it is difficult to maintain a strong moral and will to survive when you are injured. The injury itself may make it difficult to want to provide aid or seek aid. This element brings about a stark difference between the 2 aspects of Medical Aid and understanding the facts specific to both is helpful in the planning process of how to deal with both.

Ninja were masters at both First-Aid and Self-Aid. As covert warriors, they may have had to injure people through the use of poisons or traps, while on the opposite spectrum they themselves might be the victim of such detriments. Understanding how to use these tools of the covert operative meant that as a byproduct one would learn how to heal himself or a team member in the rare instance that he was part of a small clandestine group. In this same way, I feel that it is important for a person who is serious about survival or a person who spends a lot of time in the wilderness should, at minimum, have a basic education of how to provide medical aid to others as well as themselves.

COMMON TYPES OF INJURIES

Out of the 3 causes for survival, the main cause that overlaps all of them is an injury. When thinking about an injury, I invite you to think about it in a broader sense. It does not have to be a physical ailment; it can be a mental one as well. Besides just hitting your head and sustaining a traumatic brain injury, fear, shock, and anxiety can in a sense injure/ damage your ability to reason and make logical decisions. For this reason, one of the first aspects of ensuring you can survive goes back to what we talked about in Chapter 1, which is to Acclimate and Decide. This plays a role in both the aid of others and the aid of yourself. It is easier to understand in the perspective of aiding yourself if you are alone, but it is important to note that caring for a friend, loved one, or stranger can create an even greater amount of stress and anxiety. The thought of making the wrong choice could potentially cost a person their life, or both your lives, can hinder a person from making a decision. It can be an overwhelming task to make judgments during an emergency; one that requires focus, discipline, and confidence during a time that those 3 things would be extremely difficult to maintain. This is why I

It can be an overwhelming task to make judgments during an emergency; one that requires focus, discipline, and confidence during a time that those 3 things would be extremely difficult to maintain. This is why I look at the ability to properly heal your perspective by centering yourself in a calm, focused, and logical frame of mind where you can recall and act on sound knowledge is a part of both First Aid and Self-Aid.

look at the ability to properly heal your perspective by centering yourself in a calm, focused, and logical frame of mind where you can recall and act on sound knowledge is a part of both First Aid and Self-Aid. In essence, this is a deeper explanation of the mindset. A common phrase I coined for my classes is "An injury to your will can kill." There have been scenarios where people have died while in the vicinity of the items they needed to heal themselves. Sometimes the cause was because of ignorance, but other stories highlight that it is because people panic or lose their will to live because of depression, denial or fear.

"An injury to your will can kill."

The knowledge presented in this book can be used to help others, but I would like to focus on how you can use it to ensure your survival. Self-Aid is arguably one of the most important factors because you cannot improve your external survival situation or help anyone else if are not physically capable of doing so. The proverbial, "You cannot truly help others until you help yourself," could not be more applicable than in a survival situation. For this reason, we will be discussing Self-Aid a little more than First-Aid. However, it is important to note that although Self-Aid will be the primary focus of this chapter, many of the same actions and solutions will overlap First-Aid care. As we discussed previously, there are 3 common causes of a survival situation in the wilderness. These 3 causes are getting stranded, getting lost, and getting injured while traveling in the outdoors. The first 2 have caused people to die without injury because those who perished could not provide one of the essential human needs for sustaining life. Needs such as thermoregulation, hydration, food, and in some cases security, are each so important, they will be covered in their own chapter of this book. The third cause of a survival situation is injury, and it can be a standalone issue or it can additionally complicate the other two.

> **Self-Aid is arguably one of the most important factors because you cannot improve your external survival situation or help anyone else if are not physically capable of doing so. The proverbial, "You cannot truly help others until you help yourself," could not be more applicable than in a survival situation.**

Although no survival situation is planned, a major injury is an issue that is tough to truly plan for. The reason for this is because it is tough to say what type of injury you may sustain as well as the level of damage it may cause. It is impossible to prepare for everything. However, this does not mean that you should not prepare for the possibility of injuries while enjoying the outdoors. Instead, the first step in being prepared is to arm yourself with knowledge. It is important to know the most common accidents and injuries that face outdoor enthusiasts. The most common accidents and injuries are:

> **It is impossible to prepare for everything. However, this does not mean that you should not prepare for the possibility of injuries while enjoying the outdoors. Instead, the first step in being prepared is to arm yourself with knowledge.**

1. **Falls** (causing head injuries, sprains, abrasions, and fractures).
2. **Submersions** (causing drowning and hypothermia).
3. **Internal/Conditioning injuries** (causing extreme exhaustion and heart attacks).
4. **Weather-related injuries** (causing Hypothermia & Hyperthermia).
5. **Insect bites.**
6. **Animal attacks.**

Gathering knowledge of how to handle these most common injuries would be a first step in how to survive them. Knowledge is something you will never be without, however, do not make the mistake of thinking that is all it is about. It is learning how to competently apply this information that is of the greatest use. The second step to preparing for potential threats in the outdoors is to go beyond the general and learn more about the specific challenges that you could face.

A Ninja in training would learn a myriad of things. As a part of their tradition, there would be 18 skills they would have to become proficient in. Beyond this, there were additional

> **A first step in how to survive them. Knowledge is something you will never be without, however, do not make the mistake of thinking that is all it is about. It is learning how to competently apply this information that is of the greatest use. The second step to preparing for potential threats in the outdoors is to go beyond the general and learn more about the specific challenges that you could face.**

subskills they would learn. Lastly, each Ninja clan had specialties that they focused on and thoroughly trained in based on the type of missions they would often partake in. In this same manner, the person who spends a lot of time climbing should understand the injuries most common to it in the environments they

frequent. A person who spends a lot of time whitewater rafting should understand the type of issues that could threaten their safety if their raft were to capsize. More than any gadgets you can carry, the knowledge of the dangers you face and the way to overcome them with minimal items is extremely important.

HOLISTIC SELF-AID

Anyone preparing for a survival situation should think beyond what they can buy and carry. It is important to understand the essence of how to provide the type of aid needed for certain scenarios, by understanding first what it does, and then how to get that same effect out of what they can acquire from the environment.

It is important to note that having a splint, gauze bandage, clotting agent, Mylar blanket (emergency blanket), etc.; for a potential Self-Aid or First-Aid emergency is extremely useful. However, anyone preparing for a survival situation should think beyond what they can buy and carry. It is important to understand the essence of how to provide the type of aid needed for certain scenarios, by understanding first what it does, and then how to get that same effect out of what they can acquire from the environment. True emergency Self-Aid whilst in a wilderness environment is so much more than slapping a real or proverbial Band-Aid on a wound. All aspect of a person's being goes into overcoming such an event. For this reason, I teach a concept I call Holistic Self-Aid. Holistic Self-Aid acknowledges that although on the surface it may seem that you are only physically hurt, the truth is that the injury can affect you in 3 additional ways

beyond the physical, making for a total of 4 overall injuries. Beyond the body, the three additional types of injuries are to:

1. The mind.
2. The spirit.
3. The situation.

This concept of survival being more than just what is happening on a physical level is something I also touched on in Chapter 1. The Ninja recognized that our human lives were experienced and influenced on more than just the physical level but instead, there was a greater dynamic. This philosophy referenced that healing was more of a holistic dynamic where the injured individual sought to:

1. Heal his mindset.
2. Heal his spirit.
3. Heal his body.
4. Heal his situation.

This approach increases the potential for survival by unifying a person's whole being toward the task of overcoming the danger. The aspect of healing the mindset was to not let the stress of the situation hinder your logical thinking. The aspect of healing your spirit was to not let the gravity of the situation degrade your motivation or desire to act. The concept of healing your body was to take the right steps toward fixing what is physically damaged. While lastly, the aspect of healing your situation was realized through the taking of necessary actions to find or get to a safe place where further injury of any of the previous 3 aspects was minimized.

Understanding that Self-Aid is more than just what can be physically done, but is more of an overall state of being, will increase the potential of survival. Training in a way that supports this decreases the potential of not surviving due to overlooking important elements that deeply influence human existence. Those who are ignoring or fail to acknowledge the extent to which all four aspects are connected will find themselves lacking necessary resources to win the battle of survival.

NINE PROCEDURES FOR MEDICAL AID SUCCESS

Ninja had 9 Initial First Aid Procedures, called Okyu Shochi No Tejun. These procedures are still applicable to survival today as they encompass all of the most important aspects of medical aid for the average person in a survival situation. These 9 Initial Procedures are:

1. **Acclimate yourself to your surroundings** – Tenken.
2. **Decide on the best way to improve your situation** – Handan.
3. **Deal with sprains and fractures** – Kossetsu.
4. **Attend to head injuries immediately and maintain consciousness** – Ishiki.
5. **Attend to severe bleeding immediately** – Shiketsu.
6. **Attend to breathing and circulation** – Kokyu Junkan.
7. **Treat symptoms of shock** – Mahi.
8. **Treat poisoning** – Gedoku.
9. **Get help** – Kyujo.

These concepts are old but even in the modern day, will give any person in a survival situation a well-rounded scope of how to care for themselves or others. The order is flexible as each survival situation can be different depending on the activity a person is participating in. For instance, if a person is climbing than sprains, fractures, and head injuries are

more likely than poisoning. However, this also serves as a general order of the most common injuries sustained during outdoor activities overall.

The first 2 of the 9 medical aid procedures are to acclimate yourself and decide on the best way to improve your situation. Both of these

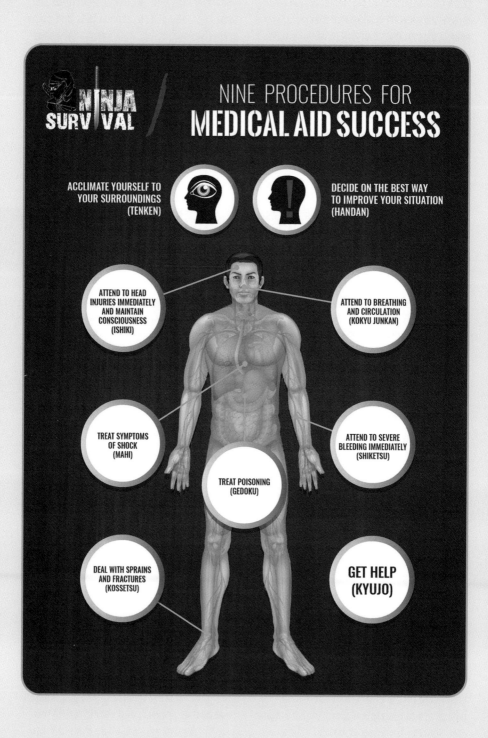

NINJA SURVIVAL

NINE PROCEDURES FOR
MEDICAL AID SUCCESS

ACCLIMATE YOURSELF TO YOUR SURROUNDINGS (TENKEN)

DECIDE ON THE BEST WAY TO IMPROVE YOUR SITUATION (HANDAN)

ATTEND TO HEAD INJURIES IMMEDIATELY AND MAINTAIN CONSCIOUSNESS (ISHIKI)

ATTEND TO BREATHING AND CIRCULATION (KOKYU JUNKAN)

TREAT SYMPTOMS OF SHOCK (MAHI)

ATTEND TO SEVERE BLEEDING IMMEDIATELY (SHIKETSU)

TREAT POISONING (GEDOKU)

DEAL WITH SPRAINS AND FRACTURES (KOSSETSU)

GET HELP (KYUJO)

steps correlate to the A.D. of the A.D.A.P.T. acronym explained earlier, and therefore, we will not go into re-explaining it (see Chapters 1 and 2).

The third step is to deal with sprains or fractures. One of the primary accidents that happen in the outdoors are trips and falls. A common result of these are sprains and fractures. Due to this fact, it is important to know how to treat sprains and fractures. A secondary injury that is caused by falls is head injuries that result in bumps, concussion or unconsciousness.

TREATING FALLS AND UNCONSCIOUSNESS – RAKKA

Because we mentioned 2 common results that happen as a cause of a person falling, we will explore some options for treating injuries that result from the 2 outcomes. Earlier it was noted, and we will primarily explore this from a Self-Aid standpoint, however, it is important to restate that what is used for Self-Aid can easily be modified for First-Aid.

Deal with sprains, dislocations, and fractures – Kossetsu.

A sprain happens when your ligament is stressfully stretched beyond your individual standard range of motion. As a result of this stress, the ligament, which are the fibrous bands of tissue that connect two bones together at your joints, is torn or damaged causing severe pain, swelling, and loss of mobility. Sprains are commonly sustained in the ankles or knees as people will often step or land wrongly, and in the wrists or fingers as people will often reach out to stop or lessen the impact of a fall. In our modern day, the common way to deal with a sprain is to use the four steps outlined in the acronym **R.I.C.E**.

1. **Rest** – Refrain from moving the injured joint and allow it time to heal.
2. **Ice** – Apply ice or another type of cold therapy to the injured joint to help with inflammation and a reduction in pain.
3. **Compression** – Wrap the injured area to help keep it stable and immobile. The wrap will also assist in reducing swelling.
4. **Elevation** – Raise the affected area above the level of the heart. The goal is to keep the blood circulating instead of pooling in the injured/inflamed area.

R.I.C.E used to be the golden standard for dealing with a sprain, however in recent years, a new acronym has been on the rise that challenges the R.I.C.E process. It is called M.E.T.H, and no there is no pun intended as there is no drug use recommended here. The acronym **M.E.T.H.** focuses on:

1. **Movement** – Continue to minimally use the affected area. However, do not overuse it, instead monitor how it feels and rest when needed.

2. **Elevation** – As in the R.I.C.E method, raising the affected area can aid with circulation. This is not a necessary step; however, it will tremendously aid in the minimizing of swelling in the injured joint.

3. **Traction** – Gently pull to elongate the area. This should not be done more than a few seconds.

4. **Heat** – Apply heat for no more than 30 minutes to encourage blood flow.

> If you are in a survival situation alone and need to get to safety or need to stay alive in a particular area as you await rescue, it is hard to refrain from using an injured joint and consistently icing it.

I personally like M.E.T.H better, because if you are in a survival situation alone and need to get to safety or need to stay alive in a particular area as you await rescue, it is hard to refrain from using an injured joint and consistently icing it. If you are in a cold environment, icing can dramatically decrease your temperature which decreases your ability to thermoregulate properly. In my opinion, it is more realistic to try to avoid overuse when trying to survive instead of non-use. Using the injured area as much as you can to stay mobile/move without major pain will be of better service to you as with another common phrase I say in my classes, "Mobility equals Survivability." In addition, wrapping the injured area could be of some help in this scenario, but only to provide some support as you move. The acronym itself does not suggest wrapping because it hinders blood circulation, which is important for the healing process, and it can also decrease sensation in the area. This is why I mention wrapping it lightly to only provide support during use, but then unwrapping it when not in use. Elevating the injury at night when resting is feasible in both scenarios. However, it is much more efficient to do at night near a fire where you can also apply wrapped warmed stones from the fireside for heat therapy to the injured area as well as traction during the time you are reheating the rocks.

Another type of injury that can commonly occur as a result of a fall is a Dislocation. A dislocation, also called Luxation, happens

> A dislocation, also called *Luxation*, happens when a bone is knocked or jolted out of its normal position in the joint by some type of trauma. In lucky cases, a dislocated bone could move back into its proper location, which is called Subluxation. If this happens using the M.E.T.H. method described earlier, it will help with the healing process.

when a bone is knocked or jolted out of its normal position in the joint by some type of trauma. In lucky cases, a dislocated bone could move back into its proper location, which is called Subluxation. If this happens using the M.E.T.H. method described earlier, it will help with the healing process. However, if the dislocated bone does not self-correct, then your second option in a survival situation will be to try to relocate it. This relocation through manual manipulation without surgery is called Closed Reduction (also Reduction) and it should be done as soon as possible if you are going to attempt it. The longer a bone is dislocated the more it will swell. The swelling will impede the process of relocating the bone to its proper positioning. Common areas that dislocate during trips, slips, and falls are shoulders, elbows, and fingers. Similar to sprains, this happens as a result of people instinctively reaching out to stop or reduce the impact of their fall, as well as people landing in a way that forces the bone out of the joint. In addition, depending on the height of the fall, or in the case of the foot being trapped while the body twists, dislocation at the hips and knees can also occur. Dealing with dislocation can be pretty scary when you are alone as well as tricky to heal. Two reasons for this are due to the heightened degree of stress and pain both of which create tension in the body, therefore making the process difficult since relocation requires relaxation of the muscles. There are several methods of reduction that can be used to heal a dislocation depending on the area affected and the resources available. Three common dislocations and methods for dealing with them are:

Shoulder Dislocation Reduction Method

A common technique used to heal this injury is known as the **Stimson technique**. The following outlines the aspects of this method:

1. Find a rock or object that weighs 8-15 pounds.
2. Wrap a rope, rag, or something similar around it and your wrist.
3. Lay flat on a raised surface with your damaged arm hanging down freely.
4. Grab or attach the rope to the wrist of the damaged arm and lift so that rock, or weighted object is off the ground and the arm is holding weight. Note: This is best if done with a relaxed arm so holding the weight is not recommended.
5. Let the arm hang for a few minutes until it relocates.

Knee Dislocation Reduction Method

1. Try applying traction and straighten the leg.
2. If traction doesn't work, slowly work the knee back in place with your hand.
3. Apply a splint.
4. Make sure the splint does not reduce mobility or put pressure on the damaged spot.

Finger Dislocation Reduction Method

1. Keep the finger slightly bent.
2. Clamp your thumb and middle finger on the end of the damaged finger.
3. Pull while using your pointer finger to push the dislocated joint back into place.
4. Place something soft in between your injured finger and a non-injured one, then tape the fingers together, be sure not to tape over the injured joint.

As with the M.E.T.H method, slowly pulling the bone away from the body to aid in its relocation is called traction. However, the Move principle should be used if at all possible since the focus is lone survival. On the contrary, if you are providing this care for someone else, then it would be feasible to immobilize the affected area with a splint or sling, thus minimizing the Move principle.

> **A fracture is the breaking of a bone in the body.**

The third of the more common mechanical injuries is a fracture. A fracture is the breaking of a bone in the body. In the outdoors, there are several types of common fractures that can likely be sustained. However, it is important to note the type and severity truly depends on the activity you are partaking in. Some of the more common fractures are:

- Collarbone fractures.
- Upper arm fracture.
- Lower arm fracture.
- Wrist and hand fracture.
- Rib fracture.
- Leg fracture.
- Pelvic fracture.

Besides the location of the fracture, there are two general designations to the style/type of fractures that may be sustained. These styles are known as an open or closed fracture. Open fractures refer to fractures that protrude through the skin, whereas closed fractures are designated as fractures that do not. Fractures are extremely difficult to deal with on your own. With the exception of an obvious deformity or protrusion, the pain alone will make it very difficult to properly assess whether a bone is fractured and to what extent. Because of the severe pain, you may not want to try to move or touch the hurt area. After a fall, the task of maneuvering your body to a position where you can reach the injured area may be extremely difficult. In addition, there are fractures such as hairline fractures that are not visible without X-rays. Obviously, if you find yourself in a survival situation, you will not have access to an X-ray, so you will have to diagnose yourself. One of the first steps of self-diagnosis is to restate the importance of acknowledging that a fracture will cause extreme pain. This pain will be more intense than a sprain, and the limb at the site of the fracture will not be mobile. You may be able to hear or feel the grinding of the fractured bone in your body but focusing on this will be hard with the added benefit of pain with every movement. Normally, there is also heavy swelling at the site of a fracture. As stated earlier, you may also recognize that there is a deformity.

> **Besides the location of the fracture, there are two general designations to the style/type of fractures that may be sustained. These styles are known as an open or closed fracture. Open fractures refer to fractures that protrude through the skin, whereas closed fractures are designated as fractures that do not.**

> **There are several things you can do that generally can assist in dealing with most fractures but please note, these are general and there will need to be additional training for more specifics on what to do for each type of fracture.**

Attending to a fracture during a situation that may have already been or will be a lone survivor scenario will be a major task. There are several things you can do that generally can assist in dealing with most fractures but please note, these are general and there will need to be additional training for more specifics on what to do for each type of fracture. The general guidelines for assessing and providing Self-Aid for a potential fracture after a fall are:

- After a fall, pause for a minute to get your bearing and to feel your body. You may be injured in more than one spot, but your attention may be called to one area or the adrenaline could cause you not to feel the pain right away.

- once you have identified a specific area that is extremely painful and you suspect a fracture, determine if maneuvering yourself to best assess the injury will cause more damage.

- If you decide you can move, position yourself. If you cannot maneuver without causing more damage, do what you can to immobilize it before moving and prepare for the pain.

- Try to assess by feeling it without removing clothing from the area of the fracture so you can properly assess it. It is normally recommended to cut away the clothing so you can do a proper assessment. However, in a survival situation destroying clothing which serves as protection from exposure may not be ideal. Removing clothes can be difficult and can cause more harm to the fractured bone, so be careful with this action. Try exposing the area using methods such as lifting your shirt or rolling up sleeves and pant legs instead of cutting if possible.

- Check to see if the muscles appear to be spasming.

- Check the area for displacement/deformity, non-displaced fracture or open fracture. If the bone has broken through the skin, you will have to deal with bleeding first.

- If you determine you have a fracture you must also determine whether it has caused damage above or below the site. Often, the bone could have damaged blood vessels and nerves causing problems with circulation. Look for signs of discoloration or a strong pulse below or above the extremity.

- If you do not have a deformity, you should splint the fracture immediately taking care to not cut off blood flow.

- If the fractured area is deformed, you will have to apply reduction to put it back into place (reduction is covered in the sprains section). You should be very careful when doing this procedure as when the bones are moving they can cause additional damage.

- For open fractures, clean the area and apply gentle traction to get the bones to recede back under the skin, then dress and splint it.

- All splints should be applied in a way that allows the injured area to rest in a natural position. This will reduce pain, help release tension, and allow for the normal flow of circulation in the body.

As you can see there are multiple aspects to dealing with sprains, dislocations, and fractures in the outdoors. It is very important that if you know you will be participating in an outing that can result in one of these injuries then, like the Ninja, you are prepared. However, as I hope you understand by now, applicable knowledge is also important.

A QUICK ASSESSMENT FOR TRIPS, SLIPS, AND FALLS

When dealing with the after-effects of trips, slips, and falls, I teach the following 9 steps as methods for self-diagnoses after falling and feeling pain in a particular area:

1. Center your focus on where you are and what happened.

2. Prepare yourself mentally and emotionally for dealing with your injuries.

3. Visibly and physically inspect the area in which you feel pain. Do you see or feel open wounds, deformities, or swelling?

4. Check and see if you can move the area. If you can, to what extent can you move it?

5. Listen and feel for bones grating or popping when you try to move the affected area.

6. Monitor if you have a loss of circulation, tingling, or discoloration.

7. Check the rest of your body for injuries you may not have noticed yet due to the dominating pain of your other injury.

8. Decide on a course of action.

9. Administer aid, begin improving your survivability, and stay mindful to monitor injury.

ATTEND TO HEAD INJURIES IMMEDIATELY AND MAINTAIN CONSCIOUSNESS – ISHIKI

It is not uncommon for people to fall and hit their head in the wilderness. Often these accidents result in minimal damage such as cuts, bruises or bumps, and in most cases, the damage stops with that. However, any type of injury, no matter how small, should be taken seriously because even the smallest damage can mask injuries that exist inside the skull. Damage to the inside of the skull is called traumatic brain injury (TBI). Traumatic brain injuries manifest themselves in different ways. The most common and easy to recognize is the state of unconsciousness. If you were unconscious, most likely you will know it, and therefore you will know that you have suffered a traumatic brain injury. However, TBIs are not always this easy to determine. The most common type of TBI is a concussion. Concussions can have a myriad of symptoms, but you can still be very alert after the concussion. The most common symptoms to assess for after sustaining an injury to your head are:

- Headaches.
- Nausea.
- Tinnitus (ringing in the ear).
- Dizziness.
- Blurred vision.
- Trouble with coordination.

Slurred speech is a sign as well, but can be hard to diagnose in yourself. However, it can aid in diagnosing a concussion in someone else. You may not always have visible or exposed signs of a head injury as sometimes bruising of the brain can happen. A very jarring fall or a jolting impact from being hit with a rolling or falling object can cause the brain to slam against the wall of the skull. This is called a Coup injury and can also lead to a concussion. In addition, a Coup can also cause swelling or bleeding inside the brain resulting in a hematoma (blood accumulation), thus hindering proper blood circulation in the brain causing death. Head injuries are deceptively dangerous. There are a variety of more

A very jarring fall or a jolting impact from being hit with a rolling or falling object can cause the brain to slam against the wall of the skull. This is called a Coup injury and can also lead to a concussion.

After sustaining an injury to the head, take time to inspect it. If there is bleeding, try to gently wrap it but be careful not to apply a lot of pressure.

serious head issues than a mild concussion such as depressed skull fractures, open skull fractures, and brain herniation. All of these are very dangerous and tough to self-treat. After sustaining an injury to the head, take time to inspect it. If there is bleeding, try to gently wrap it but be careful not to apply a lot of pressure. You should next take time to monitor for any symptoms. If you are injured to the point of unconsciousness, then the answers are simple: you will want to take it extremely easy and lay on your side with something to stabilize your head and neck opposite the side of the injury. Try not to fall asleep and pay close attention to how you feel. However, if you are not completely unconscious, what to do next can be a challenge to determine. Head injuries at any level are unpredictable. Therefore, rest and assess are your best options in a lone survivor situation. This may seem like common sense, but the issue arises with the need for fulfilling other life-sustaining tasks in a survival situation. Without a shelter, you can die in 3 hours, but with a TBI, walking around, problem-solving, and building a shelter is not conducive to assessing or aiding in your recovery. Herein lies another major dilemma in survival—which choice is the right one to make: rest and assess, or assess and progress? The medical answer for properly recovering from a TBI is to rest and avoid physical

Head injuries at any level are unpredictable. Therefore, rest and assess are your best options in a lone survivor situation.

exertion, movement, and analytical thinking, but in a lone survival situation, this may not be possible. This is truly something that each individual will have to determine based on the factors surrounding their situation.

Rest and assess, or assess and progress?

METHODS FOR STOPPING EXCESSIVE BLEEDING – SHIKETSU HO

It is likely that if you are injured in a way that would cause a survival situation, there would be a blood producing wound involved. The wound itself may not be the most severe issue at the time but could become an issue later through continued bleeding or infection. With small cuts it is important to keep them clean and unexposed. However with the average rescue of someone that is lost or injured in the wilderness being within 1 to 2 days, the chances of a small abrasion (graze) or laceration (tear) being dangerous is not likely. On the contrary, a deep laceration or impaled object could be life-threatening within the first few minutes to hours if not cared for immediately and properly. When dealing with severe blood loss, chances of survival drop drastically if not attended within the first hour. In this instance, blood loss supersedes expo-

sure as second on the list as one of the most immediate dangers to survival in the law of 3s. I call this the law of Catastrophic Damage. It would seem like common knowledge that if I sustain an injury that causes me to bleed significantly then you would have to attend to it right away. However, I have talked to many people in my classes that do not have a clear understanding of how much blood loss is too much, how dangerous it really is, and what immediate affects it has on the body. I believe that like many false notions in our society, television has had a strong impact on how people see the reality of blood loss as it pertains to functionality. Often, in the common action movie the hero is shot, stabbed, cut, etc. but yet continues to push through his injuries, performing amazing feats, and saving the day all while drenched in his own blood. Unfortunately, this is not the reality as the human body has very specific and immediate reactions to blood loss. The average adult will have about 8-12 pints of blood in their body. 15% or 1.5 pints of blood can be lost with little effect. At 2 pints (20%) there will be an increase in breathing and pulse as well as agitation, weakness, and fatigue. This is the stage where hemorrhagic, not enough oxygen is being delivered to cells due to blood loss, or hypovolemic shock, the heart is unable to pump enough blood to the body, occurs. At a loss of 2.5-4 pints of blood your body

A deep laceration or impaled object could be life-threatening within the first few minutes to hours if not cared for immediately and properly. When dealing with severe blood loss, chances of survival drop drastically if not attended within the first hour. In this instance, blood loss supersedes exposure as second on the list as one of the most immediate dangers to survival in the law of 3s. I call this the law of Catastrophic Damage.

The average adult will have about 8-12 pints of blood in their body. 15% or 1.5 pints of blood can be lost with little effect. At 2 pints (20%) there will be an increase in breathing and pulse as well as agitation, weakness, and fatigue. This is the stage where hemorrhagic, not enough oxygen is being delivered to cells due to blood loss, or hypovolemic shock, the heart is unable to pump enough blood to the body, occurs. At a loss of 2.5-4 pints of blood your body will have a severe reaction. You will become confused and disoriented; your breathing will become shallow, and you may also go in and out of consciousness. After a loss of half the blood in the body, about 4-6 liters, a person will lose consciousness and their body will not be able to maintain critical functions.

will have a severe reaction. You will become confused and disoriented; your breathing will become shallow, and you may also go in and out of consciousness. After a loss of half the blood in the body, about 4-6 liters, a person will lose consciousness and their body will not be able to maintain critical functions. Understanding this information is important, because it highlights how much blood volume you may be losing if you are injured, as well as the significance of managing blood loss.

Beyond knowing what happens when you lose a certain amount of blood, you should also understand the types of blood loss. There are 2 main types of blood loss that a survivor should be able to identify, and they are venous bleeding, bleeding from the vein and arterial bleeding, bleeding from the artery. Blood from a vein will be of a dark red color and it will flow steadily from a wound, while arterial blood will be bright red and it will spurt out in pulses with the rhythm of the heart. Both bleeds are normally easily discernible when there is a laceration, but when there is an impaled object these can be difficult to determine as the object may sit in the body in such a way that the blood is not consistent, or it may have damaged both veins and arteries. It is important to also note that signs of bleeding may be underneath the surface of the skin and may only manifest as bruising.

In a situation where you may have sustained a serious laceration or implement, you will have to try to calm yourself so that you can deliver a proper self-assessment. This is easier said than done since you will likely be in shock, and as we discussed earlier, loss of blood can cause dizziness and confusion. Having concise action steps to follow will always benefit in situations like this. The standard for checking yourself if you suspect a bleeding injury is to look and feel for bleeding that:

- Spurts.
- Oozing or rapidly and continuously flowing.
- Pools beneath the surface of the skin causing bruising.

To go a little further in depth, slowly scan your body for visible signs of moisture, discolored clothing, or obvious open wounds. Next, rub your hands over your body searching for wetness or wounds. You may also feel pain at the site of the injury.

Once you have identified an area of bleeding and have determined the type of bleeding, whether it is venous or arterial, you will want to start self-care methods to stop or slow the loss of blood. The Ninja called these steps **Shiketsu**, which were as follows:

1. Apply direct pressure on the bleeding wound – **Osae**.
2. Elevate the wound – **Mochiage**.
3. Arterial pressure points – **Shiatsu Shiketsu Ho**.
4. Tourniquet – **Shiketsutai**.

Each one of these steps should be applied in order if possible, however, depending on the injury some may not be applicable. It may be unlikely that if you were just going on a quick hike or trail run that you would have a first aid kit on you, although having a first aid kit is always recommended. Therefore, if you find a wound you most likely will not have gauze or other materials, so you will have to use a hat, bandana, or piece of torn clothing to place over the wound before applying pressure. The goal of applying pressure is to slow down the flow of blood so that the body can naturally form a clot. In a situation where the wound is to an extremity, in addition to using pressure you can elevate your extremity above the level of your heart, as a means to slow the blood pressure in that limb. This should not be done when the wound is in the torso area.

Beyond direct pressure and elevation, there is the use of Arterial Pressure Points. The Ninja were masters at anatomy. An understanding of the body, and how to harm and heal it, is paramount to aid in combating injury and illness as well as others. Pressure point knowledge was a part of their training, and they would have been masters of how to use these points by the time they were ready for field operations. Unfortunately, in today's society the average person is not aware of pressure points that can be used in aiding in the slowing of blood flow from a wound. Below, I will provide some basic pressure points that are commonly used to aid in blood flow reduction to certain areas of the body. Knowing about these areas is not enough as a person should practice finding these areas before using them. The following are 7 of the common areas that pressure points can be used to aid in the slowing of bleeding:

- **Subclavian artery** – located behind the collar bone. This is used to aid with wounds to the shoulder and upper arm.

- **Brachial artery** – located on the inside of the upper arm near the armpit between the elbow and torso. This is used to aid with wounds to the lower part of the upper arm and elbow.

- **Radial artery** – located on the thumb side of the wrist. This is used to aid with wounds to the hand.

- **Ulnar artery** – located on the pinky side of the wrist. This is used to aid with wounds to the hand.

- **Femoral artery** – located near the groin area halfway between the hip and groin on the speedo or bikini line. This is used to aid with wounds to the thigh between the hip and knee.

- **Popliteal artery** – located behind the kneecap on the back of the leg. This is used to aid with wounds to the calf between the knee and ankle.

- **Posterior artery** – located at the front top part of the foot where it meets the shin. This is used to aid with wounds to the foot.

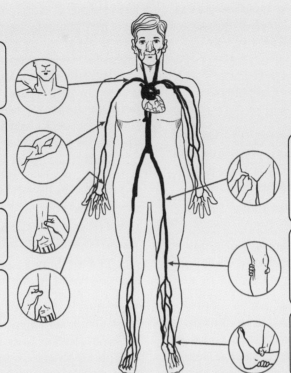

SUBCLAVIAN ARTERY – located behind the collar bone. This is used to aid with wounds to the shoulder and upper arm.

BRACHIAL ARTERY – located on the inside of the upper arm near the armpit between the elbow and torso. This is used to aid with wounds to the lower part of the upper arm and elbow.

ULNAR ARTERY – located on the pinky side of the wrist. This is used to aid with wounds to the hand.

RADIAL ARTERY – located on the thumb side of the wrist. This is used to aid with wounds to the hand.

Femoral artery – located near the groin area halfway between the hip and groin on the speedo or bikini line. This is used to aid with wounds to the thigh between the hip and knee.

Popliteal artery – located behind the knee cap on the back of the leg. This is used to aid with wounds to the calf between the knee and ankle.

Posterior artery – located at the front top part of the foot where it meets the shin. This is used to aid with wounds to the foot.

There are additional pressure points that exist in the head and neck region such as the carotid, temporal, and facial. However, these are not advised because, due to unseen or unnoticed spinal, facial, or skull injuries, you could do more damage to these areas by applying pressure.

The last and most extreme method of dealing with severe bleeding is to apply a tourniquet. A tourniquet is a device that allows for consistent constriction of an area of the body to restrict blood flow. Without blood flow for two hours or more, a tourniquet limb will sustain permanent muscle and nerve damage. Any longer than 2-3 hours and tissue death will occur, ultimately resulting in the loss of that limb. It may seem like a bad choice using a tourniquet knowing that you could lose a limb, but the alternative, which is loss of life due to blood loss, is of greater consequence.

In an unexpected survival situation, chances are you will not have a tourniquet. However, they are simple to make. To make an improvised tourniquet, take a ripped piece of clothing, bandana, or belt and tie it two to three inches above the wound. Lift the material up with one finger and twist to make a loop, making a figure 8 shape. Your arm should be in the bottom bigger loop, and your finger in the upper smaller loop. Remove your finger from the upper loop and replace it with a solid stick. Twist the stick until blood flow stops and tie the stick in place around the arm. As a final note, if possible, you should try to write or remember the day and time that you put the tourniquet on. This may help medical staff when you are found. The following is a step by step reference for self-care in a survival situation:

- Find and expose the bleeding area.
- Assess how to treat it.
- Apply pressure and elevate if applicable.
- Apply improvised tourniquet if the bleeding will not stop. Write or note the day and time you applied the tourniquet.
- Stay warm and elevate legs, unless it is a torso wound.
- Immobilize the area to minimize the chances of re-opening the wound if you have to move.

There is one last injury to note and that is an injury caused by an object that impales you. It is important to never remove an object that has impaled you unless it impedes your ability to apply self-aid or maneuver to safety. Without X-rays and a proper medical examination, it is impossible to tell what extent an impaled object is having on you internally. The object could be keeping a vein or artery from pro-

fusely bleeding. In addition, removing it can cause more damage by snagging and ripping flesh, as well as causing damage through suction that may be created while removing. For these reasons, it is recommended that you keep the object in place. There are steps that should be taken to ensure that you are protected from further injury when leaving the object in. These Self-Aid measures are:

- Control bleeding with a bandage and light pressure.
- If possible, reduce the size of the object by breaking or cutting it.
- Try to demobilize the area or at most minimize the movement of that area.

All the methods listed above will give an average person a fighting chance when injured to the point of severe bleeding. However, the stress of a situation where you are alone and severely bleeding will be overwhelming. It is hard to train and be prepared for that type of stress. The only thing you can work on is making sure that you at least know and understand how to apply the knowledge.

ATTEND TO BREATHING AND CIRCULATION – KOKYU JUNKAN

The respiratory and the circulatory system work together. They ensure oxygen enters the body and is transported to the areas that need

Without oxygen, your body will quickly begin to break down as low oxygen in your blood will lead to low oxygen in your tissues, this is called Hypoxia.

it. Air enters the lungs where it is then transported to the red blood cells and circulated through the body to aid in the production of energy and to help organs function properly. The brain, for example, uses about 20% of the oxygen that comes into the body. Without oxygen, your body will quickly begin to break down as low oxygen in your blood will lead to low oxygen in your tissues, this is called Hypoxia. There are several symptoms of

Hypoxia, which are:

- **Confusion.**
- **A sudden cough.**
- **Shortness of breath.**
- **Wheezing.**
- **Headaches.**

A common cause of Hypoxia in the wilderness is high altitude. As a person moves to higher altitudes, the air gets thinner, and thus, it is tougher to get the amount of oxygen the body needs. This is often referred to as High Alti- tude Sickness. The best way to treat this is by getting to a lower altitude. Another example is long term submersion or drowning which com- pletely removes oxygen intake. Unlike Hypoxia where oxygen is insufficient, when oxygen is not present it is called Anoxia. Both of these are often referred to as Environmental Hypoxia.

In the law of 3s, normally the first or second law, depending on the chart you are reading, state that a person can only survive 3 minutes without oxygen. To be more specific, a person will sustain irreversible brain and other organ damage in 3 minutes without any oxygen in the body. After 6 minutes without oxygen, a person will die.

TREAT SYMPTOMS OF SHOCK – MAHI

A common condition caused by a lack of oxy- gen-rich blood to the vital organs of the body so that they can function properly is called shock. There are several types of shock, such as:

- **Cardiogenic shock** – A form of shock caused by heart problems.
- **Anaphylactic shock** – A form of shock caused by an allergic reaction.
- **Septic Shock** – A form of shock caused by an infection.
- **Hypovolemic Shock** – A form of shock caused by too low of a blood volume.
- **Neurogenic Shock** – A form of shock caused by damage sustained by the nervous system.

> **A common condition caused by a lack of oxygen-rich blood to the vital organs of the body so that they can function properly is called shock.**

Because shock is a byproduct of most major injuries, understanding it and how to deal with it is an important part of basic self-aid and first-aid. Unfortunately, both methods of care are not equal when it comes to survival as treating shock in someone else is tremendously easier than treating symptoms of shock in yourself. Common symptoms of shock are:

- **Thirst.**
- **Dizziness.**
- **Anxiousness.**
- **Disorientation.**
- **Shallow but rapid breathing.**
- **Weak heart rate.**
- **Nausea.**
- **Vomiting.**

It is easy to see how these symptoms can make it difficult to provide aid of your shock, and therefore, makes it difficult to manage and care for it. Ninja field agents would often go through intense training that would induce extreme levels of mental, emotional, and physical stress to induce shock symptoms. The goal was to give the Ninja trainee opportunities to understand how to manage and function during periods of shock through continued exposure to conditions that produced these reactions. The goal was to help aid in building a mild immunity, like conditioning, that aided in helping the Ninja function beyond capabilities of the average person during times of shock. This methodology of training is similar to a psychotherapy process known today as stress inoculation. Unfortunately, the average person of today will not have this training, and thus, will have to do their best trying to overcome these symptoms in order to provide aid and stay alive until rescued. Methods for providing care for shock are to:

- Promptly and properly identify and treat the cause of shock.
- Stay calm and focused on the task and keep an optimistic attitude.
- Get in a comfortable position and elevate your legs, unless you have an injury that prevents it.
- Stay warm using layers of clothing, fire, debris, or a safe combination of these.
- If you feel thirsty and alert, sip small amounts of fluid. But if you feel nauseous and dizzy do not drink water, just rest and stay warm.

Shock is a serious issue that requires a lot of attention. As we stated earlier, it will be difficult to stay focused on properly assessing your symptoms and treat them on your own, but it is important to try your best.

Ninja field agents would often go through intense training that would induce extreme levels of mental, emotional, and physical stress to induce shock symptoms. The goal was to give the Ninja trainee opportunities to understand how to manage and function during periods of shock through continued exposure to conditions that produced these reactions. The goal was to help aid in building a mild immunity, like conditioning, that aided in helping the Ninja function beyond capabilities of the average person during times of shock.

HYPERTHERMIA – ONNETSU RYOHO

Overexposure to environmental heat conditions can cause the body's internal temperature to rise above its standard 98.6 degrees. The body has certain mechanisms to help regulate temperature. When the brain senses that the body's core temperature is rising too high then it responds, trying to cool the blood by pumping it through blood vessels at the surface of the skin. When the blood flows through the blood vessels at the surface of the skin, it cools by dissipating the heat to the cooler environment. An additional mechanism for heat dissipation is through sweat, which is another automatic response for cooling. The sweat glands release fluid from the body to the surface of the skin that then begins to evaporate. Through the process of evaporation, the liquid is turned to vapor, which removes heat from the surface of the skin. The body will continue to perform these processes as a means to cool the body until the fluid is so low that it can no longer produce sweat or when the temperature of the skin and the environment become so similar that the body cannot expel heat, a common environmental condition that causes this are times of high humidity. When the body becomes

unable to expel excessive heat, it will begin to overheat. During this overheating, the body will continue to try to cool itself to the extent of sacrificing other functions. This happens when the body sends so much blood and fluid to the surface of the skin that it detracts from other vital areas such as organs and muscles. This leads to a host of issues that slowly degrade the body's overall ability to function, a process referred to as heat illness or heat injury (known to the Ninja as **Nissha Byo**).

> Heat illnesses are common in hot environments, however, they can also happen in colder environments where people wear lots of clothing, work a lot, and do not drink enough fluids.

Heat illnesses are common in hot environments, however, they can also happen in colder environments where people wear lots of clothing, work a lot, and do not drink enough fluids. Therefore, whether in a hot or cold environment a person should stay mindful of the possibility of overheating. Heat illness has 3 main stages, which are:

> When the body becomes unable to expel excessive heat, it will begin to overheat. During this overheating, the body will continue to try to cool itself to the extent of sacrificing other functions. This happens when the body sends so much blood and fluid to the surface of the skin that it detracts from other vital areas such as organs and muscles.

> - **Heat cramps – Nissha Keiren.**
> - **Heat exhaustion – Nessha Byo Ichi.**
> - **Heat stroke – Nessha Byo.**

Heat cramps are one of the first signs of heat illness. These cramps are muscle spasms that cause pain and manifest as a result of the loss of salts from the body due to high activity and sweating. I personally have dealt with heat cramps as a soldier in the hot environments of Fort Benning, Georgia, and Fort Bragg, North Carolina. It is easy to get to this stage of heat injury, especially during the panic of trying to meet your survival needs in a lone survivor situation. Even in this situation, one has to stay aware of how the body is responding to the environment as it can easily be overlooked, and thus, make the situation worse. One should stress a good work to rest ratio in a survival situation. This will help to conserve energy and not overexert in challenging conditions. If you do become very sweaty and cramped you should stop, get to a shaded place, loosen any restrictive clothing, drink cool fluids and relax. Replacing salts is also important, but that will be hard to do in a survival situation unless you have a good food source. Beyond heat cramps the next stage of heat illness is heat exhaustion. Signs that you are nearing or are at a level of heat exhaustion is:

- **Profuse sweating.**
- **Cold and clammy skin.**
- **Fatigue.**
- **Dizziness.**
- **Nausea.**
- **Headache.**
- **Cramping.**

One should stress a good work to rest ratio in a survival situation. This will help to conserve energy and not overexert in challenging conditions.

If you begin exhibiting these signs, then get to the shade immediately. Once in the shade, you should:

- Loosen clothing.
- Wet excess clothing and place it on head, neck, armpits and across your belly.
- Lie on your back and elevate your feet.
- Refrain from any activity for at least an hour or until you feel cool and recovered.

The third and most severe of heat illnesses is heat stroke. During my army career, I saw 4 people suffer heat strokes. In every case, it ended their Combat Special Operations career. They stayed in the army, but just had to do less strenuous jobs due to the damage done to their bodies because of the heat injury. Heat stroke can damage the nervous system, muscles, and vital organs. If not treated immediately heat stroke will lead to death. However, even if steps are taken to make the symptoms of heat stroke subside, the damage is done, and the body will not be able to function at its pre-heat stroke level ever again. A heat stroke is caused when high temperatures overwhelm the body's ability to manage it. These systems become so overworked that they break down much like an overheated car. As the temperature rises in your body nearing heat stroke level, symptoms will include:

- Lack of sweating. However, in some cases you could also exhibit extreme sweating if experiencing exertional heat stroke.
- Hot and dry skin.
- Rapid pulse.
- Confusion.
- Extreme fatigue.
- Cramping.
- Convulsions.

If you begin to experience any of these symptoms, then you should:

- Move to a shaded area.
- Wet excess clothing and place it on head, neck, armpits and across your belly. If this is not enough, find a safe body of water to submerge yourself into.
- Treat yourself for shock.
- Stay inactive until you feel cool and somewhat back to normal.

No one is immune to issues related to exposure. Whilst on a survival challenge in Columbia, I had to lie in a creek several times a day even with the threat of anaconda attack due to the extreme overheating. It was a dicey judgment call that I had to make based on the fact that wetting my clothing, dumping water over my head, and drinking cool water was not dropping my temperature. You will hear me say my phrase "Survival is not Perfect, it's Survival," all the time, and this was one of those moments.

> **"Survival is not Perfect, it's Survival."**

In a survival situation, it is highly important to stay focused on avoiding getting to a point of heat stroke. As I stated earlier, once you have reached this point your body will not be the same. You will be more susceptible to heat injury than you were before suffering a heat stroke. You will also fatigue easier. This will undoubtedly hinder your ability to survive effectively.

HYPOTHERMIA – TAION TEIKA

On the other end of the spectrum from hyperthermia, excessive heat is hypothermia, low or below heat. Hypothermia is when a person's body temperature drops to a point that it can no longer warm itself and function properly. Any drop in your body temperature below its standard 98.6 degrees can be considered a stage of hypothermia. However, since internal temperature can fluctuate, true hypothermia is believed to begin at around 97.5 degrees Fahrenheit. When most people think about hypothermia they think exposure to extreme cold. The truth is that a combination of clothing conditions, like a damp shirt, mixed with weather conditions, such as wind and rain, mixed with physiological conditions, such as hunger or exhaustion, together can cause hypothermia.

> **Any drop in your body temperature below its standard 98.6 degrees can be considered a stage of hypothermia. However, since internal temperature can fluctuate, true hypothermia is believed to begin at around 97.5 degrees Fahrenheit. When most people think about hypothermia they think exposure to extreme cold. The truth is that a combination of clothing conditions, like a damp shirt, mixed with weather conditions, such as wind and rain, mixed with physiological conditions, such as hunger or exhaustion, together can cause hypothermia.**

Like with hyperthermia, the body will use certain mechanisms to aid in regulating temperature when core body temperature drops. When the hypothalamus in the brain senses a decrease in body temperature, it causes your body to respond with shivering. In addition, unlike the body's reaction to combat overheating by sending blood to the skin for cooling, it reverses the process constraining the blood in the core where it can warm the organs.

If body temperature falls to 95 degrees, the signs of decreased functionality will begin. This will create a myriad of symptoms such as:

- Disorientation.
- Cold and pale skin.
- Poor balance.
- Loss of fine motor skills.

If the temperature begins to fall lower than 95 degrees, more severe symptoms will manifest such as:

- Muscle stiffness.
- Shallow breathing.
- Slowing pulse.
- Fatigue.
- Confusion.
- Lack of care and concern.
- Shivering stops.

Due to loss of motor functions, moral, and increased degradation of reasoning skills, hypothermia can very subtly render you helpless. Since it is tough to read your own temperature in a survival situation, during my Ninja training, I was taught an easy method of how to determine if you are in a severe stage of hypothermia, which was called the "hypothermia challenge." To perform this test, just draw a line 30 to 40 foot long on the ground, and try to walk it in a heel to toe manner, much like a sobriety test. Walking the line without an issue means you are probably not in a later stage of hypothermia, but if you have trouble performing the task then you can surmise that you are in the later stage of hypothermia.

As you can see from these symptoms, hypothermia can be deadly primarily because it can affect your ability to do the simplest of tasks quickly. Due to loss of motor functions, moral, and increased degradation of reasoning skills, hypothermia can very subtly render you helpless. Since it is tough to read your own temperature in a survival situation, during my Ninja training, I was taught an easy method of how to determine if you are in a severe stage of hypothermia, which was called the "hypothermia challenge." To perform this test, just draw a line 30 to 40 foot long on the ground, and try to walk it in a heel to toe manner, much like a sobriety test. Walking the line without an issue means you are probably not in a later stage of hypothermia, but if you have trouble performing the task then you can surmise that you are in the later stage of hypothermia. To aid in reversing the effects of hypothermia, you can treat it with the following methods:

- Move to a shelter.
- Remove wet conditions, either by getting out of the rain or, when possible, removing wet clothing and putting on dry ones.
- Sit in front of a wind block with a fire near you.
- Consolidate your body by sitting on a pile of leaves, for insulation from the ground, with legs crossed and hands under armpits.
- Nest in a pile of leaves, like an animal in a nest.

None of the above suggestions are perfect or foolproof. If you have waited too long to begin taking action, many of the physical and mental functions needed to perform these tasks may be degraded to a point where you cannot complete them or may not care to try. For these reasons, the best way to deal with hypothermia is to clearly and honestly assess your situation then take steps to prevent it. Just clarification on what is meant by clearly and honestly assess your situation, it is easy to misjudge what you need in a survival situation. I once was on a survival adventure with a friend. After a day of travel, we had a long debate on whether we wanted to focus on shelter or fire for our campsite for that night. He wanted a fire, but I explained I believed it could rain that night and I did not think it was a good idea to go for fire. I felt shelter would be best since it would protect us from the rain, we can stay warm using one another's body heat, and we could rest for our next day's journey. He was so adamant about the fire that I gave in and said okay. Later that night the sky opened up and rain poured violently from above. Although we tried to keep the fire going, we did not have enough wood to keep it lit in a heavy rainstorm. Our fire went out two hours into the storm and we spent the rest of the night cold and wet. Since the day was hot we both had light ponchos but that night was extremely cold and so we sat hugging each other under our ponchos trying to stay warm. It was a miserable night, and the next day we were so exhausted we cut our adventure short and decided to go home. This is what I mean by properly assessing your situation and condition. In a lone survival situation, you only know the condition of the moment you are in. You are already in a survival situation so do not gamble with your life. Pay attention to your condition, the conditions around you, and set yourself up for success.

TREAT POISONING – GEDOKU

In a truly unexpected and unprepared survival situation, dealing with poisoning is very difficult. The Ninja people had a deep understanding of herbology and how to use nature to heal. They knew uses for many of the flora in their environment. They understood if plants and herbs could be ingested, used raw and when they needed to go through a process to use. This was learning that was passed down from generation to generation. To them, the wilderness was the only drug store or care clinic they knew, and therefore, if there was an ailment, they often knew what could be used as the cure. In addition, as with the balance inherent in everything, the Ninja also understood what plants, herbs, and toxins from animals could be used to poison and kill.

Today, people often have little knowledge as to what is poisonous and what is not. From plants to insect and other wild creatures, knowing how to identify what are the poisonous and venomous dangers in the wild are not common skills of the modern man. Many people mistake the two words using the word poisonous as a term to describe venomous. However, they are not the same, and it is important to understand the difference. A poison is a substance that once it enters the body whether, through ingestion, absorption, or breathing can cause illness or death. On the contrary, venom is toxic fluid that is injected into the skin by a bite, sting or stab. Both poison and venom have a similar effect when in the body, but both enter the body in different ways. In both cases, if you are not prepared with the proper knowledge of what and how to identify what can be used from the environment to nullify the effects, or if you do not have the proper cure there will not be much you can do. The good news is that, for the most part, the majority of poisonous and venomous plants and animals that people encounter are not normally fatal. In most cases, the symptoms take hours to days to completely manifest, and when they do, they cause extreme discomfort, pain, swelling, and other ailments, but they are not normally fatal. However, I did not state that there are a number of people who die each year from plant poisons as well as insect and animal stings. Fortunately, when it comes to plants, fatal poisoning is normally due to ingestion of a plant, but as written in the food section of this book, you should stray away from eating plants in a survival situation unless you can absolutely identify them, even then for a survival situation that is less than 30 days, this should not be attempted.

Unlike poisoning from the ingestion of plants or contact with harmful plants, which are normally in your power to avoid, animal encounters are not purely in your control. There are a number of deaths from encounters with venomous animals every year. For the most part, this number is low, but it is because of access to medical assistance. In an unexpected survival situation, chances are the person will not have first aid equipment on them, nor will they just be able to rush to the nearest hospital. Therefore, knowing what dangers exist in

> A poison is a substance that once it enters the body whether, through ingestion, absorption, or breathing can cause illness or death. On the contrary, venom is toxic fluid that is injected into the skin by a bite, sting or stab. Both poison and venom have a similar effect when in the body, but both enter the body in different ways.

the wild and what to expect if encountered is good knowledge to have.

The most common irritants and dangers are:

- **Poison ivy, oak and sumac.**
- **Chiggers.**
- **Bees, wasps, and hornets,**
- **Ants.**
- **Spider bites.**
- **Scorpion stings.**
- **Snake bites.**

Poison Ivy

Poison Ivy, Oak and Sumac – These plants are responsible for contact poisoning. They all produce oil called urushiol, which is a chemical compound that irritates the skin and sensitive areas of the body. Once a part of the plant is damaged and the oil touches your skin, it will cause a reaction that normally results in an itchy rash. Even if not directly exposed to the oils from these plants, it is important to know that the oils can exist on clothing for a long period of time. Therefore, it is possible to later transmit the oil to parts of your body. Both poison ivy and oak have leaflets that grow in 3s. A good phrase to remember is the old adage "If there are leaves of 3, leave it be," is something that can help with proper identification. However, sometimes poison ivy can develop as a furry vine on a tree. Poison Sumac is more of a tree or shrub and it can grow 15-30 feet in height. The leaves of Poison Sumac are oval and grow in opposite pairs. Learning how to identify these plants is not only important because of the rash they could cause, but more detrimentally, is the issue that can be caused through inhalation. Sometimes a person who has failed to identify these plants could accidentally place them in a fire. This is a mistake as the smoke produced from this is poisonous to inhale and could be fatal.

Oak

Sumac

As stated earlier, natural remedies exist in the wild to aid with rashes, such as Jewelweed or Witch Hazel leaves, but you truly need to be versed in plant identification and medicinal skills to find and use these plants. A rash in all cases normally takes a few hours to a day to develop, however, if you suspect you may have been exposed, refrain from touching your mouth, eyes, nose and other sensitive areas of the body to avoid spreading the oil to these areas. If you develop a rash, it is also important not to scratch it as you could open a wound and infect it with the oil. In a lone survival situation, it is best to wrap the affected area and not touch it. If the itching becomes hard to ignore, you could try putting cool mud on it as a means to sooth it. Note that this is not a full proof remedy.

Chiggers – These are tiny parasites that bore under the skin. They are not particularly harmful but they are very demoralizing and irritating. I have had chiggers several times in a situation where I did not have items to properly get rid of them and treat the symptoms, and it was almost unbearable. Chiggers are too tiny to be seen by the naked eye, and they often live around brush and water. They are most active in the spring with a lifecycle of about 60 days to a year. Chiggers will normally bite around the ankles, back of the knees, and in the crouch or waistline. They do not burrow in the skin and they do not drink blood. Instead, they attach themselves to the skin with their mouth, and like flies do for their food, Chiggers secrete saliva that breaks down the skin to a liquid that they then suck up. Chiggers will normally be brushed off when the area they are in is wiped or scratched, but the area will continue to itch for days after due to an allergic reaction your skin has to their saliva. Other than the torment they cause, very few people could actually have a reaction that causes them to feel ill. Normally people will just scratch the irritated area to the point of creating open wounds, which is the main concern in a survival situation.

Bees, Wasp, Hornets, and Ants –

These insects are generally referred to as hymenoptera, often identified as winged and social insects. In the United States, these insects are responsible for the most deaths a year than any other due to their aggressive swarming nature. Ants kill close to 10 people a year while bees, wasp, and hornets are responsible for nearly 60. It is speculated that the difference is that ant nests are easy to spot and to get away from once disturbed, whereas bee, wasp and hornet nests are sometimes harder to spot and harder to escape once disturbed due to their ability to fly. If attacked by ants, move away from the area and wipe the ants away with a leaf or piece of material. If they are on your clothing, after moving to a safe area, remove the clothing and shake them out. If attacked by bees, wasps, or hornets immediately move from the area as fast as possible. Try not to swing and swat at them as this will agitate them more. If you have a jacket or covering, use it to cover your head and any exposed portion of your upper body. Once you get far enough from the hive they should stop the pursuit. In normal society, it is estimated that the average adult can survive hundreds of stings or bites and still live, however, due to allergic reactions,

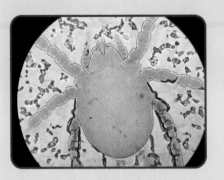

Chigger

Wasp

Ant

Black Widow

Brown Recluse

just one or a few venomous stings or bites from these insects can kill. Over a million Americans have allergies to insect stings and bites with symptoms that can range from swelling, hives, nausea, and difficulty breathing. Without the proper treatment, which is often a shot of epinephrine, a person will not be able to recover from anaphylactic shock. In a lone survival situation, there is not much you can do if you have a severe reaction to a bite or sting. However, if you have a mild reaction, such as swelling, pain, and irritation, you should sit, rest, and monitor yourself. Remove any stingers that may be visible with your fingernail or knife and cover the area to protect it from exposure. Often people who are allergic to stings will carry an Epi-Pen. If this is you then you should administer it immediately.

Spiders – Spider bites are not that common as spiders will not bite unless provoked. Spider bites are normally accidental and not fatal. The fatality rate of spider bites is only about seven deaths a year. There are about 3,000 species of spiders in the United States and many are venomous, however, few have venom that is toxic to humans. In the U.S., there are 2 types of spiders that cause the most trouble, which are Black Widows and Brown Recluse spiders. The Black Widow is shiny black with a red hourglass shape on her abdomen. It is one of the most venomous out of all the spiders in the U.S., however, their bite is rarely fatal. In normal society, less than 1% of the people bitten by a Black Widow will die from its bite. Those most vulnerable to death are the elderly and children. Normally, a Black Widow will only inject a little venom upon biting, which will cause pain, nausea, muscle spasms, and other issues, but it is possible for someone surviving in extreme scenarios to recover without medical help. If you can, always seek medical attention.

The Brown Recluse is a small brown spider

Scorpion

Bark Scorpion

Copperhead

that has a violin shape on its back. A bite from a Brown Recluse is not fatal but it can cause a lot of damage. In a short amount of time, the bite will turn red, become puss filled, and then the flesh around it will start to deteriorate and die. If not treated, the wound will grow as the flesh continues to die which is called necrosis. Keeping the area covered so it is not exposed to the elements is the best thing you can do to ensure foreign material does not enter the wound. However, without immediate medical attention, the wound will worsen.

Scorpions – There are 90 species of scorpions in the United States. Mostly, all of these scorpions are not dangerous with the exception of the Bark Scorpion from Arizona and its border areas. This is the only known highly venomous scorpion that is dangerous to humans. Scorpions like to live under logs, rocks, bushes, and debris and will not normally sting unless threatened. Once stung by a scorpion you may feel burning, pain, and tingling at the sight. You may begin to sweet or feel nauseous. Get to a safe place sit, stay calm, and monitor how you feel. Eventually, symptoms should subside.

Snakes– Out of almost 8,000 venomous snake bites a year, less than ten of those people will die. This is normally due to receiving the proper medical attention but also because venomous snakes will dry bite or inject a small amount of poison when biting. There are 4 species of venomous snakes in the United States, which are rattlesnakes, copperheads, cottonmouths and coral snakes. All will bite when threatened but most will try to avoid human contact, or in the case of the rattlesnake, give a warning when they feel someone is invading their space. One of the most aggressive of the venomous snakes is the cottonmouth. However, it is not responsible for the majority of the bites every year. Out of the nearly 8,000 bites a year in the U.S., most of them are by copperheads. Copperheads are the Ninja of the

All snakes should be avoided in a survival situation. The only time this may not be an option is if they come to your site, or you are over 3 weeks into a survival situation and need food, but even then I would caution against it.

If you are bitten by a venomous snake, you will likely have a reaction at the site right away. You will feel burning, swelling, and pain. You may often get blisters and feel tingling. These are signs that venom has been injected into you. Another way that you may have been bitten by a poisonous snake is by the look of the bite.

snake family with camouflage that is so good they normally hide in plain sight. They often do not move when approached and they do not give a warning when they feel threatened. Instead, they strike and strike often. Luckily, they do not often inject a lot of poison, and therefore, you can likely survive the bite. All snakes should be avoided in a survival situation. The only time this may not be an option is if they come to your site, or you are over 3 weeks into a survival situation and need food, but even then I would caution against it. If it is at your site and you must kill it, make sure you know that even a dead snake can still bite out of overactive reflexes, and its venom is still active even if its head is severed from its body, which is why burying the head is recommended. One way to tell if you are dealing with a venomous snake is if they have a big triangular head. This is common among pit vipers but not coral snakes. With coral snakes, a good saying to remember is "Yellow touching red

can make you dead, red touching black there's no venom in that." If you are bitten by a venomous snake, you will likely have a reaction at the site right away. You will feel burning, swelling, and pain. You may often get blisters and feel tingling. These are signs that venom has been injected into you. Another way that you may have been bitten by a poisonous snake is by the look of the bite. If you see a series of smaller teeth marks forming an half oval with two bigger puncture marks towards the top of the oval, these may have been caused by the fangs of a venomous snake. The best ways to deal with venomization is to stay calm because panicking will cause your heart to beat rapidly, and thus, the toxin to circulate faster, keep the bitten area below the heart, and splint the limb if possible. It is important that you do not try to cut the area bitten, suck out the poison, nor should you put a tourniquet on. After you take the steps recommended, your best follow up action is to get help.

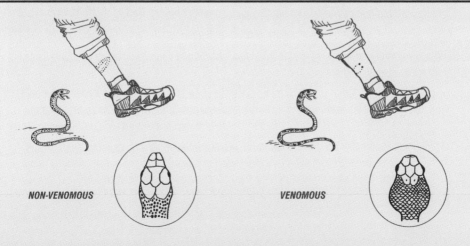

NON-VENOMOUS

VENOMOUS

HOW TO AVOID BITES, STINGS, AND IRRITATION

The Ninja had a saying "Where ever there is danger, do not be there." This simple phrase has a lot of depth to it and this is part of the higher levels of what is known as Ninja Invisibility. Understanding the characteristics, traits, and habits of that which may cause you harm and then ensuring that you are not there, is one of the most important skill sets in all aspects of survival.

Understanding the common animal and insect threats that can be faced in a survival situation is one aspect of being prepared. Another is how to avoid them altogether. The Ninja had a saying "Where ever there is danger, do not be there." This simple phrase has a lot of depth to it and this is part of the higher levels of what is known as Ninja Invisibility. Understanding the characteristics, traits, and habits of that which may cause you harm and then ensuring that you are not there, is one of the most important skill sets in all aspects of survival. Using this philosophy, a lone survivor can more effectively navigate his environment in a way that will not cause him further harm, if he is already injured, or injury if he is healthy but just lost. Some methods of how to do this are as follows:

- Wear long clothing and avoid areas with lots of debris, tall grass and foliage if possible. This may be difficult because you may need to use these materials for a shelter, so be careful.
- Use a walking stick to tap the ground as you walk, to move unknown brush, and disturb any debris you may use.
- Hit with a stick, or kick, and shake logs, branches, and rocks before touching them with your hand. Never lift or investigate with your hands first.
- Use an improvised rake to gather debris, spread and regather at least once before picking it up with your hands.
- Clear and inspect the ground of any place you plan to sleep. Also, visually inspect a 10-foot radius around the area to ensure nothing dangerous is nesting nearby.
- Use smoke to smoke out your shelter before sleeping in it.
- Use ash from your fire to spread around your shelter in a perimeter. Ash is a natural deterrent for many insects and animals.

GET HELP – KYUJO

The majority of our society has turned to the internet, pills, and quick walk-in urgent clinics to keep us healthy with no desire to gain the knowledge we need on our own.

All self aid and first aid are focused on one thing and that is keeping yourself, or someone else, alive and capable or, at minimum, medically stable until official medical care can be provided. The body is a machine with many moving parts and functions. It can be simple or complicated, or both at the same time. Most people are not medical professionals, and few have a desire to be well versed in Self-Aid concepts, and even fewer in first aid concepts. The majority of our society has turned to the internet, pills, and quick walk-in urgent clinics to keep us healthy with no desire to gain the knowledge we need on our own. However, if you desire to spend any

time in the wild, you should hone your understanding of, at minimum, the basics of how to stay healthy, get back to health, or sustain your life until you can find help or it finds you. Medical knowledge may seem daunting but in reflection, most adults in society have encountered a number of illnesses either first or second hand. We have all gained a basic knowledge of healing over the years of being sick and being acquainted with sick people, therefore with just a little practice one can be adequately prepared for many, situations. The goal is not to become a wilderness medicine man/woman but instead, it would be just to stay alive until help arrives so that you can get proper medical attention.

Medical knowledge may seem daunting but in reflection, most adults in society have encountered a number of illnesses either first or second hand.

CHAPTER
4

SURVIVAL SHELTER MAKING

ZANZON HO HINANJO

As discussed in the previous chapters, the Ninja saw the natural realm as a represen-tation of their own makeup. Because of this they only needed to look within and around themselves as a means to decipher the challenges set forth by survival. This lesson was one of the most valuable lessons taught to me by my Ninjutsu teacher Stephen K. Hayes.

If you look around our modern society, you can see what one of the most important needs is housing, or to those who under-stand survival, climate control. Developers are building at an astonishing rate all over the United States. The two most important needs for human survival is the ability to escape direct contact with the elements and to regulate climate for one's own comfort. As we understand from the law of 3s, 3 or fewer hours of exposure can kill, and this was the initial concern for man in the past. But now in the modern world, our ability to thermoregulate has become weaker due to the myriad of ways that we have developed for artificial environmental control. From our cars to our beds, showers, and homes, every-thing has temperature control. These are a few examples that highlight the importance of thermoregulation in the life of everyday humans outside of just survival. I witness this first hand every time I have a class as youth will often come to my survival camps and, in 75-degree weather, mention how they cannot survive and are going to die without

> **We are simply weaker now than we were in the past as our tolerance for shifting weather and our ability to regulate our temperature is not exercised enough.**

air-conditioning. We are simply weaker now than we were in the past as our tolerance for shifting weather and our ability to regulate our temperature is not exercised enough. For these reasons, understanding what makes for the best methods of regulating your core body temperature is important and, as you can see from our society, the best method is to have some sort of insulated structure/shell.

Here's a question; I want you, the reader, to take a moment and list five things you think that I have with me at all times when hiking. I am sure you are guessing, and most of you might guess some things correctly, but some may not be so close. Since I am a survival instructor, it would be a lot easier for you to imagine what I would have, than for me to

> **If you look around our modern society, you can see what one of the most important needs is housing, or to those who under-stand survival, climate control. Developers are building at an astonishing rate all over the United States. The two most important needs for human survival is the ability to escape direct contact with the elements and to regulate climate for one's own comfort.**

> **There is no way for me to know what you could have on you and what you will not if you are in a survival situa-tion. The one thing that is a lot more certain is that, unless you are in a nudist colony or on Mars, you will have clothes on, and you will be in some sort of natural environment.**

imagine what you will have with you in the outdoors. I am not going to be foolish enough to think that I can tell each of you what to take with you outdoors. I am ashamed to say it, but I remember putting a survival box of gear in my wife's car only to find it in the garage one day. When I asked her why she took it out of her trunk she said it is because she needed space in the trunk and forgot to put it back. The point here is, anyone can make suggestions on what you should have with you, but no one can force you to take it with you. From this perspective, the one certainty is that no survival instructor in the world can tell you what you will have on you in the event you find yourself in a random wilderness survival situation. The keyword in the previous sentence is "random," there is no way for me to know what you could have on you and what you will not if you are in a survival situation. The one thing that is a lot more certain is that, unless you are in a nudist colony or on Mars, you will have clothes on, and you will be in some sort of natural environment. However, in the case of tents, tarps, and biveys, there is no way to be certain you would have any of these. Because of this, I believe it is important to know how to use your landscape in conjunction with your clothing as a means to find or create shelter.

I spent several nights in high thirties temperature on the side of the Himalayan mountains in India with nothing more than a debris covered and filled shelter. It rained, it was windy, and it was cold most of the time, not once getting above the mid-sixties. There was nothing about the situation that was comfortable, but I was able to stay alive. By the way, did I mention I was naked?! I was on an extreme survival challenge and, as far as survival situations go, I was in the worst of the worst situations that I could imagine. Although for the most part this adventure, if I could call it that, this was self-imposed. I found that the thing that saved me was the proper applica-

tion of shelter building knowledge.

A common discussion in the survival world is, what is more important—shelter or fire? A common answer since the discovery of fire is that it depends. However, the point of that phrase is "Since the discovery of fire." Before the discovery of fire, man survived primarily in trees, caves, and in any other natural cover/ shelter they could find. This was the case for a long period in human history. It was not until later that man discovered fire. The importance of fire cannot be down played, as it is credited with being responsible for different aspects of human evolution. The ability to cook food, provide light at night, deter animals, give warmth, and increased options and capabilities that improved their survivability. However, one thing still remained: fire alone cannot protect you from dying of exposure to both the elements and predators.

> **The importance of fire cannot be down played, as it is credited with being responsible for different aspects of human evolution. The ability to cook food, provide light at night, deter animals, give warmth, and increased options and capabilities that improved their survivability.**

The importance of shelter cannot be understated. Shelter serves 2 primary functions which are:

- To protect you from overexposure to the elements which help you thermoregulate and keep your body's core temperature at 98.6 degrees.
- To give you a sense of security.

Every human body is constantly trying to maintain core temperature by regulating the body's heat gain and heat loss. Through the use of the hypothalamus, the brain senses changes in temperature from signals sent by temperature receptors on the body, and then it adjusts, sometimes using mechanisms such as sweating, shivering, etc., to help keep the body's core temperature as close to 98.6 degrees as possible. The body does have some flexibility in core temperature dynamics, but it is very slight. The range of flexibility normally falls within the scope of 98-100 degrees Fahrenheit. The body is always seeking homeostasis (a balanced state) as without this equilibrium that body becomes at risk of dying from either hypothermia or hyperthermia. Without proper thermoregulation, the body dies, and one of the main barriers to proper thermoregulation during survival is exposure. The term exposure itself says it all when it comes to why people have problems regulating temperature. To be exposed means to have a lack of cover, protection, and security against an outside force or situation. Having no barrier means that you are subject to those forces having a greater impact on how your body operates. In most aspects the greater the exposure, the greater the effect, therefore, the greater the effect the harder it is to counter it. The way I have found best to teach this concept is to liken it to the idea of bench-pressing weights. When you are in control you may only put on weight that you are capable of handling. This means you can regulate it much easier. However, if your trainer or friend is in control, they may put on more weight than you can handle, which could lead to a failure in being able to push the weight. When you are exposed to the elements, then you are at the mercy of how much Mother Nature will subject you to. However, if you take control by taking steps to minimize the effect/exposure, you may be able to manage the weight and handle what you are subjected to. In survival, a shelter is obviously not the solution for everything as people have frozen to death in tents. However, its importance cannot be understated. People have existed in some of the most extreme conditions with shelter alone, whereas the same cannot be said with just fire alone. It is worth highlighting that the combination of both shelter and fire are as important as a combination of food and water to the human body. They support one another and help

> The body is always seeking homeostasis (a balanced state) as without this equilibrium that body becomes at risk of dying from either hypothermia or hyperthermia. Without proper thermoregulation, the body dies, and one of the main barriers to proper thermoregulation during survival is exposure.

> Having no barrier means that you are subject to those forces having a greater impact on how your body operates. In most aspects the greater the exposure, the greater the effect, therefore, the greater the effect the harder it is to counter it.

> Importance of the shelter cannot be understated. People have existed in some of the most extreme conditions with shelter alone, whereas the same cannot be said with just fire alone. It is worth highlighting that the combination of both shelter and fire are as important a combination of food and water to the human body. They support one another and help to fortify the likelihood of surviving extreme cold conditions.

to fortify the likelihood of surviving extreme cold conditions. With that mentioned, it is also important to note that many homeless die year after year from lack of shelter even if they have a fire. This is because having a fire only provides radiant heat, which can warm your surface temperature faster than it can warm your core temperature. However, you can go out during extremely low temperatures and see many homeless individuals surviving through the use of layered blankets and clothing, which are a form of shelter. One reason that a person could die while standing or sitting in front of a fire is that standing in front of a fire can make them too hot on their fire facing side, while the part of them that is not facing the fire gets cold. Like a rotisserie, people will then rotate to warm the non-exposed area. When the weather is cold enough, what can often happen is that as this rotating

process occurs your core temperature gradually drops. This is sometimes tough to understand as it may seem that your outer layer is warm. The best way to think about this is to think about the idea of a frozen turkey where the outside is cooked faster than the inside. On the outside, it looks prepared, but when you cut into it you find frozen, cold or soggy uncooked meat. As your core temperature drops, you are less and less capable of functioning and improving your conditions until eventually, you succumb to hypothermia.

There are 5 ways that cause the body to lose or gain heat. These culprits have varying degrees of effect on the human body depending on the environment, the level of activity and adequacy of shelter (clothing or structure). The 5 ways that the body loses and gains heat are:

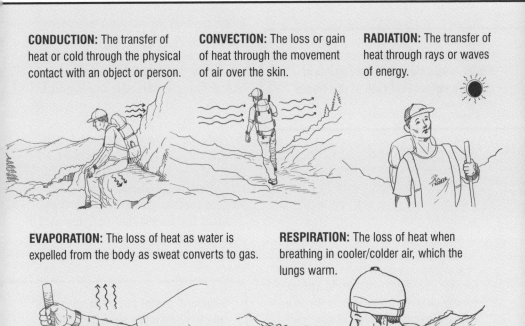

CONDUCTION: The transfer of heat or cold through the physical contact with an object or person.

CONVECTION: The loss or gain of heat through the movement of air over the skin.

RADIATION: The transfer of heat through rays or waves of energy.

EVAPORATION: The loss of heat as water is expelled from the body as sweat converts to gas.

RESPIRATION: The loss of heat when breathing in cooler/colder air, which the lungs warm.

Unlike a fire, a proper shelter can protect you from the harmful effects that come with these 5 aspects of thermoregulation and that is why shelter is so important. A shelter can have 2 primary purposes, which are **protection and insulation**. In a true random survival situation, it is hard to say which one you will need but understanding the difference is important. A shelter that provides a protective barrier is one that only provides protection against direct sun, wind, or rain. However, protective barriers won't always provide proper insulation. Therefore, having a shelter that serves as an insulated barrier, would mean that it is capable of retaining radiant heat such as that from a fire or your body. An easy example of a protective barrier would be the idea of using an umbrella to provide shade, while stripping down to your underwear and zipping up in a thick sleeping bag would be an example of insulation.

> Having a shelter that serves as an insulated barrier, would mean that it is capable of retaining radiant heat such as that from a fire or your body.

A well-designed shelter, even if crudely built, can provide you with the ability to protect against improper regulation of the 5 ways the body loses and gains heat, and thus, help survive a myriad of conditions. Proper shelter with good ground insulation will keep you from losing or gaining heat through a hot or cold ground. Proper walls and good insulation can block cold or hot air from blowing directly on you causing harmful temperature change through convection. A good shelter can protect from the direct rays of the sun, which affects the body's temperature through solar radiation. A shelter providing adequate temperatures in warmer weather,

as well as cooler weather, can keep the body from sweating or keep the sweat from being cooled too rapidly causing a strong fluctuation in body temperature as sweat evaporates. Lastly, a well-insulated shelter can retain body heat warming the air before it enters the lungs, which aids the lungs in their efforts to warm cooler air during the process of respiration.

Shelter comes in 2 major forms. These forms are **material and structural**. The material form is clothing. Although your body has certain mechanisms and features that help regulate temperature like fat and hair for insulation, clothing serves as an easily manageable way to help with thermoregulation. By simply putting on more clothing or taking them off, you can easily control the aspects of thermoregulating your body temperature. The second form of shelter is structural. This form of shelter is what people normally think of when they think about the term. Structural shelter has 2 sub-categories which are **naturally formed or man-made**. This, of course, can further be broken down into **habitable or inhabitable**. Naturally formed shelters can be caves, rock cliffs, tree hollows, tree trunks, and exposed root beds from a toppled over tree. A man-made shelter can be abandoned cabins, mills, old concrete formations, and maybe old junk vehicles. I have been on hikes in remote places and stumbled across stone fireplaces that are still standing in the ruins of an old cabin, and even cars with vegetation grown all over them.

> Structural shelter has 2 subcategories which are naturally formed or man-made. This, of course, can further be broken down into habitable or inhabitable.

Understanding the above aspects of shelter which breaks it down into 2 categories, material and structural, a person in a survival situation can competently strategize and successfully thermoregulate through the recognizing of what I call the **Trifecta of Survival Shelter**. In this trifecta, I highlight that proper shelter can be accomplished in 3 ways, which are to:

- **Wear It.**
- **Seek It.**
- **Build It.**

This Trifecta of Survival Shelter serves as an easy way to retain how to plan for providing proper shelter from exposure when in a survival scenario.

WEAR IT

As we mentioned earlier, your first line of defense besides the natural mechanisms in your body are the clothes on your back. A good rule to consider is to always wear more layers than you need. The old saying "It is better to have it and not need it, than need it and not have it," is of great importance in this situation. Having an extra layer or two that you can take off when you get hot is better than needing extra clothing so that you can get warm but not having them. However, it is important to know that all clothes are not created equally. It is dangerous to think that since we have clothing, we will be able to thermoregulate efficiently and enhance our possible survival. When judging clothing there are 2 terms that we want to understand, and they are *hydrophobic and hydrophilic*.

"It is better to have it and not need it, than need it and not have it."

Hydrophobic means that a material has an ability to repel or transfer water and not retain or absorb it. This quality is sometimes referred to as "non-polar," and it helps pull sweat away from the skin and expels it easier. Hydrophilic is just the opposite, meaning that a material has a propensity to absorb and retain water quality, sometimes referred to as "polar." Some clothing repels and expels water quickly while others absorb and retain it. Depending on material quality, different clothing have different strengths and weak-

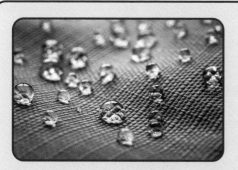

Hydrophobic means that a material has an ability to repel or transfer water and not retain or absorb it. This quality is sometimes referred to as "non-polar," and it helps pull sweat away from the skin and expels it easier. Hydrophilic is just the opposite, meaning that a material has a propensity to absorb and retain water quality sometimes referred to as "polar."

nesses when it comes to survival. To make things simple, let us use the four clothing material types that are common among average people:

Cotton – Cotton can be very helpful in a survival situation for things such as starting a fire, filtering water, and even bandaging wounds. One thing cotton is not particularly good at is providing quality thermoregulation. Cotton is an absorbing material and it retains moisture. So, for the very reasons that it works well on wounds, cotton can aid in destroying your thermoregulation when worn as an item of clothing. Cotton can lose roughly 80-90% of its insulating qualities when wet, and since moisture is easy to come across in the outdoors through sweat, rain, and accidental submersion, etc. it is important to understand that cotton is not something that should be worn during outdoor events in cold or unpredictable climates.

> Cotton can be very helpful in a survival situation for things such as starting a fire, filtering water, and even bandaging wounds. One thing cotton is not particularly good at is providing quality thermoregulation.

Wool – For the same reason that wool is good for a sheep's thermoregulation as an insulating coat, it is also good for humans. Wool has many great qualities for regulating temperature in all types of environments. Wool can absorb 30-60% of its weight in moisture and still feel dry. This also does not affect its ability to keep you warm as wool has tiny air pockets that naturally exist in the fabric. This helps retain your body heat for cold days but does the reverse on warm days, due to its breathability, it can conversely allow moisture from your body to easily evaporate. Similarly, birds will fluff their feathers in cold

> Wool has many great qualities for regulating temperature in all types of environments. Wool can absorb 30-60% of its weight in moisture and still feel dry. This also does not affect its ability to keep you warm as wool has tiny air pockets that naturally exist in the fabric.

temperatures to create air pockets between them to aid in trapping heat. Wool naturally contains lanolin, which is an oil secreted by sheep to aid in the shedding of water. This oil helps wool stay water resistant, however, it also absorbs moisture and can pull it away from the skin. This dual ability to both repel and absorb makes it a good as either a base layer or an insulating outer layer. Another great quality of wool is that, although it is a natural material like cotton, it is not very flammable, which is of great benefit when trying to nestle next to a fire to stay warm or using the fire to aid in drying out the material. Wool can, however, be very itchy and this causes many people to not use it, especially as a base layer. This can easily be solved by wearing a different material underneath to minimize skin irritation.

Synthetics – 2 of the more common synthetics are *polyester and nylon*. It is common for a person to have a jacket or shirt made of these materials, and thus, they are fabrics that I commonly talk about.

Polyester is an acrylic fiber made from oil. It is cheap to make as it is essentially plastic, and is often used in the production of clothing for outdoor use. Unlike wool, it is a lightweight material that is not bulky and, due to its synthetic nature, it is also resistant to rot and mold. Polyester does not absorb water, it

Polyester is a lightweight material that is not bulky and, due to its synthetic nature, it is also resistant to rot and mold. It does not absorb water, it is hydrophobic and as a base layer, it moves water away from the skin to the surface of the fabric where it can evaporate. It does not pull energy from the body to dry it out. This means that it feels warmer in colder climates.

is hydrophobic and as a base layer, it moves water away from the skin to the surface of the fabric where it can evaporate. It does not pull energy from the body to dry it out. This means that it feels warmer in colder climates. Polyester is heat resistant, but if it catches fire it melts quickly since it is a plastic-like material making it problematic around fires. Nylon is also flame retardant, but polyester is more resistant to heat.

Nylon is also made from oil like polyester, but it is often more durable and weather resistant. Nylon is mostly hydrophobic like polyester but slightly hydrophilic meaning it absorbs water and therefore unlike polyester, it can take longer for nylon to dry. This quality also causes the body to use more heat energy to warm, making nylon feel colder when it is moist, which is an issue in colder weather but can be beneficial in warmer weather. Because of its

Photo: Jnn (Wikipedia)

As one version of an environmental layer, Ninja would have worn was Mino as protection against rain and snow. This was a tightly woven rice straw cloak that covered the whole body. As you can imagine, wearing natural material would give the added benefit of camouflage, thus aiding the Ninja in protection from the elements as well as his enemy.

Nylon is mostly hydrophobic like polyester but slightly hydrophilic meaning it absorbs water and therefore unlike polyester, it can take longer for nylon to dry. This quality also causes the body to use more heat energy to warm, making nylon feel colder when it is moist, which is an issue in colder weather but can be beneficial in warmer weather.

durability, nylon works well as an outer layer to protect against windy and wet conditions. Even though it absorbs a little water, nylon can expel this water fairly quick and easy, therefore not compromising its thermoregulatory qualities as a protective outer layer.

Beyond understanding the quality of the materials that outdoor or active wear is made of, people often buy their gear based on key terms written on the label such as water resistant, wicking, or breathable, without understanding the true nature of what this means. I have had people come to classes with water resistant jackets when the days for the events called for heavy rain, and then are surprised when they are drenched all weekend. One thing I learned when using a poncho as a shelter was that it was porous, and if you touch it from the dry side while it was wet on the other side, water would pass through. That is good to know when you have a low spot in your tent collecting water that you decide to use your hand to push up to expel, and then find yourself miserable as that area allows water to pass through the poncho for the rest of the time you are under it.

Now that we understand the types of common materials used for outdoor clothing, lets discuss a few of the key terms that you may see around:

Wicking – Means that a material does not absorb moisture. Like a wick in a lantern, the material draws the oil (moisture) from the base up to the tip of the wick where the flame is. This process allows the flame to burn more of the oil than the material. Similar in concept, wicking material pulls moisture away from the skin and transfers it by way of evaporation to the atmosphere. Wicking ability is a good quality to have in a base layer, but understand that, although it will dry faster than a non-wicking material, it does not mean that

it will be immediate. Wicking takes time and, during lots of activity, you will sweat faster than the material can expel it.

Breathable – Means that material allows moisture vapor transfer. As warm moisture vapor is expelled from the body it is attracted to the cooler air outside of the material. Breathable waterproof material is great and provides the benefit of letting moisture pass through it, getting it from the body but at the same time keeping moisture from the environment getting through it. Sometimes, the breathability and air permeability are stated as the same thing, however, in a more detailed view, breathability deals with how a material releases heat and moisture, whereas air permeability refers primarily to how well air flows through a material. It is important to note that you can get a good waterproof material that is breathable but having a material that is high air permeable means that it will have a low waterproofing rating.

Non-breathable – Means that a material does not allow moisture vapor transmission. This can cause overheating and dehydration in hotter climates and excessive sweating and extreme cooling in colder climates. It is important to have a means of ventilation (ventilation pits) when a material is non-breathable.

Water Resistant – Means a material is able to resist the penetration of water to some degree, however, not entirely. Materials made to be water resistant can withstand light rain but not heavy exposure and wet conditions.

Waterproof – Means a material is able to withstand heavy exposure to rain and wet conditions. It is important to understand that there are varying degrees of waterproofing. Saying that an item is waterproof does not mean that it is under any condition. There are ratings for waterproofing, and these ratings are determined under certain controlled conditions. There is another added benefit to waterproof clothing, which is that it normally provides protection from the wind as it serves the dual purposes of also being windproof.

These are some of the more common terms that you may see in association with outdoor gear. After first having a good understanding of the capabilities of the material, understanding the key terms that may be associated with them, also ensures that if you have or find a material that highlights these terms, you will be able to effectively use them for the right environmental conditions.

Knowing what to have, what it is capable of, and how best to us it was an important skill for the Ninja as they did not have synthetics, and once on a mission, what you could find or what you had was instrumental in their survival. Understanding the true qualities and capabilities of the tools and materials in their possession or environment meant that they could create solutions on the fly. To the lost trail walker who did not plan for being injured, I cannot overstate enough that "Knowledge is King, Application is Queen, and Together they rule." You may not always have the right stuff, but if you can improvise based on sound understanding you can be successful.

> **After learning what types of clothing is best to wear and what types are best to stay away from, it is important to know how you layer them.**

ing what types of clothing is best to wear and what types are best to stay away from, it is important to know how you layer them. A simple example that I use to help my students relate layering to everyday life is to think about it in terms of going to bed at night. You have your pajamas, which is your base layer, then your blanket, which is like an insulating layer, and finally your home, which insulates as well but has an even greater purpose of protecting against direct exposure to the natural elements. This same concept is how you should perceive the layering of your clothing when you are in the wilderness. You want a base layer that removes water away from the body and help warm the air barrier that exists between the material and your skin. Next, you have a layer of insulation that, like the sheets and blanket in your home, they can be added or removed to assist with regulation of body temperature. Finally, there is the protective layer which assists with deterring the elements. This would be articles of clothing such as waterproof or resistant coats or jackets.

> **The strategy for how you wear your clothing is called *layering*.**

Now that we have established the importance of the type of clothing you wear, lets examine how you wear your clothing. The strategy for how you wear your clothing is called *layering*. As we mentioned before, having multiple layers of clothing that can be removed or added gives you some control over your ability to thermoregulate. However, after learn-

> *Not having access to the best of materials, such as the highest quality silks and kinds of cotton like the Samurai upper class, Ninja would have relied heavily on this concept of layering. They may have even stuffed their clothing with dry dead grass as a means to retain body heat during a mission. Layering is one of those golden concepts that spans the test of time.*

SEEK IT

This is a very important aspect of providing shelter because if it can be accomplished it is very efficient. In survival, your energy and caloric expenditure is very important to manage. Think of a scenario where you have little charge on your phone in a place where you have no signal, but you really need to make an important call. For a person that likes to surf Facebook, Instagram, and check emails every 10 seconds, conserving battery life so you can get to an area to make this call means minimizing the use of these apps to ensure you use the battery for the most important task. This idea can also be applied to survival. If you can cut out a step and conserve your energy for the tasks ahead then that is a much better choice. This is why being able to properly seek and identify natural features in the landscape surrounding you that can serve as a shelter is a valuable asset. These types of shelters are called Natural Shelters because they naturally exist in the landscape. Sometimes building a shelter from scratch with natural materials can also be called a natural shelter, it just depends on your instructor's preference. Highlighting the fact that there may be an injury involved in a survival situation, finding a natural shelter also increases the importance of not having to carry and maneuver a lot of materials for building a shelter. Much like we discussed earlier, not only will the injured person's body have to compensate for the injury, thus causing extra stress on the body which burns more calories, but they could also subject themselves to further damaging the injury or causing a new one. Think of how tough it would be trying to carry a 7' long x 4" diameter pole for your shelter if you have a damaged knee or ankle. Now imagine trying to do that several times before you lose sunlight. Knowing what is

needed for proper shelter, how to find it, and how to fortify, enhance, and secure it is paramount in a true survival situation.

For the Ninja, finding Natural Shelter was also very important, for not only calorie expenditure, but also because of the impact on the environment. For a Ninja on a mission, this was less about the betterment of the land and more so to aid in their ability to leave little evidence of their movements and presence in a particular area. The Ninja formed an observant eye for seeing natural features in the landscape that can aid with thermoregulation as well as concealment.

There are many different natural features that can be used as natural shelters, however in my time of teaching and wondering in the woods, I have found 5 to be the most common:

- Fallen Trees or Saplings.
- Exposed Roots of a Fallen Tree.
- Cliff and Hill Overhangs.
- Caves.
- Abandoned or Dilapidated Structures.

With little to no improvement depending on environmental conditions, these natural shelters can provide the necessary protection from the elements. A fallen tree or sapling can serve as a good ridge pole for a lean-to or A-frame shelter. If the trunk is big enough, you may just be able to sit or lay under it for protection from the rain or heat from the sun. Exposed root base of a fallen tree could serve as a windbreak or fire reflector. Depending on the thickness and spread of the roots, a hollow cocoon

Natural shelters

Windbreak   **Natural shelter tree**   **Fire reflector**

Natural shelter

Cave shelter

Taking shelter in a cave

of shelter could exist where you would only have to add some cover and insulation in order to complete a decent natural shelter. Cliffs and hill overhangs can provide good protection from rain or sun, whereas caves can provide both protection from the rain and sun as well as the wind.

Natural Existing Shelters are a blessing in a survival situation; however, there are some concerns when using an existing shelter. The main concern that spans all of them is that if it can make a good place for you then it may be likely that another living creature has surmised the same thing. From 4 legged animals to slithering creatures and tiny critters, there could be an array of harmful or dangerous living hazards that can further degrade your survival situation. When considering a natural shelter, it is important to check for signs of living things. Look for tracks, scat (feces), and remains of food as a sign that something was there. If there are no visible signs, next get a long stick to poke around and clear the ground of any debris. Look for movement or signs of life. As the last test, you may want to set up a small fire near the location and put punky wood or living material on it to create lots of smoke. Wave this smoke into the interested area, if there is something that is living there, it should be agitated and irritated by the smoke and at least try to reposition itself. I remember when I was attending the army Survival, Evade, Resist and Escape (S.E.R.E) school we had a young soldier hide in a small depression, only to find that it was home to fire ants. He lived but only because he was able to get immediate help.

> **Natural Existing Shelters are a blessing in a survival situation; however, there are some concerns when using an existing shelter. The main concern that spans all of them is that if it can make a good place for you then it may be likely that another living creature has surmised the same thing.**

Photos: Aaron Phillips

Abandon cabin

Abandon concrete building

Outside of living hazards, there are also structural and airborne ones. You will want to ensure that the fallen tree is structurally sound and is not rotted. You may want to put some weight on it, or poke into it with a knife or sharp stick to ensure that there is no rotting. You also want to look at the trees surrounding you. The fallen tree may have died and there may be other dead trees around that could be a hazard. When checking a cliff or overhang, you should inspect for cracks in the rock or loose easily disturbed dirt in a dirt overhang. Another thing to understand is that if you use fire near a rock cliff, similar to using fire on a moist rock, the heat could cause it to expand rapidly which may cause some of the overhang to break off and fall making it a hazard. In caves, there is the potential of fallen rocks as well as flooding and poor air quality. Caves are damp and moist, and therefore, they are breeding grounds for fungi and bacteria. Caves can also have a buildup of carbon dioxide. When inhaled, these fungi, bacteria, and carbon dioxide can all cause different issues, so monitoring yourself is paramount. Caves are a catch 22 situation, as they can provide good shelter, but there are so many potential

risks that you really have to consider your options. Stay near the entrance of any cave if you decide to take shelter in one and always stay alert.

In addition to natural shelters and frames, you may also stumble across man-made structures. In the average survival situation, there are few places that a person will venture that someone else at some point in time has not gone. This may mean that there are some remnants or remains of a structure. I have been on several hikes where I have come across old abandon cabins, concrete buildings, or walls. Although often times not complete structures, in an extreme situation they could be used to shield against wind, rain, or direct sun. They normally will not provide good insulative qualities, but can reduce your level of exposure. The obvious issue with these structures is that they are abandoned or dilapidated. Therefore, they have normally deteriorated to a point that they can be unstable. This can pose a great risk to you, and therefore, strong consideration and discernment should be used when deciding whether to use these locations.

BUILD IT

Photo: Sarah Bartell

The life of the Ninja was not one of abundance, but instead humble and meager resources. Therefore, they became adept at thinking outside the box as a necessity. Whereas Samurai would have an abundance of resources, the Ninjas lack of resources nurtured what came to be an abundance of resourcefulness.

If the clothes on your back are not enough to protect you and you cannot find or build up a natural feature within your environment to create shelter, then your next option is to build it completely from scratch. Because of the uncertainty of a survival situation's dynamic, I often focus on teaching people how to make a shelter with nothing but the landscape, and then we build from there. It is important that people understand how to properly construct from nothing for, in my opinion, this raises their confidence to a new level when they have items to use. However, the reverse is not the same. A person taught using unnatural materials will normally feel uncertain without those tools and may lack the creativity to see

the potential in the environment around them.

The road of building from nothing is not an easy one and, just to reiterate, if you can avoid it you want to, especially in a survival situation. Remember, this is not a fun survival camp or a by choice outing for growing your skill sets. This is an uncertain survival situation that abruptly interrupted your life and is a threat to your very existence. Everything at this point truly matters, so choose wisely. Knowing you need shelter is important, but not as important as the thought and energy that will go into the build. Making these decisions have to do with several factors which need to be considered. I call them the 4 Root Factors of conceptualization, and they are as follows:

- **Time – Jikan.**
- **Conditions – Joken.**
- **Landscape – Fukei.**
- **Positioning – Basho.**

Time

The importance of time cannot be understated. The amount of time you have before the sun goes down is paramount to your build as it will become extremely more difficult, if not impossible, to continue building during the night time. If you have a flashlight, trying to search for the proper materials will be difficult and if you do not have a light it will be nearly impossible. I would not recommend walking around with an improvised torch as ignited debris or material can fall from the torch and light the foliage below on fire. There is also the potential hazard of falling while carrying the torch which is also a danger for obvious reasons. If you are injured, searching about in the dark will increase the chances of new injury or further damaging your existing injury. There is one other very overlooked injury-producing factor: and that is there will be several nocturnal animals and critters lurking about. Some may see you as prey, and others may just be searching for insects or animal prey. Moving about could mean alerting hunting animals to your presence and digging through debris could easily set you up for a bite or sting from something lurking about in the brush or debris. This can be even more problematic if you cannot see the critter to identify it which could make it difficult, if not impossible to determine how to treat the wound.

Although dangerous to a person in a modern survival situation, the Ninja would feel at home in the darkness. For the same reasons that we would not want to work at night, the Samurai would normally avoid searching at night. This made it primetime for the Ninja to move

> **Like nocturnal animal hunting their resting prey. In this same way, the Ninja would use the night to his advantage, operating on an opposite schedule than the rest of the world gave him the element of surprise.**

around. Like nocturnal animal hunting their resting prey. In this same way, the Ninja would use the night to his advantage, operating on an opposite schedule than the rest of the world would give him the element of surprise.

Knowing not to build at night is one thing, and if you have a watch to tell you the time and when the sun will go down, you can plan for nighttime a lot easier than if you do not. However, if you do not have a clock, you will have to determine your time. One easy method of doing this without any materials is to use your hand and the sun. I call this the ***Hand Clock Method*** and it is important to note that I did not create this method of time telling. The steps for using the Hand Clock Method are:

1. Get to a place where you have a clear line of view between the sun and the ground.

2. Place your hand up palm facing you with all fingers extended, excluding the thumb.

3. Start with your pinky at the horizon and place the other hand where the pinky will sit directly above the pointer finger.

4. Follow this process until you reach the sun.

5. Each finger represents 15 minutes; therefore, one hand represents an hour.

6. The number of fingers you can fit in the space between the ground and the sun will determine the time before sundown.

It is important to note that this is not an exact science as with most things in the survival realm. As people's bodies are different, so are their finger sizes and this obviously will distort your numbers. Also, if you are using the top of a ridge or mountain as your base, you may not have a clear understanding of the height from the sun to the ground on the other side of the mountain, and therefore, you can only guesstimate. You will have to account for being off by 30 minutes or more, but this method is better than not having any idea. It is always best to plan for less time than to plan for more.

Now that we have explained how to determine time without a watch and why nighttime shelter building could be a serious detriment, let us discuss how this fact would affect our choice of shelter category. There are two main shelter category types, which are *short term and long term*. The factors that will dictate choosing to construct one over the other is the amount of time you have, the resources that you have available, the environment, and the length of time that you believe you will have to stay in that location.

Short-term (Immediate shelter)

When time is low, and the risk of exposure is high, a short-term shelter is the normal go to method. It is common knowledge that if you are lost or stranded you should try to stay in one location and wait for rescue. As rescuers look for you, it could make it more problematic if you continually change your location. However, this does not mean that there are times that you may want to change locations. To clearly explain the concept of why use a

> **When time is low, and the risk of exposure is high, a short-term shelter is the normal go to method.**

> **Short term shelters are meant to solve short-term problems. As they are normally created in a short timeframe during unexpected circumstances, short-term shelters will often not provide a high quality of protection and will not stand the test of time.**

short-term shelter, let's use the scenario that you are lost, and have tried to find your way back to safety, but it's late in the day. You use your watch, or the hand method of telling time with your fingers described earlier, and you realize the sun will be gone soon. You may realize that you are not in the best location for a shelter, but due to the time constraints, you have to start building where you are or you are going to have a night of unprotected exposure to the elements. This is a situation that I was in while on one of my extreme survival challenges. My partner and I were dropped off in the mountains of India where we only had 3 hours to build a shelter that would help us survive the night. We also had no shoes which slowed us down tremendously (as it mimicked an injury). We needed something that would get us through the night, but we knew the next day we would have to make something that was much more sustainable. In this scenario, I described the factors that went into deciding to build a short-term shelter.

Short-term shelters are not meant to protect you for long periods of time and, in most cases as the name suggests, they are just temporary. I often say short-term shelters are meant to solve short-term problems. As they are normally created in a short timeframe during unexpected circumstances, short-term shelters will often not provide a high quality of protection and will not stand the test of time. They do have the potential to become long-term shelters if you decide your location has the requirements to be a good spot to wait for rescue. If this is determined, you would then

> **Think of short-term shelters as hotels or motels, yes you can live in them for a long period of time, but that is not their primary function nor is it ideal. Short-term shelters are essentially transient temporary shelters.**

begin to enhance and fortify your shelter to ensure it gives you the proper protection from the elements. Think of short-term shelters as hotels or motels, yes you can live in them for a long period of time, but that is not their primary function nor is it ideal. Short-term shelters are essentially transient temporary shelters.

Long-term Shelter

The second type of shelter is a Long-term shelter. Your home or apartment is an example. This is a little more elaborate when you are building as it will require more thought and materials to properly build. The goal of the long-term shelter is to give you enough protection and comfort so that you can survive until rescue. Think about the planning and resources that go into a semi-permanent move versus a short visit. This is the mindset you should have when building a long-term shelter. Your shelter should be in a location that will have good resources for the build as well as

> **The second type of shelter is a Long-term shelter. Your home or apartment is an example. This is a little more elaborate when you are building as it will require more thought and materials to properly build. The goal of the long-term shelter is to give you enough protection and comfort so that you can survive until rescue. Think about the planning and resources that go into a semi-permanent move versus a short visit.**

your sustainability. Sustainability will consist of things like drinking water, fuel for your fire, etc. In the survival challenge I mentioned in the short-term shelter section, my partner and I stripped our short-term shelter and built a long-term shelter closer to water and in a place near rocks that we used to build a chimney. We were dealing with extreme night temperatures in the high 30's and we had no clothing. We knew we had to build something that would keep the rain and cold air out, the heat in, and something that would be comfortable enough for us to move around in but not so spacious that it would require excessive energy to heat. We lived 18 days in that shelter before we moved to an extraction point.

Condition

When it comes to survival, the word "condition" is a loaded one. This is because there are several factors in which it could refer to.

First is your condition. How healthy are you at the time you decide to build a shelter? Are you dehydrated; do you have an injured limb, and if so, is it a leg or arm? If it is a leg injury, it will hinder your mobility whereas an arm or hand injury will affect your ability to manipulate and carry.

Second, is the condition of the environment. Is it cold, hot, wet and cold, etc.?

Third, is what is the condition of the living environment? Are there animals that are a threat to you, or is there a particular insect that likes to lurk at night looking for a warm living organism to investigate? I remember being in a survival class where a person partaking in the challenge woke up in pain due to a scorpion sting received after the scorpion crawled into their debris hut. When dealing with a short-term shelter you may not have time to address all of these, however, when building a long-term shelter you will want to think through as many of these as possible. The conditions that exist in your survival situation will vary, but use the A.D.A.P.T. method to decide the best course of action and continue to evaluate your choices as you move through your build.

Landscape

The materials in the landscape around you will be a strong influential factor in what type of shelter you can build. After properly assessing the time you have, type of shelter to build, the condition of the environment, and your mental and physical condition, next you will have to determine what type of material you can use in your build. It is important to assess this properly as I have personally been in a situation where I thought I was going to have enough material only to fall short towards completion. This is not something you want to happen while you are in a survival situation. When calories and water are sparse, possibly dealing with an injury, and the threat of a night exposed to the elements, the last thing you want is to do a lot of work only to realize you cannot finish. Depending on what you choose to build, always determine what you think you need and add on twice as much. If you do not see the proper amount of material in your immediate area then choose a different type of shelter or look for another area. However, it is important to reiterate my saying "Survival is not Perfect, it's Survival." This means that you may not have enough time to find another location or build the ideal shelter, and thus, you may have to go with what you can make with what you have.

When calories and water are sparse, possibly dealing with an injury, and the threat of a night exposed to the elements, the last thing you want is to do a lot of work only to realize you cannot finish.

Positioning

When building a good short-term or long-term shelter, be sure to carefully consider positioning. Not just where you choose to put your shelter but how you choose to place it is important to the functionality as well as its ability to be distinguishable by those searching for you. Proper positioning will help make a shelter insulated, comfortable and secure for your survivability. For the Ninja, shelter positioning was broken down into 3 primary categories, which were:

- **Location (Foundation) – Jiban no basho.**
- **Visibility – Kashi.**
- **Direction – Hoko.**

For the Ninja on a mission, the location of their shelter was important because it would need to be in a place that deterred searching or inquisitive enemy scouts. The Ninja also wanted his shelter to be hidden or camouflaged in the natural landscape as a means of hiding in plain sight. The more it could look like a part of the natural environment the better. When I was in the army Survival School, this was known as a hide site. Lastly, the Ninja would want his shelter to face in the direction of the wind as it would allow him to smell potential threats better. In addition, this would also allow him to hear better as sound waves travel faster with the wind, giving him the potential to be alerted to his adversary sooner. As discussed earlier, these were methods of the Goton-Po whereby using Dotonjutsu, an understanding of terrain to deter his enemy, and Mokutonjutsu, the use of vegetation to conceal or deter investigation into a particular area.

On the opposite spectrum, the person trying to survive would have a different motive than that of a Ninja, and would use the same understanding but to his or her benefit based on wanting to survive long enough to be found or find help. Therefore, the shelter would not be hidden or facing in wind. Remember in the Ninja dynamic of survival, staying hidden more often than not meant survival, but in a modern survival scenario staying hidden is counterproductive.

Location, location, location is the name of the game when it comes to building a good shelter. You do not have to be a survivalist to know what are some of the key considerations you should account for when it comes to choosing the proper location. Just look at modern society. When choosing a place to live, we often look for places that are close to resources (near stores that provide essentials), safe from predators (good neighborhoods away from crime), low instances of natural disasters (places not prone to floods, storms, etc.) and places not prone to accidental disasters (areas with dilapidated infrastruc-

> **Location, location, location is the name of the game when it comes to building a good shelter. You do not have to be a survivalist to know what are some of the key considerations you should account for when it comes to choosing the proper location.**

ture that present potential hazards). The Ninja called determining the location of building a shelter in a way to keep it protected from specific threats as *Hogo*. As I mentioned before, man is, for the most part, the same as we were in the ancient days, and therefore, there are certain needs that we cannot transcend. We can look into our modern city or suburban lives and see clues of what we need to ensure our survival. However, even though we have clues around us, education is still important. For a more technical way to determine a proper location for building a shelter, here are four of the first determinations one must make before settling on a particular build site:

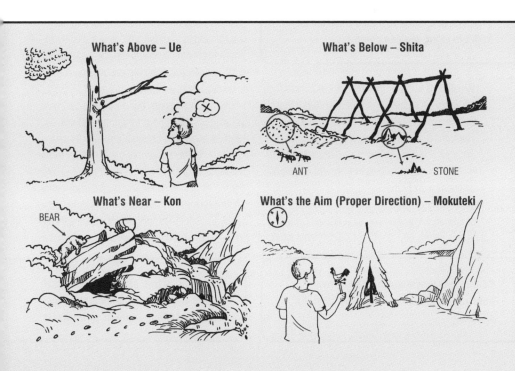

What's Above – Ue

What's Below – Shita

ANT   STONE

What's Near – Kon

BEAR

What's the Aim (Proper Direction) – Mokuteki

These 4 factors easily recalled as A.B.N.A. (Ab-Nah) are the main considerations that will aid in building a proper survival shelter that should serve 2 main focuses, which are to keep you alive and to get you found. Here is a brief explanation of each of these 4 factors:

What's Above – Ue

– Be sure not to build in a location under or in the path of a dying or dead tree. The tree or its limbs can break off and fall on you or your shelter. A secondary consideration is to make sure your shelter is visible from the sky. Since we are discussing survival, it is important you build in a location that is easy to see from the sky if you can control it. However, you may be in a location that has a thick canopy and this is not possible. As a side note, you may want to find a spot near your shelter location that is more open in which you can set up a signal for rescue.

> A secondary consideration is to make sure your shelter is visible from the sky. Since we are discussing survival, it is important you build in a location that is easy to see from the sky if you can control it.

What's Below – Shita

– As discussed earlier, what is below you is also important. Building on an insect mound can be a mistake you cannot recover from. Sweep and clear the area first before building. Another consideration is to ensure that the ground is free of vegetation and other debris as well as being level. Often overlooked is how disruptive it can be to have the head of a deeply buried rock sticking up into the middle of your shelter, hindering your ability to sit or lay comfortably. In addition, being on uneven or slanted ground can impede your rest, especially since many people are used to sleeping on flat areas. Comfortability within your shelter will help you de-stress in an already stressful situation. The Ninja recognized this importance of having comfort within a shelter and called it *Anraku*.

What's Near – Kon

– Another strong determining factor of shelter location is to properly evaluate what is near it. Waterways are one of the main aspects to consider. Think about the swell, rising, and receding of the tide. If your shelter is too close to a waterway it can flood your location in strong rain or with the rising of the tide. The same is true of areas where flash floods are common. Look around for signs of rushing water or watermarks. Also, be aware that the closer you are to water the more likely you are to have an encounter with the wildlife as they will also be coming to the water to drink and, in some cases, looking for potential prey. This also goes for animal trails. If you are near a well-traveled animal trail, you are likely to encounter wildlife. When dealing with caves, cliffs, or steep rocky hills ensure you are not in an area that is prone to falling or sliding rocks. Setting up on the top of hills can give you more visibility but could subject you to more exposure to the elements like the sun, rain, and wind. Wind chill can drop the temperature 15-30 degrees as well as blow away pieces of your shelter. Since colder air sinks and heat rises at the base of mountains or in valleys it will get colder at night as the cooler air collects at the lowest level.

> Comfortability within your shelter will help you de-stress in an already stressful situation.

> The same is true of areas where flash floods are common. Look around for signs of rushing water or watermarks.

What's the Aim (Direction) –

Mokuteki – The direction your shelter is facing is also another important consideration. The Ninja would want to face their shelter openings with the wind so that they could hear potential threats lurking about. Although this can also be important in a modern survival situation in regard to potential predators, it is more important to focus on facing your shelter away from the wind in order to protect from exposure to the cold. Placing your shelter in the proper direction can enhance comfortability and decrease harmful exposure. Another consideration is sun exposure as

> It is more important to focus on facing your shelter away from the wind in order to protect from exposure to the cold. Placing your shelter in the proper direction can enhance comfortability and decrease harmful exposure.

facing your shelter east will give you immediate sun at dawn. Another advantage is that although storms can come from any direction, in the U.S. they most often travel from west to east.

THE 4 QUALITIES OF A GOOD SHELTER – YOI HINANSHO NO YOTTSU NO SHISHITSU

If you are in a survival situation, things are already bad and the last thing you want to do is make them worse. Therefore, I am a big proponent of making sure I take the extra care to do things right in the timeframe I have for building a shelter. Overlooking important details in your build is a sure way to make a bad situation worse and take a major hit to your moral in the process. No one wants to be

> If you are in a survival situation, things are already bad and the last thing you want to do is make them worse. Therefore, I am a big proponent of making sure I take the extra care to do things right in the timeframe I have for building a shelter. Overlooking important details in your build is a sure way to make a bad situation worse and take a major hit to your moral in the process.

hunkered down in a shelter when the temperature drops, a rainstorm begins and then you find out you should have spent more time on making it windproof and waterproof. I personally have lived this, and it will literally make you want to punch yourself, because not only will the suffering be bad, but mentally knowing that you could have done something about it will really destroy your will. To avoid this, understand your environment and plan well for the unexpected. Ensure that you have a quality shelter with the time and resources you have available. There are 4 main qualities I focus on when making a good shelter, and they are:

Waterproofing – Making sure your shelter can shed water is important. This can be done with thick layers of vegetation stacked on your shelter frame at least 2 to 3 feet thick starting from the bottom of the shelter and working your way up like shingles. This is normally done with dead loose vegetation or with living broader leaf vegetation. On slanted roofs, it is always good to have a 45–60-degree slope if possible, to both provide cover and proper rain shedding.

Windproofing – Some mistake this as the same a waterproofing, but it may not always be the case. For instance, waterproofing with leaves could protect against water but not when it comes to the wind as high winds could blow the leaves away. Therefore, in addition to having lots of leaves to resist water and air permeability, you may also want to add sticks and twigs to keep the wind from blowing away the leaves.

Climate control – Like any good house, a good shelter will be able to retain or dissipate heat.

Ground insulation – In addition to insulation above, a good shelter will also have good insulation covering the ground where you will sit or lay. This is important as the ground can pull the heat out of your body through the process of conduction.

YOUR BODY AS A TEMPLE/TEMPLATE

The Ninja saw a reflection of themselves in nature and all aspects of nature in themselves. As mentioned earlier, this served as a guide for them during operations. I have found this to hold true even in shelter building. Using the design of the body as a way to remember how to build a shelter was a trick, I learned from my Ninja training, but I have found it serves others well in helping them to remember how to construct a proper shelter. Using the heart, spine, ribs, muscle/fat and skin, a person in a survival situation has a perfect concept for how to remember the needs and the design of a quality shelter. Each of the above body parts can be linked to a piece of a shelter in the following way:

- **Heart** – The heart symbolizes the human being in the shelter as it is housed within the body structure and is protected by it.
- **Spine** – The spine symbolizes the ridgepole or center pole of the shelter in which all the other pieces of the shelter rely on to maintain structural integrity and stability.
- **Ribs and Skeletal System** – The ribs and skeletal system is symbolic of the frame which makes up the walls and roof of a shelter.
- **The Muscles and Fat** – The muscles and fat of the body are symbolic of the insulation of a shelter. The leaves and bows that allow your shelter to retain heat and keep you protected from the conduction of the earth help to maintain your core temperature like the muscles and fat of the body.
- **The Skin** – The skin is symbolic of the waterproofing qualities of a tarp, bark, or banana leaf (or another broadleaf) on the roof of your shelter.

Your Body as a Temple & Shelter
TEMPLATE

Heart

The heart symbolizes the human being in the shelter as it is housed within the body structure and is protected by it.

Spine

The spine symbolizes the ridgepole or center pole of the shelter in which all the other pieces of the shelter rely on to maintain structural integrity and stability

Ribs and Skeletal System

The ribs and skeletal system is symbolic of the frame which makes up the walls and roof of a shelter.

The Muscles and Fat

The muscles and fat of the body are symbolic of the insulation of a shelter.

The Skin

The skin is symbolic of the waterproofing qualities of a tarp, bark, or banana leaf (or another broadleaf) on the roof of your shelter.

Following your own body as a guide helps in the recall of important features of a shelter build. Because most people have a basic understanding of these parts of the human body, retention of this information is easy and efficient.

BASIC SHELTER CONSTRUCTION TYPES – SHURUI

The mind is one thing people will always have with them. If you can teach people how to understand their needs and how to satisfy their needs based on what is around them, they have a better chance of always being prepared. This is because you prepare their mind and hearts.

As with all methods presented in this book following with the concept of the Ninja lesson of applicable knowledge that is versatile, effective, efficient, and requiring minimum material, I focus on teaching how to do more with little to nothing. Taking into consideration that it is not enough to just be prepared by having the proper gear and believing people will follow that guidance, I would rather teach as though the person will not heed my words of gear and equipment preparation. After years of teaching, I can tell you that people more often than not know they should be prepared, but they do not always make it a priority to get or carry what they need the whole time. Often, people rescued from survival situations were reported as being underprepared or, in some cases, did not know how to use the gear they had or even forgot they had it on them. So, if preparation in regards to gear is not the answer to how people can better be prepared, what is? I believe it is to empower the mind. The mind is one thing people will always have with them. If you can teach people how to understand their needs and how to satisfy their needs based on what is around them, they have a better chance of always being prepared. This is because you prepare their mind and hearts. This is very evident with shelter building. As discussed in an earlier chapter, exposure to extreme elemental conditions can kill you in 3 hours or less. A shelter is the one thing that most mammals are capable of constructing with minimal resources as a means to ensure survival, whereas the same cannot be said for many of the other aspects of survival. Squirrels cannot start fires, purify water, nor bandage injuries, but they can build a nest to survive through extreme conditions. The Ninja method of shelter building would simply be to build it quickly and efficiently based on the natural resources surrounding him. In this spirit, there are 4 types of shelters that I believe are easy and effective for helping a person survive. These 4 shelters are:

1. Cocoon or Nest Shelter.
2. A-Frame Shelter.
3. Lean-To Shelter.
4. Wikiup Shelter.

Squirrels cannot start fires, purify water, nor bandage injuries, but they can build a nest to survive through extreme conditions.

Using the guidelines from the 4 root factors (time, condition, location, and position), a person can normally find that one of these four shelters will be suitable and easy to construct in a wilderness location. After choosing whether to make a long-term or short-term shelter based on a proper evaluation of your condition and the conditions around you, choose one of the following and begin.

Cocoon/Nest Shelter

This is one of the easiest shelters to construct as it requires few materials to build. The Cocoon Shelter is one that you can make with very limited time if you find yourself lost and the sun going down. You will not need poles or any type of structure for support, all you will need is loose or light vegetation. Collecting dead leaves, pine needles, bark, ferns, and dead grass are several examples of this. You will need to get enough material so that you can make a pile of it at least 3 to 4-feet tall,

5 to 6-feet wide, and 4-foot longer than you are tall. The reason for the excess material in width and length is to allow the insulation to extend well beyond the reach of your body. If you move or a gust of wind blows, you want to ensure that a piece of your body does not become exposed. Anyone in an urban or suburban community has seen this type of shelter during fall as it is the same as the huge pile of leaves you see on many people's lawn. Essentially, what you are creating is a giant sleeping bag or, as the name suggests, a cocoon or nest. To help fortify your cocoon you can add twigs and branches on top of it. This will provide weight and pressure to the top layer and eventually create a retaining layer that will help keep the top and side material from blowing away or sliding off when you move. Another way to add to the protective quality of this shelter is to try to construct it in front of a natural wind block (tree, boulder, mound) and under the canopy of a tree, which will help displace rain and assist in keeping it from

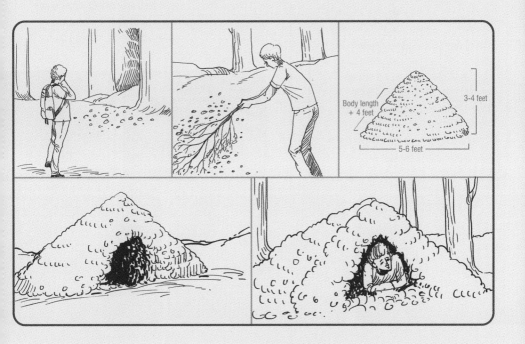

Nest Shelters

There are two ways to collect debris for building a shelter. One way is to use your feet to sweep debris into a pile and the other is to create a rake using a living small diameter sapling with three smaller branches extending from it in a pitchfork formation.

saturating your nest. Once your nest is built, you want to shimmy into it backward as a way to keep your face exposed. Make sure you have plenty of material below you so you can stay insulated from the ground. Remember that through conduction, the ground can absorb a lot of your heat.

One of the downsides of cocoon shelters is that it can require a lot of energy to collect the material. If you do not have a rake or jacket in which to compile the materials with or on so that you can move them to your location, then it may be best to build your shelter in a location that has all the materials around it. Doing this may mean you have to choose a location that may not be the best for building a comfortable shelter. If you have a mechanical injury, this can impede the process of walking back and forth or picking up loads of material. It is also important to stress extreme caution when digging through piles of vegetation as this is where critters will live and they may bite or sting your hands, thus making your situation worse. Because of this, it is also important that you tuck your pants into your socks and cover up as much exposed skin as possible when moving into this shelter. Even with the possible downside of extensive travel and movement, the cocoon shelter is still very effective to build when you have limited time and resources.

A-Frame Shelter (leaf or debris hut)

Second on my list of shelters to build is an A-frame shelter. I used a combination of an A-frame shelter and a cocoon shelter to survive 4 nights in the Himalayan mountains in high 30-degree weather with no clothes on. Through the insulative qualities of the debris I was nestled in and the protection from the rain the A-frame cover also provided. I had a more controlled environment in which to regulate my body temperature at a steady 98.6 degrees and that heat warmed the immediate area around me while the debris retained most of the warmth. Because of this, I was able to survive conditions that would have killed people with more than what I had.

An A-frame is shaped like an "A," hence the name. The shelter can be raised at both ends of the ridge pole/spine at the front and rear of the top of the "A," or one end of the ridge pole can be seated on the ground. Often times, the ridge pole of the A-frame shelter can be found in nature as a fallen or broken tree limb (this is discussed in the "Find It" section of this chapter). If you cannot find a naturally produced ridge pole in the environment, then you will have to create it.

Follow all the steps that we discuss in the location assessment section of the 4 Roots of Shelter building. After you do, you can begin building your shelter. Because of the need for fewer materials, we will discuss the building of an A-frame with one end of the ridge pole seated on the ground. This means that you will not need to find as many longer sticks to serve as the ribs/roof, and side framing of the shelter.

- Find a tree with a natural "V" or "Y" shaped opening in the trunks. If this is not available you can find 2 or 3 stout/ticker branches shaped like a "Y," and lean them against each other, interlocking the "Y"'s to create a tripod.

- Next, you will get a thick straight sapling or fallen tree that is about 2-4" in diameter, something similar in diameter to your shin and calf. It will also have to be several feet longer than you are tall. I normally allow 2-3' extra at the top of the pole above the head area for stabilizing on the support tree and still have at least a foot clearing between it and my head. I also allow 1-2' past my feet allowing for ease of movement while lying down. This is called your ridgepole/spine, and for me personally, a 9-11' ridgepole works well. It is important to check the strength of this pole once set into the "V" or "Y" shaped of your tree. Use your body weight by pressing or hanging from it. The ridgepole is the spine of your shelter and has to be as strong as possible as it will bear all of the weight. Sit your ridge pole at an angle that allows it to slope a foot away from your toes with you lying on your back. You do not want to kick it while moving in your shelter.

- After you have hung your ridgepole, you may want to take the opportunity to lay under it and mark the area that extends one foot beyond your shoulders. Draw this line all the way down to the end of the ridge pole. Now you should add your insulating layer to the ground. You can also add poles on the ground that follow the line as this will help keep your debris compiled much like a bed frame (I call these bedding poles). It is easier to do this now before

your shelter ribs are placed as they will restrict your movement.

- Next, gather straighter sticks that are 1-2" in diameter, half or the full size of the average wrist, that can be used as your shelter ribs (roof beams). Lay them on your ridgepole at a slope of 45 degrees so that they set a foot past the borders of your shoulders on each side or on the outside edge of the bedding poles.

- Start stacking them from front to back at an overlapping forward facing angle so they interlock. If you cannot find enough to completely cover both sides of your shelter, then you can use the weaving method to hold the few rib poles down. Then you can put twigs and smaller branches over the gaps before adding debris.

- After the gaps are full, you can now add the leaves or debris for exposure protection. Start from the bottom and build to the top. Continue to pile on roofing until it is at least 2-3 feet, the length of the tip of your middle finger to shoulder.

- It is optional, but you may want to make a door or find a piece of bark that can block the wind or help keep out the cold.

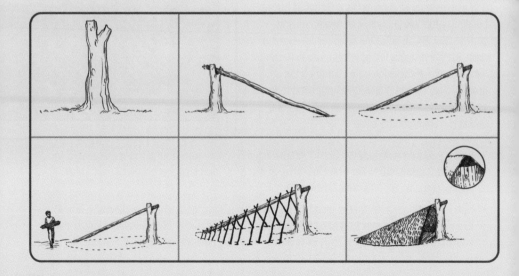

> *Be sure to close off one side of the shelter completely so that you only have one entryway. The only time you will not do this is if you need to entries for two people or if you want to make an area for the heat of your fire to move into without blocking your entrance.*

The downsides to an A-frame shelter are that it takes a lot of energy to gather bigger materials for a stable structure as well as the insulating materials. It is also not the safest when wanting to add fire. Lastly, this shelter impedes your senses because within it you have a limited field of vision, hearing is, and sense of smell.

Lean-To Shelter

Half of an A-frame shelter with both ends of the ridgepole off the ground is essentially a lean-to shelter. Basically, you would follow the steps of building a raised A-Frame Shelter but you would leave one side of the A-Frame exposed. The advantages of this are that it is quicker to build, but it also leaves you considerably exposed since it is open on one side. This shelter is good for hotter environments and warm wet environments where you just need to get out of the rain, wind, or direct sun. This shelter gives good air flow and allows you to use your senses a lot more effectively to look, listen, and smell for rescues and predators. With no added modern fortifications such as sleeping bags, Mylar/space blankets, etc. this shelter is not great for providing protection from the cold with the exception that a Lean-To does allow for the safer use of fire. Since the fire is exposed and away from the shelter it is less likely to catch the materials on fire. When a heat reflector wall is added, it further supports warmth in

colder environments even though the front of the shelter is open. Be mindful that if you use this method in a cold environment you will have to gather lots of both shelter and fire materials. In a situation where you may be injured or trying to conserve energy, this may work against you. This is a choice you have to make in your particular situation armed with the facts of your individual needs. The following are the proper steps to creating a proper lean-to shelter.

- Follow all the steps that we discuss in the location assessment section of the 4 Roots of Shelter building.

- Next find 2 trees that are directly across from each other and are 3-feet farther apart than you are wide (only if you will build the shelter long with your head at the front and your feet extending to the rear like an A-Frame), or 3' more apart than you are tall (if the shelter will accommodate you lying across between the 2 trees with 1 tree at your head and the other at your feet).

- Basing this build off the assumption of having limited resources, 2 natural ways to hang a ridgepole without cordage is to find 2 trees close to one another that might have a natural V-shape opening in the trunks. If this is not available, you can find 2 stout/ticker branches shaped like a "Y" and lean them against the 2 trees at a slight angle. Sharpen or angle the bottom of the Y-supports and press them securely in the ground to ensure their base does not slide when you apply the ridge pole and the ribs (roof beams).

- Next, you will get a thick straight sapling or fallen tree that is about 2-4" in diameter (something similar in diameter to your shin and calf). It will also have to be several feet longer than you are tall. I normally allow 2-3' extra at the top of the pole, above the head area for stabilizing on the support tree and still having at least a foot clearing between my head and the support tree. I also allow 1-2' past my feet allowing for ease of movement while lying down. This is called your ridgepole/spine and for me personally, a 9-11' ridge pole works well. It is important to check the strength of this pole once set into the "V" or "Y" shaped of your tree. Use your body weight by pressing or hanging from it. The ridge pole is the spine of your shelter and has to be as strong as possible as it will bear all the weight of your shelter. Sit your ridgepole at an angle that allows it to slope a foot away from your toes with you lying on your back. You do not want to kick it while moving in your shelter.

- After you have hung your ridgepole you will gather straighter sticks that are 1-2" in diameter (half of the full size of the average wrist), that can be used as your shelter ribs

(roof beams). Lay them on your ridge pole at a slope of at least 60 degrees. You will need enough shelter ribs that can give you an even spread across the beam. In the interest of time and possible injury, I suggest an odd number of shelter ribs/roofing beam branches and then using long thin living branches, at least ½" in diameter, to weave in-between the shelter ribs using the "over and under." This is a simple plain weave to help create rigidity in the structure keeping the rib branches in place. Do this with an even spread from the top of the shelter to the bottom.

- At this point, placing your bedding material is a good idea so that you can get the material to the far back of the shelter by reaching through the shelter ribs. Place a bedding pole in the front of the shelter and along the sides of the shelter, and then stack a pile of debris in this frame.

- Next place twigs and smaller branches over the gaps of the shelter ribs so they create a mess like covering over the holes.

- After the gaps are full, add the leaves or debris for exposure protection. Start from the bottom and build to the top. Continue to pile on roofing until it is at least 2-3' thick on the shelter ribs, the length of the tip of your middle finger to your bicep or shoulder.

- Now that you have exposure protection, you can begin your fortification by gathering fire materials, building a fire pit and a reflector wall.

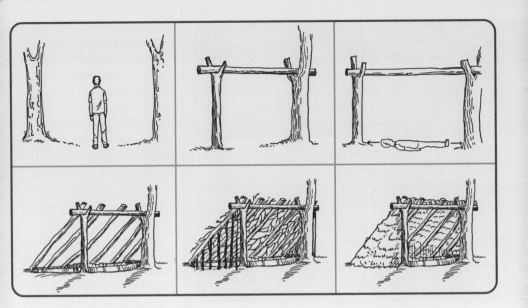

Wickiup Shelter

Out of the 4 shelters, the wickiup shelter although easy to construct when healthy, it can be difficult, energy consuming, and therefore inefficient if you have an injury or limited natural resources
in your surrounding area. Essentially, a wickiup is a tepee style shelter which, in its primitive form,
can be made primarily from longer poles/sticks. Often, they are made by placing sticks in a circle
with a wide base and weaving
them at the top so they lock
into one another creating a
cone-like shape. The best
way to start this process
is to find three poles with a
Y-shape, cut them and interlock the tops together making a tripod shape. Once the
tripod structure is together,
dig a hole for each foot. Next,
check the structure to see if it
can support your weight, lean
longer straighter poles around
the tripod. You will leave a
small triangle-shaped opening
for the door and then insulate
it the same way you would
the A-frame or lean-to shelter.
Wickiups can be made using

Finding three poles with a Y-shape

Making a tripod shape

Digging a hole for each foot

Checking the structure

Leaning poles around the tripod

Placing debris

An opening for the door

Bedding

less structural poles, but you would still need to use the weaving method mentioned in the lean-to shelter section to ensure structural integrity, and then the twig method to ensure that your debris has surface to rest on so it will not fall through an opening. Once you have your structure and twig shell you will place debris starting from the bottom and moving to the top. Lastly you will add debris for bedding on the inside boundaries of the shelter until the bedding layer is to a suitable thickness.

As I mentioned the Wickiup is a good shelter but it can be demanding without lots of natural resources or minimal artificial materials. For this reason, I do not often recommend it as a go-to in an unexpected survival situation.

Keep in mind that with all shelters you want to ensure they are not too tall or too short. The goal is to have it high enough for you to crawl into and sit-up comfortably and to provide enough slope for water shedding. Like a modern house the bigger the square footage the harder to manage climate control.

Keep in mind that with all shelters you want to ensure they are not too tall or too short. The goal is to have it high enough for you to crawl into and sit-up comfortably and to provide enough slope for water shedding. Like a modern house the bigger the square footage the harder to manage climate control. Not only can our bodies generate heat, but in a small enough space we can heat our surrounding environment. The same goes for using a fire, the bigger the space and the further away, the harder it will be to heat.

SHELTER FORTIFICATIONS

With all of the shelters mentioned above, you can add fire to the equation to fortify the thermoregulatory capabilities. However, you have to keep in mind that you are essentially in a big tinder box, and therefore, one floating ember or coal shooting out of the fire as a result of wood popping, and you could be trapped in a flaming prison. It is often recommended that a fire is placed at least 10 feet from a shelter, but in my experience, even with a reflector wall, in a cold environment getting enough heat to stay warm is hard at this distance unless you have a big fire, which is a lot of work. Also having a bigger fire would defeat the purpose of having the fire 10 feet from your shelter as the size would produce more embers that are hotter and can travel further.

Finally, another highly overlooked aspect of shelter is security. This is not a required aspect, but it is one that can be useful in protecting you from annoying or dangerous pests in a short-term situation and potential predators in a long-term survival situation. In the short-term scenario using ash from a fire to surround the outside of your shelter and the inside perimeter will deter many pests from entering your shelter. I mentioned putting it on the inside perimeter to protect the ash from

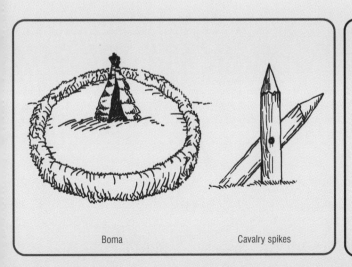

Boma   Cavalry spikes

Cavalry spikes, also called Cheval de frise, are x-shaped spiked structures that can be placed around the perimeter of your shelter to help deter curious or deadly predators. These can be made by sharpening sticks and placing them, with the point facing out, around your shelter.

washing away in the rain. For bigger predators one method that worked well for early man was the use of thorn bushes or vines to encircle their sleeping or shelter areas in concentric rings. This structure was known a boma and it is still used in Africa today (these can be taxing to make as the spikes will often stab and cut the handler). If thorn bushes are not available another method used during war time to deter cavalry was the use of cavalry spikes, also called Cheval de frise. These are x-shaped spiked structures that can be placed around the perimeter of your shelter to help deter curious or deadly predators. They can be made by sharpening sticks and placing them, with the point facing out, around your shelter. I do not recommend this type of barrier for short-term shelters, but if the threat of big predators is high, they should be considered in a long-term stay-in-place scenario. The issue with this is that they take time and calorie consumption to build. One should carefully weigh the potential choice of adding this to their list of to-dos in a survival situation.

CHAPTER 5

FUNDAMENTALS OF SURVIVAL FIRE

CHAKKA

The Ninja saw no object or methods that would assist him in accomplishing his task as "off limits." Survival was of the utmost importance because his continued operation meant the survival of his community. Therefore, Ninja would often equip themselves with the tools they would specifically need to survive. Much in the same way, the modern outdoor enthusiast should also make sure they bring with them the tools and gear they feel they would need if things went wrong. Since it was first harnessed hundreds of thousands of years ago, fire has been an important aspect of survival. The controlled and repeated use of it has even been credited with aiding in aspects of man's behavioral and biological evolution. Fire undoubtedly serves many purposes as it allows for cooking, purifying water, providing warmth, light, and security. Fire is not always essential to every survival situation. Sometimes there are situations that dictate that you do not need it, for instance, if the weather conditions allow for stable thermoregulation or if you are injured in a way that hinders movement or you are trying to conserve energy. Keeping a fire going the whole night takes a lot of resources and energy. Hobbling or running around trying to gather enough firewood to last the night will burn a lot of valuable calories, as well as increase the chances of further injury or cause one. Another reason you may not need fire is that you may have access to fresh water, and thus, you will not need to purify any. Even though you may not always need it, which is evident by the fact that man survived for many years without it, fire does play an important part in the fortification of one's survivability especially if it is a long-term survival situation.

I have people survive overnight on their own. While preparing, I watched people scramble to gather firewood and not get enough tender and small kindling material to start it before the sun went down. I have also had students stay awake all night attending to a fire in moderately cool weather only to find themselves exhausted the next day and incapable of performing at a high level. Survival is a series of fluctuating circumstance that requires an open, flexible, and clear-thinking mind. It also requires a capable body. For this, you have to reason based on your particular circumstances. I never teach that fire is a must in my classes, just like I do not always teach that shelter is a must. It always depends on 3 factors:

1. The circumstances.
2. Your needs (physically, emotionally and mentally).
3. Your capabilities.

Always weigh these carefully and always be conservative. For example, if you know rain is coming and you do not have the experience or physical capability due to injury or fatigue to keep a fire going and there is nothing to shelter a fire, then it is probably not a good idea to build one. However, if you are in the same circumstances and there is a cliff overhang, you can set up under it, then maybe, building the fire is a good option.

For the sake of this chapter, let us say your circumstances, needs and capabilities dictate that fire is something to have. It is important to know that, "The less you have to do under

As with all aspects of survival, it is important to truly understand your situation and what your needs are. I have often hosted classes where

Fire is not always essential to every survival situation.

Survival is a series of fluctuating circumstance that requires an open, flexible, and clear-thinking mind.

Me teaching some youth how hard it is to keep a flame going in the rain.

duress, the more likely you are to have success." This is another one of my personal quotes, and the point is based on some of the human responses to stress we discussed in Chapter 1. Simply put "Survival is Survivable when it is Simple." Just to reiterate, having the proper equipment will always be better than having to start from scratch. Provided of course you know how to use the equipment. Following this principle, when it comes to fire the first and foremost step is to always have a modern means of fire starting with you. No matter what you are doing outdoors, you should have a lighter, a pack of waterproof matches, and a ferrocerium rod (fire steel), or if you really recognize the importance of having a good fire when you need it, you should carry all three. In addition, having good tender material is also paramount for supporting

fire as it moves to its next phase of growth. Unfortunately, having all of these things does not guarantee fire production in the wild. I have hosted many classes where I run a simple ten-minute fire-starting drill, and people fail all the time. For the drill, I give a person or a group a waterproof match and ask them to gather materials and start a fire, then sustain it for one minute with what they collected during the collection and preparation phase.

"Survival is Survivable
when it is Simple."

"It's not how much you have,
but how you use what you know."

It is rare that I have had the majority of the group succeed. Often the people run around gathering the wrong types of material from all the wrong locations. They then set their firebase up in a way that will not support the proper fire growth based on its behavior, and then they struggle to get the fire going or keep it going for up to a minute. This is a perfect example of how having good tools at your disposal does not mean that success is guaranteed. I hope you are getting this point as I have now talked about it several times in this book. Another one of my personal maxims is, "It's not how much you have, but how you use what you know." The best way to prepare yourself is to always be thinking about what I call the Three Tenets of Preparedness:

- **Knowledge first** – How do things work, what can keep it from working, and how to fix it.
- **Application second** – How do I get what I need to make it work, how do I make it work.
- **Gear last** – Prepare with equipment that can help you achieve success easily in multiple tasks but know how to repair and create similar equipment when needed.

Are you getting the repeating message of, "You can have everything you need and still fail?" This lesson also highlights the impact stress has on being methodical and using good reasoning skills. In addition, students learn how the conditions in the wild can impact their fire making potential. Wet conditions decrease the chances of finding material dry enough to burn, cold conditions make it difficult to manipulate the material and fire-starting devices (flicking a lighter, striking a match, etc.), and fading light without the aid of a flashlight makes it difficult to see materials for processing, organizing and igniting.

As you have noticed with other processes within this book, I like to use the Ninja methods of relational learning as a means to teach and help participants retain information. Therefore, I relate growing fire to stages of human growth. The one thing all people have knowledge of is how people grow and, on a foundational level, what people need to grow. In my classes, I teach youth to adults, and they have all been able to learn and retain my methods of teaching based on this presentation. In the human life cycle, there are 4 commonly known stages of development. These stages are:

1. **Infancy** – At this stage, humans are totally dependent on caregivers and they have restrictive and specific dietary needs.
2. **Childhood** – In this stage, human beings begin to develop independence and the character traits of self-confidence to aid in exploration and growth as they explore how to operate in the world.
3. **Adolescence** – At this stage of human development, youth begin going through physical changes and they begin to find their identity. The exploration of their identity grows their independence and confidence as they recognize their ability to influence the world around them.
4. **Adulthood** – At this stage of human development, a person is mostly self-sustaining but operates in more of a symbiotic relationship with the community and environment around them. They influence the environment and the environment influences and provides for them.

In each of these stages, the human being grows more resilient and capable of operating on their own. In a similar way, a fire can be related to these stages. In my survival program, I have developed a list based on these stages of development with one additional stage. These stages help in giving a clear understanding of fire development for easy recall and sustainable success. The 5 stages of progression are:

1. **Conception** – This is the stage of bringing the necessary elements together to achieve an initial spark and ember.
2. **Infancy** – Is the stage of birthing a flame and the initial feeding of that flame with a tinder bundle.
3. **Childhood** – At this stage, the flame grows to an intermediate size where it can burn wire to pencil size kindling, but is still fragile.
4. **Adolescence** – This is the point of growth where the flame can burn thicker fuel and becomes more stable. It is fragile and can still easily be extinguished, but it can provide the essentials of warmth, light, and can be used for cooking and purifying water.
5. **Adulthood** – This is the stage of the flame where it is big enough, hot enough, and strong enough to operate in a symbiotic style relationship with the individual using it for surviving. Very little attention is needed at this phase as a person just needs to add fuel at a slow but consistent rate.

The Five Stages of Development as I call them are a good overview of how to grow a fire from heat to flame. However, as I said, these are just a general overview. With each stage of development, there are sub stages that contain their own process and are essential in understanding how fire operates, and thus, how to create it. I call these steps the 6 Fire Building Essentials, and they are:

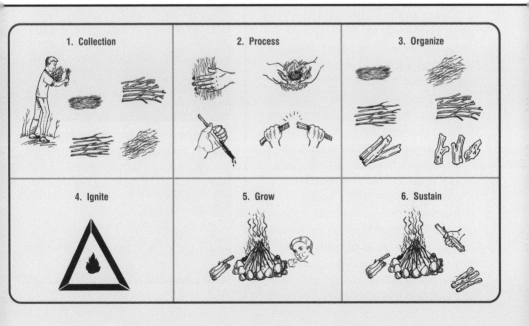

COLLECTING MATERIALS – ZAIRYO ATSUMERU

In the Collection stage, you will need to be able to identify and gather what materials you need to start a good fire. I teach that there are 4 collection focuses on building a fire during a survival situation. Of the 4, 2 are optional while the others are mandatory. These 4 stages of material collection are:

> 1. Friction Fire Kit Material – Masatsu hi no zairyo atsumeru
>
> 2. Gathering Tinder Material – Doka-sen no zairyo atsumeru
>
> 3. Gathering Kindling Material – Maki no zairyo atsumeru
>
> 4. Gathering Fuel Material – Nenryo no zairyo atsumeru

The first 2 stages I list are optional because, as I mentioned in an earlier chapter, some causes for a survival situation are people getting lost, stranded, and injured. In many of these cases, people had items with them as they were trekking in the wild or site seeing. The chances are these individuals have some sort of fire starter (match, lighter, ferrocerium rod) and basic tinder, but there is a chance that they do not or maybe these items were lost or damaged. In one story I remember reading, an adventurous hiker decided to lay down his bag and go for a run to a scenic overlook. He thought he marked his bag well but when he tried to return to it he could not find it. This would be an example of the importance of knowing how to gather the materials for a friction fire kit and tinder is. We will discuss how to make a friction fire kit

later, but for now we will focus on the means of collecting materials for the three primary stages of building a fire.

Tinder

If you do not have a modern tinder product such as tinder tabs, your first step will be to collect good tinder for your tinder bundle. Good tinder is material that is light, fluffy and can easily be set to flame by a spark or smoldering ember. Materials such as dry grass, certain types of inner and outer tree bark, and different dry and fluffy weed tops make good tinder.

important to note that certain plants like poison ivy, oak, and sumac, even if dead and dry, should not be handled or burned in a tinder bundle as the smoke can be hazardous. Bird's nests are great examples of tinder as they are dry bundles of dead leaves, grass, and plants. The bird's nest design also makes for a good fire-starting resource as the indent in the nest used to hold the egg creates a good pocket for shooting a spark or placing an ember. It is a good technique to set up a tinder bundle in this way even if you do not have an actual bird's nest. As a final note, if you cannot find dead grass making a feather or fuzz stick out of the inner bark of a branch or scrapping fine shaving off of it are good options to try. It is important to note that any branch that is wet will have to be shaved to remove the wet outer layer first.

It is important that you gather tinder from high areas. Tinder material absorbs moisture easily and the ground retains moisture, therefore, gathering from the ground means that you will be gathering material that may also be moist. By gathering high, you are likely to get materials that have had the opportunity to be dried because of minimally obstructed exposure to the sun and the breeze of the wind. This is also helpful for a getting a good feather stick because sticks lying on the ground can receive excessive moister exposure, which will cause water to penetrate deeper into the stick. In addition,

Birds nest

There are materials that could look like good tinder material but are not; materials such as hair, fur, and feathers. In addition, it is also

I tell my students to try to gather a grapefruit-sized bundle or the size of a ball formed by cupping your fist in your other hand. However, if you are in a true survival scenario and find a good source of tinder, try to collect as much as you can while you can. Even if it is wet you can dry it out over time for use later.

look for areas that are not in the shade if you are in a wet environment. Shade makes it harder for moist areas to dry since there is little sunlight exposure. Another factor to consider is the time of day. In the morning there may be a lot of moisture in the air settling on the materials you wish to gather. Therefore, gathering later in the day when the sun is up and has had a chance to dry out some of the prime materials is best.

Lastly, an important factor in gathering tinder is to make sure you gather enough. Remember, tinder is supposed to catch fire easily. It is fluffy and light which means it will burn fast. The function of it will be to provide a flame with enough heat to combust your smaller kindling. If you do not have enough material you run the risk of your fire burning out before this can happen. This will have a negative effect on your moral, especially in a survival situation and is something you want to avoid.

Kindling

Next, you will want to collect kindling. Kindling is dry twig and sticks that require small amounts of heat to ignite. Potential kindling should be tested for dryness by attempting to snap ends of the sticks you are interested in using. There should be little to no flex before snapping and the sound made should be clear and loud enough to discern a sharp breaking/snapping sound. If the sound of the twig/stick breaking is dull and low, it may mean that the wood is saturated or still living. This is not good kindling and should not be used. Kindling should vary in size from small to large. The purpose is to allow the fire to consume material that will aid in its ability to grow bigger and hotter, which as a result allows it to burn bigger material. Think about a fire like your muscles. In order to get stronger, you start with light weight and proper diet for your caloric need. As you get stronger you gain more muscle, which allow you to lift heavier weights but also require you to increase your caloric intake. This is what is happening with your fire as you use different sizes of kindling to grow to a new level of fire strength. A good frame of reference for identifying kindling size

progression that allows for positive growth, are the following:

> 1ˢᵗ **level – Wire size.**
> 2ⁿᵈ **level – Skewer size.**
> 3ʳᵈ **level – Pencil size.**
> 4ᵗʰ **level – Thumb size.**

Beyond the size of the diameter of your kindling, the next important aspect is in regard to length. You will want your kindling sticks to be about the length from your wrist to your elbow. This will give your fire enough time to build as it burns through the material in a fuse like fashion. Also, since fire likes to burn in an upward direction this will give it material to feed on as it searches for more material to consume.

Lastly, as with your tinder, you will want to have enough to really ensure that you can build enough heat to move to the next step of your fire, which is the fuel stage. In order to ensure they have a point of reference; I teach my students to gather at least a rolled up sleeping bag or padded mat in diameter worth of kindling. If you fail to have one of these and cannot remember the size, grabbing both wrist and forming a circle with your arms will give a good relative perspective of how much you should gather.

Fuel

The purpose of tinder and kindling is to get a flame and to grow the heat level of that flame to a point that it can burn larger material such as thicker branches and logs. These thicker branches and logs are considered fuel, which is the next and final stage of the fire material collection. There are 2 types of wood fuel and they are Hardwoods and Softwoods. Hardwoods are ideal for fuel because they burn hotter, longer, and produce better coals. Hardwoods grow slower and therefore they are denser. A good way to identify them is they have broader leaves that they shed every autumn and winter. Softwoods usually remain evergreen year-round as they are conifers and they tend to be easier to light since they contain different types of resin, for instance the pine resin in pine trees. Softwoods burn faster and produce less heat. Whether hard or soft, start with using dry wood that is split. Unlike the other stages, once you build enough heat in the fuel stage you can begin to burn green living logs that are split or whole.

Before jumping the gun and trying to set a log on fire, remember we have to build in steps. First collecting the properly sized fuel to burn. Proper fuel diameter should start at the thickness of your wrist and forearm. Next, you can move to the size of your calf. Again, using dryer fuel in the beginning is important.

The length of your fuel can vary but you want to make sure the fire is manageable. Unless you know rescue is near, you are not looking for a bonfire. Besides, you do not want to take the chance of burning down the woods around you. Thus, you will want to get fuel that is about the length of your arm or shorter. If the logs are too long, they burn at the bottom and topple over out of your fire ring, or if you lay it flat it could burn through the middle, seesaw and roll off the fire.

> If you are in an extremely cold environment and you do not have a shelter or other means of staying warm, you may want a full night's worth of fuel especially since the coldest part of the day is just after dawn.

In regards to the amount of wood you need, you will want to collect enough wood to last you most of the night if you are in a cold environment. If you are in an extremely cold environment and you do not have a shelter or other means of staying warm, you may want a full night's worth of fuel especially since the coldest part of the day is just after dawn. However, do not be fooled, this is easier said than done especially if you are injured. If this is the case, there is a good possibility you may not be able to collect enough wood. Therefore, you should be looking at other alternatives to say warm. Remember the type of wood you choose will also have an impact on how much you need. If you gather hardwood then you will need less because it burns longer and gives off more heat. This will also

mean your trips for wood may be more taxing as the wood is heavier. However, if you gather softwood then you will need more as it will burn faster, and you will use more if you need more heat.

> Remember the type of wood you choose will also have an impact on how much you need. If you gather hardwood then you will need less because it burns longer and gives off more heat.

These are just a few guidelines on why, how, and how much when it comes to selecting good material for a fire. I mentioned earlier how to find these materials in a moist environment, but if you are in a very dry environment these issues may not be of concern. The main thing to be aware of is that the collection of proper materials is important. You should be able to identify these materials based on the environment you are going to or operating in. Whether it is a snowy, wet, dry, or humid environment, the fire building process is a stepped process where one step helps you ascend to higher. It is important to remember this as it is the foundation of successful material collection.

PROCESSING MATERIALS – ZAIRYO KAKO SURU

After gathering the materials to start a fire, the next step is to process it. This means prepping it to a stage that is optimal for fire production. For instance, if you are using cedar bark to start your fire, the first step would be to twist, ring, and roll it to a point that you can get thicker, tougher pieces of bark out. What you have left is the hairy and fibrous material

that will easily catch flame from a spark or ember. Next, as I mentioned in the gathering section, forming the bark into a nest-like shape will further increase the chances of the tinder holding the spark or ember, which also assists in the ignition process.

For processing kindling, it is good to separate

it into piles of similar diameter sized pieces as mention in the gathering section. Next, you will want to process each pile into the proper lengths. Lastly, if some of the twigs or branches are wet, then you may want to scrap off the bark to expose the dry portion of the wood.

For the processing of fuel, you may have to slit the fuel into smaller manageable pieces. This may be extremely difficult if you are injured. If you can, look for pieces that are already the size you need. If you cannot find the size that will fit into your fire pit/ring, then you can use a method of burning to separate the log in two pieces.

As I stated earlier, you do not have to split wood in order for it to burn if you have enough heat. However, splitting the wood helps facilitate the process of burning by exposing the more flammable inner portions of the log. It is important to note that tree bark is actually mildly flame resistant but stripping the bark of logs that you wish to burn would be asinine. The main point is to split fuel if you can by cutting, burning through or break-ing it. The goal is trying to produce smaller pieces that are easier to handle and burn.

There is another step to processing material that can sometimes be overlooked. Prepping materials for future fire production is also an important aspect. An example of this would be the gathering of moist tinder and small kindling and putting it close to the fire so that it can dry. This prepares it for burning at a later time, possibly when you move to a new location.

> **It is important to note that tree bark is actually mildly flame resistant but stripping the bark of logs that you wish to burn would be asinine.**

Processing your material is as important to fire as cooked or properly prepared food is for the body. Neglecting this step could make your effort to get a healthy fire going impossi-ble or difficult to maintain.

ORGANIZING MATERIALS – ZAIRYO SEIRI SURU

A very underrated stage of fire building is organization. The last thing anyone wants when dealing with a survival situation is los-ing material or damaging it after collecting and processing. I have seen so many people overlook this stage in my first years of teach-ing that I decided to make it a part of my lesson plan. I too was not immune to this in my early learning. During the stress of a sur-vival situation, your faculties may be dimin-ished. You may be dealing with a loss of light, diminishment of fine motor functions, or an injury. This will make it difficult to concentrate and find things in a moment's notice when you need them. I remember being so excited after igniting my tinder bundle in an extremely cold and moist environment, I scrambled to keep the flame going by throwing the burning bundle into my fire pit and gathering up my scattered pile of kindling to feed the flame. In the process, I dropped my black ferrocerium rod into the dirt and did not even notice. It was not until the fire was roaring, and I thought all was right with the world, that I settled down enough to realize that I had lost my fire steal. Immediately I was thrust back into panic mode as I searched for it most of the night. It was another day before I would find it, and I was happy I did, but the added stress, time, and energy could have all been saved if I had just been organized and had taken my time. I have seen people knock their lighter into the fire, burn themselves, inadvertently drop their kindling onto a wet ground and much more. These are all issues that you do not need if you are in a survival situation and can be easily solved if you just take a little care to arrange your fire material in a way that allows you to be methodical. The best way to do this is to make sure everything has a place that is close enough to your working area but is not jeopardized due to that closeness, like knocking your lighter in the flame, or hindering the timely feeding of your flame due to your materials distance, for example having your kindling so far away and so spread out that by the time you get it together your tinder bundle has burned out. The strategy of making sure everything has a place to be removed from and returned to is crucial. Set things up so you can be efficient and your

process will be effective. If you are in a survival situation, chance has already interrupted your life in a negative way. Do not make your situation worse with silly mistakes. Organize your fire making materials in an assembly line so you can smoothly move from one phase to another.

Another important aspect of the organization is fire containment. Fire can burn a dry or semi-dry forest at an incredible rate. There is an obvious hazard when using fire and the last thing you will want while already trying to make the best of your survival situation is to find yourself, your shelter, or environment in a blaze due to poor placement and management of your fire. This is why taking the extra time to ensure the fire is contained is very important. In addition to containing it from spreading because of human error, there are also natural occurrences that can cause the fire to spread. Some of these occurrences are wind and, if there is moisture in your wood, the rapid heating of it will cause the water to evaporate causing the wood to pop sending tiny hot embers out into the surrounding area. Also as the wood is consumed, the logs will shift and can sometimes roll out of the fire. These are just a few additional reasons why your fire should be contained. There are many methods of containing a fire, but 3 common ones are as follows:

> Organize your fire making materials in an assembly line so you can smoothly move from one phase to another.

1. **Rock, earth, or log sidewalls – Mizo Gata.**

2. Natural indention or pit – Ana Gata.

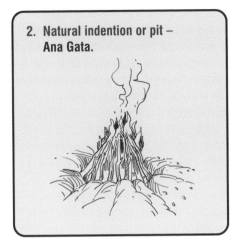

3. A platform built with sticks and dirt – Shiki Gata.

With all containment methods, the surrounding area for the fire should be cleared of any flammable material. This perimeter should be at least three feet from the fire. Be sure to also monitor if there is any material above the fire area that can be ignited if it heats up or if a floating ember rises up into it and catches it on fire.

Rock, Earth, or Log sidewalls – Mizo Gata

This method is the most commonly used, and it also has many beneficial functions. You can use dry stones that are not close to a body of water to make a fire ring, a big log, or several logs to surround the fire or a natural dirt mound/wall. This will not only serve as a boundary for your fire but, these methods can serve as wind protection or as a heat reflector (**Netsu hansha-ban**) much like a fireplace.

Natural indention or pit – Ana Gata

If you can find a natural recess, hole, or indentation in the landscape, it can be used to help keep a fire contained. However, this can also hurt your fire if it rains as the pit can naturally hold water and saturate your firebase to the point of extinguishing it. One other concern is that this pit could restrict air flow. The restriction of airflow can easily be fixed if you dig a small trench on the side of the pit much like a keyhole fire pit.

A platform built with sticks and dirt – Shiki Gata

For situations in which the ground is very moist or you are in a swampy area, it is best to build a platform for your fire. This will get it off of the damp or wet ground initially improving your ability to start and grow your fire. To build a platform, first, clear the area and make sure the ground is as flat as you can get it. Then place two bigger green sticks (living branches) parallel with a gap in between. You can also use dead wood, but they will catch fire sooner and your fire could burn through and not be able to withstand the moisture of the ground. The gap underneath will allow for better airflow, thus promoting the growth of the fire. Lay a layer of sticks similar in size going perpendicular to make a platform for your fire. Then you can start the process of starting it. There are more detailed ways to make fire, especially if you are in low standing water or snow. This would require that you make a higher platform similar to a table a few feet off the ground. You will need to add mud or a layer of sand, or gravel-like rock, on top of the platform base to keep the fire from burning through.

IGNITING MATERIALS – ZAIRYO O HAKKA SA SERU

Once you have your materials gathered, processed, and organized, the next step is to ignite your tinder. The ignition process is never one hundred percent predictable in a survival scenario. Because of injuries, weather conditions, lack of materials, or damaged/inoperable equipment that may be present getting flame is never guaranteed. Of course, there are a lot of things that you can do to enhance the odds of creating fire but nothing is ever certain. There is one thing that is important and that is the knowledge of understanding how fire happens. Without understanding the fire process, it is tough to create and keep it alive.

For the sake of proper education, I would like to highlight two aspects of properly igniting a fire. The two aspects are:

- Understanding the ignition process.
- Applying the steps to get ignition.

The ignition process is never one hundred percent predictable in a survival scenario.

Understanding the ignition process, known to the Ninja as *Chakka Ho*, means that you have to understand what we in the modern world call the fire triangle (*Hi sankakkei*), also

the combustion triangle. The fire triangle is a diagram and teaching method that highlights the 3 main ingredients that must be present in order to obtain visible combustion known as fire. These 3 elements are heat, fuel, and oxygen. When a fuel source such as wood is heated up, the energy of this heat is stored in the fuel and then reacts to oxygen. If enough heat and oxygen reaction is created the result is combustion. Once a fire is achieved, the chemical chain reaction will continue to occur until one of the three elements is removed. In a survival situation, the two most common elements to be removed are heat due to rain, or fuel due to lack of materials to burn.

As I stated earlier, it is important to have modern means of lighting a fire with you when you go outdoors. Items such as matches, lighters, and at minimum a ferrocerium rod, or fire-steel, should be a mainstay in your survival gear. However, what happens when you do not have these items or they are damaged? Understanding how the ignition process in regard to what fire needs will help you in creating it. Using a primitive fire-starting method would be important to know in this situation, but first, you will need to know how to create the fire making materials needed. Besides using the obvious methods above, I teach new students how to create fire through the friction of natural materials. This is known as the *Friction Fire Method* and it is important to restate, friction fire is not a sure thing. Finding the right materials that are in the right condition (non-moist, straight, and the proper type of wood) is difficult in environments you may not be completely familiar with. It is also important to highlight the physical and mental condition of the person trying to collect these materials. If the person is injured and grimacing from pain with every step because of a damaged knee or ankle, trekking around looking for materials will not be something they will want to do for long as the pain will be demoralizing. Even without injury, I have seen seasoned survival instructors, myself included, go to an unfamiliar area or even familiar ones, and struggle to start a friction fire, sometimes not at all and others only after multiple tries. It is also important to note that the process of making a fire by friction can burn a lot of calories, which may be in short supply during a survival situation. With that said, let us return to what friction fire is, and how to create it. Friction Fire is a fire that is made as a result of taking two pieces of solid combustible material, such as wood, and rubbing/grinding them together in a strategic way where you can achieve maximum friction through speed and pressure. This friction will grind the wood at the point where the two pieces meet and will create char dust/powder (punk). As the char is created, it is simultaneously heated until it is at a point where it reacts with oxygen enough to create an ember. The ember can then be transferred to your tinder bundle. Once the ember is lightly enclosed in your tinder bundle, methodical streams of air can be added through blowing, fanning, or waving the bundle. This will raise the temperature of the ember to the point where it can ignite the tinder around it.

The type of wood used is important as not only should it be dead and dry as mentioned earlier, but it is also preferred that the wood is somewhat soft (like a Cedar or Poplar). The Ninja would have had access to a variety of woods as Japan is one of the most heavily forested countries. Japan's forest contains both Deciduous (harder woods) and Conifers (softwoods) such as Spruce and Fir. In the Iga Province of Japan (now Mie Prefecture), one of the main regions for Ninja Clans, there were also Hinoki cypress, cedar, and other quality softer trees for making fire. The way to check if the wood is soft is to cut or scrape off a patch of the bark exposing the wood. After exposing the wood, press your fingernail into it with generous pressure. If there is an indentation left in the wood from your nail then it is a soft wood, if there is barely any indentation

then you are dealing with a harder wood. It is a common discussion about whether both kinds of wood should be soft, or one hard and the other soft. There is good success to be had both ways, but I often have success with both the spindle/plow and the fireboard being soft, whereas I have known people to have more success with a harder spindle or plow and a softer hearth board. However, as I mentioned earlier, if you are lost, stranded, or injured spending a lot of time trying to find two different styles of trees when you are not an expert may not be efficient. Finding a soft tree and using it for both the spindle and the board is acceptable and works well as long as it is dead and dry, but be sure the wood is not decomposing or rotting. An easy way to think about softwood or hard and soft combinations and the amount of energy required to make the fire is that "Soft is Easy, Hard is Tough" (all my opinion of course). There is one combination that will not work no matter how hard you try and that is the combination of two hardwoods. Using a hardwood spindle or plow on a hard hearth board will eventually produce a hard and shining drill hole or troth that will not produce char dust and the heat needed to create a coal.

"Soft is Easy, Hard is Tough."

In addition to understanding how fire is created and the steps for creating it, you will also have to understand what the best method is for igniting it in a survival situation. The Ninja referred to these lighting methods as *Hakka Ho*. Because you may be dealing with a possible injury, limited time and resources or all three, I often teach my students the methods of friction fire that require the least pieces to create. These 2 basic friction fire methods are:

1. **Fire Plow – Masatsu hi.**
2. **Assisted Hand Drill – Kirimomishiki hi.**

The advantage of these methods is that they both can be made from the same piece of wood or tree, they require little refinement work, and if the pieces are sourced properly they do not require a lot of manual dexterity to fashion. In every class, I get one person that mentions the Bamboo Fire Saw, which is indeed another good choice if the others are not available to you. The Ninja had an abundance of bamboo available to them, so using the Bamboo Fire Saw method would have been of great value to them. However, for the purposes of modern-day survival, it is likely that you will not have access to bamboo in most outdoor locations, whereas softwood is more common to be around. In addition, it is also tough to operate a Bamboo Fire Saw without using most of your fingers, whereas the fire plow and the assisted hand drill primarily requires your thumbs and palms. In my opinion, this fortifies your survivability by allowing you to do more with less.

THE FIRE PLOW – KASAI SUKI

The Fire Plow is a very old method of creating fire by friction. Some believe that since it only requires two sticks and nothing else, it would have likely been a method that was first used by many indigenous cultures through the ages. This method is known to be used throughout Polynesia and other surrounding areas. The premise of the fire plow is primarily the same as that of all friction fire methods, which is to use human energy to rub one stick on another by moving it back and forth at a high rate of speed. It sounds simple, but since the modern American has not grown up using this method for their livelihood, it is harder than imagined. Below I will provide the

knowledge of how to find, design, and produce fire with a Fire Plow.

The Materials Needed

The first step in starting a fire plow friction fire is to gather the 2 pieces you need to make it. The 2 pieces that make up a fire plow are:

- Plow.
- Plow board (Flat board).

Both the plow and the plow board should be a dead dry wood that is soft. If possible, try to use the same piece of wood for both pieces. When using softwood, it is important to remember to avoid resinous woods as it will increase the difficulty of creating an ember. The resin when heated will become liquid and, as a result, will pull some of the heat away from the point of friction.

Prepping The Materials

Once you have collected the pieces needed to make a fire plow, then you have to refine the materials. Mostly, you will carve or whittle the shapes you need to create, which can be done with a knife or sharp rock. The defined steps on how to create a fire plow are:

- Find one piece of softwood that you can break into 2 pieces; one for your plow and the other for your plow board. I have found it to work best to have both pieces be made of the same wood. However, if you cannot get both pieces made from the same wood, then make the plow from hardwood and the fire board from softwood.
- For your plow, take the smaller piece of your wood preferably circular, with a

diameter of ¾" to double that amount, somewhere about the width of 1 to 3 fingers side by side, and a length of 8-12", about the distance from the end of your palm to the tip of your middle finger.

- Carve a 45-degree angle at the tip of the plow. Then carve a bevel near the tip back to the spine. This will allow for an area for your char dust to collect when plowing.

- The plow board should be made the same piece of wood as the plow or at least a soft-wood. The plow board should be about 2-4" wide, half the width of your hand or the full width of your hand, and a length that is about 14-24" long, or the length from your elbow to the tip of your middle finger, once for 14" and twice that length for 24". Please note your board can be shorter or longer depending on your size and comfort.

- Carve a light groove/troth in the wood with your knife or sharp rock that is about 6" long, from the tip of your thumb to your pointer finger when your hand is configured like an "L." Your groove can be about ¼ of an inch or half a finger wide. If your troth is too big, it will be harder to condense the heat.

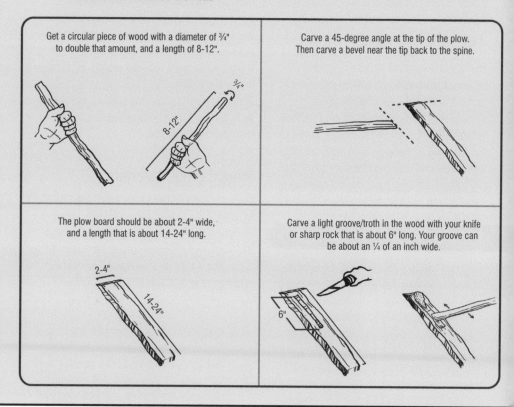

Get a circular piece of wood with a diameter of ¾" to double that amount, and a length of 8-12".

Carve a 45-degree angle at the tip of the plow. Then carve a bevel near the tip back to the spine.

The plow board should be about 2-4" wide, and a length that is about 14-24" long.

Carve a light groove/troth in the wood with your knife or sharp rock that is about 6" long. Your groove can be about an ¼ of an inch wide.

Using the Materials

After you have created the pieces you need, now it is time to endure the hard part. You actually have to use it to make your fire. Friction fire can be very fun and rewarding under normal cir-cumstances as well as difficult. However, trying to produce it in the woods while lost, stranded, or injured will by no means be fun. This is why I said to endure. In either case, the steps to using your materials to start a friction fire are the following:

- Place the Plow Board down in the way you intend to use it. There are many ways to secure the plow board but you want to be sure to choose a method easier for you, especially if you are injured. One way is to sit on one end and try to the hold the tail end with your feet for stability. This will alleviate having to extremely bend some of your joints if you are hurt. You can also sit sideways on the head of the board and secure the tail end with a rock to keep it from moving. This will make the plowing strokes more difficult but if one of your legs is injured it may be the most comfortable way for you.

- Pick up your plow and configure your hands in a triangle shape fashion with the plow in the gap so it can rest on the thumbs and press up on your overlapping pointer fingers near the Joint.

- Place your plow point in the head of the groove you made with the rock (the head will be the side closest to you). Start pushing back and forth while giving moderate downward pressure. Your strokes should be short, moderate in speed, and smooth at first.

- Slowly speed up as you start to see smoke. When you start seeing a steady plume of smoke and a good pile of char powder growing, stroke faster a few more times.

- When you have had a constant plume of thick smoke for a few seconds, and you feel confident you have an ember, stop and check. If the char powder keeps smoking you likely have an ember. Take your time and fan it a little bit to let it grow.

- Tip over your plow board into your tinder bundle transferring the coal to it.

- Slowly and methodically blow the ember into a flame.

MAKING AN ASSISTED HAND DRILL

The hand drill is also a very ancient method of creating fire by friction with evidence stretching back to Africa over 150,000 years ago. Like the fire plow, since it also requires only two sticks, it is believed that it may have been one of the first and most common used techniques for creating fire. The premise of the hand drill is to take a dry spindle like stick, place it on a flat piece of board shaped wood, and rotate it clockwise and counterclockwise with your hands so that its tip drills into the board creating hot char powder through friction. As with all methods of friction fire, this is easier said than done and unlike the fire plow, there is a considerable amount of skill needed to properly keep the spindle drilling at a high rate of speed.

The standard Hand Drill method takes a lot of skill as there is a particular technique done with the hands in order to get maximum back and forth circular movement for drilling into the fireboard with the spindle. Learning this method is infamous for creating blisters and cuts on the hand and leaving the person depleted and exhausted. These issues degrade your potential survivability; thus, they are not welcomed in a survival situation. However, this does not negate that having to collect only two pieces of material is more efficient and beneficial than having to collect more. In that same vein, the more pieces you have, the more that can be lost or damaged. The best solution I have found is the *Assisted Hand Drill*. This allows you to protect your hands as well as save time and resources. You only need to add cordage to your materials list and that is it. In my opinion, it would be rare that the modern person will ever be in the wilderness without some sort of cordage, whether it is using your shoelaces, strips of your belt or clothing.

Therefore, it is safe to assume the amount of work to get this would be minimal and not worth fretting over. Now that I have given a little background on the Hand Drill and why it is one of the second things I teach my class participants, below I will describe how to find, design, and produce fire with the Assisted Hand Drill.

The Materials:

- Drill (spindle).
- Fireboard (hearth board).
- Pressure cord/cordage (thong, root, shoestring, hoodie string, twisted/braided bark).

Prepping the Materials

- Find a straight, dead plant stalk that is about 12 -24" long, or an easy reference would be from the crease of your arm to your middle knuckle, or the back of your elbow to the tip of your middle finger. It should be about a 1/2" in diameter, the size of an average pinky finger. If possible, try to create a drill that is pithy in the center, which means it is soft and spongy in its core. Again, if you are in a true survival scenario and find softwood to use, try it. You do not want to spend a lot of time moving and looking around if you have a material that would work if you just tried it.

- Shave the outside of the spindle to remove any protrusions that may injure your hands. Traction is important when drilling so do not make it smooth. You just want to make sure it will not damage your hands.

- Carve the head of your spindle where it will meet the fireboard so that the edges have a gentle curve.

- For your fire board, you will need to get a soft wood that is at least double the diameter of the spindle. 1.5-2" or the width of 2 fingers should work. However, it depends on the size of your spindle.

- Baton the wood on both sides to get a flat slab of wood that will sit stable for your fire board. You may want it long enough to hold down between each leg if you are injured, about 16". Your fire board should be at a ½" to ¾" thick or the width of your thumb.

- Use a knife or the point of a rock to drill a starter hole in the fireboard, about a ½" from the edge. Once the starter hole is big enough to keep your drill in place, start drilling with your spindle, slightly deepen and widen the hole. Be careful not to drill to deep you just need to go about a 1/8".

- Next, you will need to make a char dust collection gap in the side of the fire board. Starting from the corner of the wood beside the whole cut a pie shaped notch with the point of the pie going towards the center of the circular indentation you made in the previous step. Make sure the notch is big enough to let oxygen in but not so big that the char dust cannot condense enough to consolidate the heat, which will eventually raise the temperature enough to produce an ember (coal). Size of the gap is important because if you make it too skinny the char will overflow out of the top and spill over the sides and not compact properly, whereas if the pie cut is too big it will fall out of the hole and not compact enough.

• The pressure cord/cordage (thong) can be a root, shoelace, hoodie string, twisted/braided bark, or a piece of clothing. You can notch the end of your drill to place your cordage in or, for a more secure method, you can tie it around your spindle using a prusik knot. With the two free running ends, tie loops to put your thumbs in.

• Place a leaf or a piece of material under the pie notch to catch the char dust and then the ember. This will allow you to easily transport the coal to your tinder bundle once it is created.

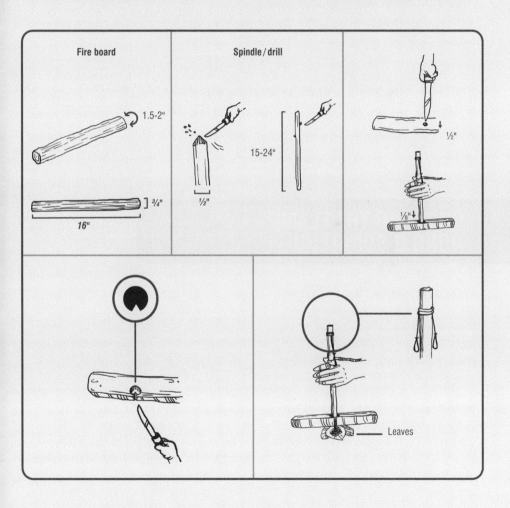

Using the Materials

- Set up the fireboard in a way that is comfortable for you based on your size, injuries, or experience. Make sure to put the coal catch (leaf, bark, or other material) underneath the pie notch.
- Next, put your thumbs in the loops and then put the spindle in the indentation you made on the fire board.
- Now that you are positioned properly start rubbing your hands back and forth with the spindle between them while providing downward pressure with the use of the thumb loops. Be sure to use more of your upper body to create pressure than your arms, this will minimize the effort needed and the energy consumed.
- Slowly speed up as you start to see smoke. When you start seeing a steady plume and a good pile of char powder growing, stroke faster a few more times.
- When you have had a constant plume of thick smoke for a few seconds, and you feel confident you have an ember, stop and check. If the char powder keeps smoking you likely have an ember. Take your time and fan it a little bit to let it grow.
- Pick up the base material used to catch the ember and transfer your coal to the tinder bundle.
- Slowly and methodically, blow the ember into a flame.

GROWING THE FLAME – HONO O SODATERU

Once you have made a flame with your tinder bundle, the next things you will need to do is grow the flame to a stage where you can burn fuel. Growing the flame just requires that you add to the fire the wood you prepared in the processing phase, in the order that you arranged it during the organizational phase. If you have followed the fire building essential steps properly, your fire will have the fuel it needs to grow. Besides adding wood, there is one more thing you may need to add in order to grow your flame and that is Oxygen. As your materials start to burn, depending on the type of wood, any moisture it may still contain, or the moisture in the air, the fire may have challenges maintaining heat and staying lit. If this begins to

happen, then you will need to blow air into it. A common mistake that I see in my classes are when students try to add air by blowing down on the fire. Since fire likes to burn up blowing down with air is counterproductive. Blowing down also pushes surrounding air away from the fire, which in essence smothers it. The best way to feed a fire air is from below or at its base. This promotes the upward movement of fire by giving it more energy from below. One way I like to explain this to my students is to think of feeding fire what it needs to the way a human feeds. In this example, I relate the wood or fuel to water in that it enters the fire from the top like a person angling their head back to drink fluid. Next, I relate adding oxygen to the fire like the way a person angles their mouth down or level to eat. Believe it or not, that seems to stick so much so I decided to add it to this book.

SUSTAINING THE FLAME – HONO O JIZOKU SA SERU

As a fire goes, or better yet grows, through the stages of burning your tinder and then kindling, it will eventually get hot enough to burn fuel. There is a cycle to this process for which heat burns fuel, fuel burning gives off gases that mix with oxygen, which then creates more heat for burning more fuel. As we discussed in Chapter 1, the Ninja saw this as one example of the natural order of transformation. As each juncture supports the other in a natural series and destruction, the result impacts the environment with light and heat. This process was part of the Gyo-Go theory which was more than a method of building sustained fire; it was a foundation of many aspects of survival.

As the heat of your fire increases, you will eventually be able to burn bigger logs including logs that are not dead (green logs). These logs will burn slower, and thus, will require less attention and monitoring. This is paramount in a survival situation as it can afford you time to work on another aspect of your survival needs, or it can give you time to relax

a little and get some needed rest.

FIRE LAYOUTS

Besides just serving the purpose of making you warm, different fire layouts highlight different functions. Certain fire formations can give off more light, burn longer, or generate more heat. Understanding different ways of constructing your fire to achieve certain goals based on your needs is a valuable skill. Because the Ninja often operated covertly, they would often learn and use a series of concealed fires. However, their Katonjutsu training also dealt with using fire for distraction, concealment, signaling, and sabotage. To do this effectively, the Ninja needed intimate knowledge of how fire operated and how to manipulate it. The Ninja referred to this deliberate setup to serve methodical purposes as *Tsumi Kata*. In the modern day, we have 4 primary ways of setting up the main body of the fuel burning stage of your fire, with each designed to produce a particular result:

. Tepee Fire – **Sankakusui Gata**	2. Pyramid Fire – **Kasane Gata**	3. Star shaped/Indian Fire – **Hoshi Gata**	4. Log Cabin/Platform Fire – **Igeta Gata**

Tepee Fire – Sankakusui

Tepee fires are the most common type of fires. The design is cone shape and looks like a tepee, hence the name. The wide lower base allows for good oxygen circulation. They are good for giving off light and for rapidly boiling water, or cooking beans hanging from a tripod. Since fire likes to travel up and the structure formation comes to a point, the fire converges on the apex creating a focal point for heat radiation.

Star Shaped/Indian Fire – Hoshi Gata

Star Shaped fires are good for when you do not have a lot of material and you do not need a lot of light and heat. It burns long, although you do not have a lot of material, especially if you use harder woods for fuel. The design of a star shaped fire is one where the logs are laid in a circle like the spokes on a wheel so that they converge in the center. The center conversion is where the fire burns and, as the converged tips of the logs are burned, the logs are pushed into the fire from the back end. I like this for survival situations where the person may be injured because they do not have to collect a lot of fuel material. However, this is all dependent on the injury. If the person's leg is badly injured, it may be more difficult to pull a few big logs over to a fire than it would be to gather a light bundle of smaller fuel.

Pyramid Fire – Kasane Gata

Pyramid fires are great long-lasting fires and they produce a lot of coals for residual heat, cooking, and use in starting additional fires. The pyramid fire construction is similar to that of the log cabin fire, however, there is no hollow center. This fire is constructed by lying a series of similar width and length logs side by side in the same direction. Next, in a different direction crisscrossing the first layer, lay another shorter layer of logs on top. Follow this procedure with the next layer, and you have a pyramid fire construction. As the wood burns below gases are released (sometimes referred to as wood gas). Often most of this gas escapes into the environment in the form of smoke but in the case of the pyramid fire this gas is captured by the fire above as it travels upward into the flame. As the wood burns and forms coals they fall below aiding in the ignition of the lower levels and producing more gasses. This process makes for a great fire that provides long-lasting heat with minimum effort.

Log Cabin/Platform Fire – Igeta Gata

Log cabin fires are named as such because they resemble a log cabin in their design. This type of fire gives off lots of light and heat. This fire is designed with lots of fuel built in and so it burns long. Due to its open design in the center, it gets good air flow for sustained burning. In addition, since the center is hollowed out as logs burn, they fall into the center creating a combination tepee- log cabin hybrid, which also promotes consistent burning. To build a log cabin fire start by placing 2 logs of similar size on the ground parallel with a separation in between them. Take two more logs and place them perpendicular across the first set with one log at each end. Follow this pattern until you reach the desired height. Place your tinder bundle in the center and make sure the corners are close enough to catch fire by the tinder bundles when it is ignited.

After you have constructed the fire you wanted, ignited it, and achieved a level of sustainment, you can use your fire to fortify your ongoing ability to thermoregulate in multiple ways. One way is to ensure you use the fire to dry out other tinder and fuel for easy ignition for later use if your fire goes out or you move location. Another use is to heat dry or mildly wet rocks. In regard to rocks with moisture in them, do not put them directly into the flames. The rocks will have to be kept at a distance so they can slowly release moisture and dry out as they heat up. These rocks can then be used as a source of warmth when you are tired of tending to your fire and you allow it to die down in strength.

TRANSPORTING A FIRE – HI O HAKOBU

As the last note, in order to conserve energy an efficient way to aid in your survivability would be to reuse coals from your fire. Even

> Even in a fire that has gone out, the embers can continue to slowly burn for a long time under the ash. The ash will act as an insulator that will restrict airflow and allow for the coals to burn slower.

in a fire that has gone out, the embers can continue to slowly burn for a long time under the ash. The ash will act as an insulator that will restrict airflow and allow for the coals to burn slower. When I did an extreme survival excursion in the Himalayan mountains, I used the coals from the previous night to restart my fire for several days. As we stated earlier, starting a fire is hard work especially if you are injured, therefore, using whatever you have at your disposal to make it easier is paramount. In addition to just using the embers to restart the fire in a single location, you can carry the ember from one place to another. With the use of bark, punk/rotting wood, or

Damp grass, leaves etc.

Dry punk wood

Heavy bark such as birch

Live coals

Move coals to tinder bundle and blow to flame

damp tinder (grass, bark, or leaves) wrapped in a burrito/cigar style, roll it around the embers you harvested from your fire, you can then transport it from one area to another. Like the ash, in the previous example, the punk wood and damp grass (not saturated) gives the embers something to slowly consume and stay alive. Once at your new location, follow the steps of setting up your fire area, prep your tinder bundle, place in it your ember and blow it to flame.

> **"Two is one and one is none."**

I hope that if one thing is clear in this chapter, it is that fire is important to have, but it is not easy to create, grow and sustain. Anything you can do to prepare for the possibility of having to start a fire in an emergency is paramount. Therefore, if you have a lighter you should have two, following the old saying "Two is one and one is none" concept. However, like a good Ninja, you should make sure that you are well adept at understanding how to produce fire if things do not go according to plan, and you find yourself needing a fire, but your equipment is missing or damaged. Always make sure to prepare your kit and your wit!

CHAPTER
6

SURVIVAL WATER COLLECTION AND PURIFICATION

SHU SUI

The Ninja understood that water was an essential building block of life. The Genin (Ninja guerrilla warrior) was an endurance athlete in every sense of the word as he would often be sent on dangerous missions in harsh conditions behind enemy lines with little to no resources. As part of this, coupled with growing up in the harsh mountain regions of Japan, those that would be called Ninja were intimately and actively aware of the needs of the human body, and how to ensure its survival and optimal performance in non-optimal conditions. Using the Go-Gyo concept of how the five elements transform and work in accordance with one another, the Ninja understood how Sui (water), transformed and aided the body through the processes of carrying oxygen and minerals throughout the body; helps in the process of breathing; aids in thermoregulation; and helps break down food and remove waste as well as protect organs and lubricates joints.

> Using the Go-Gyo concept of how the five elements transform and work in accordance with one another, the Ninja understood how Sui (water), transformed and aided the body through the processes of carrying oxygen and minerals throughout the body; helps in the process of breathing; aids in thermoregulation; and helps break down food and remove waste as well as protect organs and lubricates joints.

Like the Ninja, having a basic understanding of this knowledge, the modern person thrust in an unexpected survival situation can improve his/her situation and stay alive long enough to find rescue.

THE IMPORTANCE OF WATER

Water consumption is one of the most important aspects of human survival. When I say the word survival, I am not just referring to an unforeseen or unfortunate circumstance of being lost, injured, or both in an outdoor environment. The word survival simply refers to both in our daily lives and in an emergency. It is well documented that most people in America live in a state of mild dehydration. Between our love of soft drinks, sugary juices, and coffee we often lack the desire to drink plain water and, in many cases, we ignorantly believe that since all the aforementioned beverages have water in them, we are receiving proper hydration. As mentioned in an earlier chapter, depending on age, most people's body contains 50-75% water. Because all of the major organs contain a high content of water, as well as the cells in the body, it is often recommended that men drink 13-15.5 (3+ liters) cups of water a day and 9-11.5 cups (2+ liters) for women. The common eight, 8-ounce cups that is referred to when discussing water consumption is a minimum number that is easier to reach than the best

> It is well documented that most people in America live in a state of mild dehydration.

Because all of the major organs contain a high content of water, as well as the cells in the body, it is often recommended that men drink 13-15.5 (3+ liters) cups of water a day and 9-11.5 cups (2+ liters) for women.

The body is so in need of water that even a loss of as little as 1% can impair cognitive functions. On average, the human body loses 2-3 liters of water a day. This can result in a loss of about 25% of our physical efficiency.

recommendations, and therefore, it is often an attainable recommended baseline. Since most people are under-hydrated, they lack the knowledge of waters importance to overall health or simply do not prioritize it. The bigger the amount to drink, the less likely people will take action. It is also important to note that exact water consumption needs for each individual are difficult to determine because people's bodies and activity levels are different. Regardless of the science, the one thing that is certain is that without water, the body will slowly start to lose its functionality until it ceases to function. The body is so in need of water that even a loss of as little as 1% can impair cognitive functions. On average, the human body loses 2-3 liters of water a day. This can result in a loss of about 25% of our physical efficiency. These 2-3 liters are lost through natural processes such as:

• Sweat.
• Respiration (as air gathers moisture from the lungs and is exhaled).
• Urination.
• Defecation.
• Digestion.
• Stress.

Through the natural processes of the body, our functionality is naturally becoming less efficient, and therefore, it is important to replenish it with water regularly. This being the

guidelines for a normal daily situation does not account for the extreme and high-stress conditions of a survival situation. During a survival situation, extreme emotions, physical and environmental conditions enhance the need for water. Situations such as:

• Injury.
• Excessive exertion.
• Exposure to the cold.
• Exposure to heat.
• Illness.

All these can contribute to extreme water loss. For these reasons, water is one of the first things you would need to acquire for surviving more than a day or two in the wild. When the water you take in is not enough to replace the water your body uses or loses, then dehydration occurs. Symptoms of dehydration are:

• Fatigue.
• Dizziness.
• Headache.
• Loss of skin elasticity.
• Dry mouth.
• Thirst.
• Confusion.

The above are overall symptoms, but each phase of dehydration has a specific set of indications that can allow a person to understand more accurately their level of dehydration. It is important to consistently monitor yourself in a survival situation for the previously listed symptoms. However, one of the best ways to not get to these stages is to consistently watch your water intake, and as activity increases or the conditions become more extreme, drink more water. In addition to staying mindful of water intake, it is also important to monitor urination frequency and color. It is vital to ensure that you are urinating regularly but not excessively as excessive urination could mean over hydration and that your urine is light and not dark in color, which may be hard to determine without a toilet. Lastly, do not wait until you are thirsty before you drink water. By the time the body alerts you that it needs water, you are already dehydrated. As a general rule of thumb, below are some percentages of water loss and the effects on your body. Knowing this information helps in understanding the extent of your dehydration in a situation.

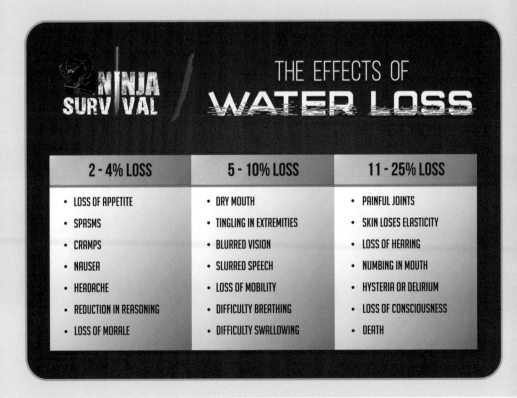

THE EFFECTS OF WATER LOSS

2 - 4% LOSS	5 - 10% LOSS	11 - 25% LOSS
• LOSS OF APPETITE	• DRY MOUTH	• PAINFUL JOINTS
• SPASMS	• TINGLING IN EXTREMITIES	• SKIN LOSES ELASTICITY
• CRAMPS	• BLURRED VISION	• LOSS OF HEARING
• NAUSEA	• SLURRED SPEECH	• NUMBING IN MOUTH
• HEADACHE	• LOSS OF MOBILITY	• HYSTERIA OR DELIRIUM
• REDUCTION IN REASONING	• DIFFICULTY BREATHING	• LOSS OF CONSCIOUSNESS
• LOSS OF MORALE	• DIFFICULTY SWALLOWING	• DEATH

WAYS TO AVOID EXCESS WATER LOSS

- **Scheduling** – Choose the right time to work. Working during the hottest time of the day or when exposed to extreme weather conditions will only deplete you faster and work against you. Choose a time where the temperature and conditions are less extreme if at all possible. You are in a survival situation and, in some circumstances, there may not be an ideal time.

- **Impose Limits** – Only do what is necessary. If it does not directly enhance your situation, do not spend the time and energy on it. Always evaluate your situation. You may have thoughts that something was a good idea but realize it is taking more time, and physical and mental resources than expected. If you impose a limit to the work you perform this will help you manage better.

- **Consume Less** – It is best to cut back on food consumption when water is low as it requires water to digest.

- **Replace** – Do not conserve water. Water is better in you than in your canteen or the landscape. People have been found dead with water in their canteens or vicinity. However, be careful not to over drink as well. Drinking too much water can flush your system of sodium,

swell your cells, and cause other harmful effects that may lead to death. This process of over hydration is called Hyponatremia.

- **Think It Through** – You may become restless, confused, and desperate, but hold on to the facts. Never drink your own urine and never drink sea water. Distillation is a process that could make these potable, but you will need proper equipment that is not often had in an unprepared survival situation. Also, think about things you can do to allow your body to conserve water. Some of these things are like keeping your body covered in hot climates as a way to reduce sweating. This may seem counterproductive but, as discussed in the shelter section, not only can clothing protect you from direct exposure to the elements it can also pass and aid in the evaporation of water. This process cools the air between the skin and the material, which in turn helps cool the body.

HYDRATION ALLIES

The body has over 2 million sweat glands and, contrary to what some may think, sweat is made of both water and electrolytes, therefore water loss means loss of electrolytes. With low-intensity work where sweat production is low, some electrolytes can be re-absorbed through the skin. However, during intense sweating, this process does not take place. The average person can lose about 15 grams of body salts per day. The body will begin to exhibit issues once it reaches a loss of 20-30%. In normal society these are replaced with vitamins, a balanced diet, and drinks specifically made for salt replacement, such as Gatorade. However, in the wild, especially in a survival situation, this can be hard to obtain.

So, what exactly are body salts and why are they important? A better term for body salts as referenced in survival are electrolytes. Electrolytes are chemicals that when mixed with water conduct electricity. Since many of the functions in the body require electrical impulses or currents to function, electrolytes help foster and regulate the movement of

The average person can lose about 15 grams of body salts per day. The body will begin to exhibit issues once it reaches a loss of 20-30%. In normal society these are replaced with vitamins, a balanced diet, and drinks specifically made for salt replacement, such as Gatorade.

electricity through the body as well as in and around the cells. To be more specific, electrolytes help in the following functions:

- Regulating fluid levels.
- Regulating Ph levels.
- Transmitting nerve signals.
- Regulating the heartbeat and function of muscles.
- Regulating cell function and blood clotting.

Lack of improper regulation of these functions can cause serious illness and even death. On a survival excursion to the Jungles of Columbia, due to the extreme heat, I decided to make sure I stayed hydrated. I maintained a high rate of water consumption, but because this was a survival trip, I had few food resources. Eventually, I began cramping and

since I thought the culprit was dehydration, I naturally drank more. A few days later after a massive full body spasm, I realized it was not that I was dehydrated, but instead I was over hydrating and flushing out my system of electrolytes faster than I was able to replace them.

Contrary to what many may think, the word electrolytes refer to several minerals the body needs to ensure proper regulation of vital systems. It can refer to:

- Sodium.
- Potassium.
- Calcium.
- Bicarbonate.
- Magnesium.
- Chlorine.
- Phosphate.

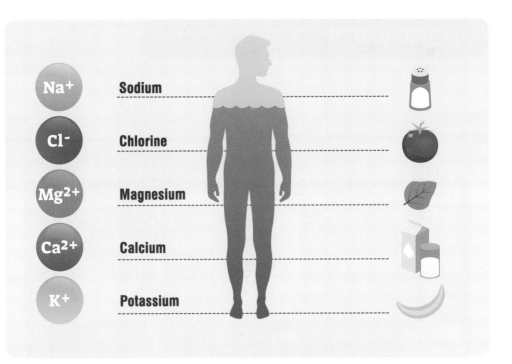

Both over hydration and dehydration can cause imbalances in electrolytes. In a survival situation, since clean water is not always abundant, dehydration is often the culprit.

Several symptoms of electrolyte imbalance are:

- Irregular heartbeat.
- Fatigue.
- Muscle cramping.
- Muscle spasming.
- Convulsions or seizures.

It is easy to notice that many of the symptoms of electrolyte depletion are similar to dehydration symptoms and that is because, as we mentioned, they are connected. The easiest way to replenish electrolytes in a truly unexpected and unprepared survival situation is through fruits, plants, and animals. Bananas are a good source for replacing potassium, whereas figs are a good source of calcium. Coconut water is full of electrolytes, as well as certain leafy greens like spinach. When it comes to animals, eggs are a good source of calcium and other electrolytes in addition to animal blood and meat. It is important to note that depending on the area, finding the proper edible plants and fruits can be difficult, and therefore, you want to be careful as eating the wrong thing could create a multitude of new issues. For this reason, having to treat an electrolyte imbalance can create a real issue.

In colder weather, your body will burn through more water than anything else. It will make you urinate more. It is also important to know not to eat snow, and that cold water will drop your core temperature. This will make you not want to drink water, but it is important that you still do.

FINDING WATER

Besides the obvious water sources such as streams, springs, rivers, etc. which can be seen or heard, there are less common ways to find water that is important to know if you are in a survival situation. All life needs water, and therefore, strong signs of life are a good indicator of how to find it. Your power of observation is one of the strongest allies in helping you find water. Below is a list that highlights some of the ways you could become aware of a possible water location:

Possible Water Source

- **Using animal trails** – As animals travel to and from the water they will naturally create a path. Several paths coming from different locations will often converge at a point like spokes on a wheel either where water is or near where it can be found.

- **Watch the birds** – Birds will often go to water in the mornings or circle it in the sky.

- **What's the bug situation** – Mosquitos and flies are often a sign that water is nearby.

- **Understand water's movement** – Like all things on the planet water moves with gravity, and thus, it flows downhill to low lying areas.

- **Look for dense vegetation** – Plants need water to survive. Thick vegetation in one area can mean water is near. It is important to know that sometimes vegetation is not the best sign of finding water because some can draw water from deep within the earth through its roots.

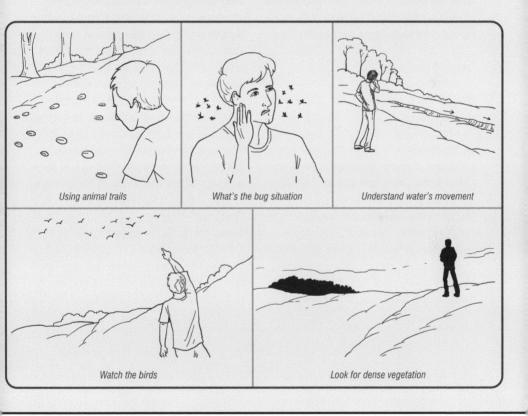

Using animal trails

What's the bug situation

Understand water's movement

Watch the birds

Look for dense vegetation

I remember talking with my Ninjutsu teacher, Stephen Hayes, and asking him about an experience that he describes in his book about training in Japan with the grandmaster. He describes that he and his seniors were running during a late-night training session on a golf course. He explains that he could barely see in front of him and following along with the group was difficult. Suddenly, his feet felt wet and with each step he heard a splash. To his surprise, he became aware that he was standing in a pond. At that moment, he hears a shushing sound come from the darkness and he realized it was one of his seniors. The sound turns to a voice that says, "your being too loud."

Hayes responds "I can hardly see. How was I supposed to know this water was here?"

The voice replies from the darkness, "you are not supposed to see it; you are supposed to smell it."

I was a young bright-eyed twenty year old when I read that book and could not wait to ask him about that story. "Could the Ninja really smell the water and know when it is near?" I asked.

"Yes," he responded.

"What is that special skill called and when do I learn it?" I asked.

He smiled and said, "It was not a special skill with a special name. To the Ninja, this was just something that developed as a natural part of living in the wilderness. The more time they spent in connection with nature, the more the characteristics and qualities of nature began to reveal themselves. Like spending a lot of time with a person eventually you learn how they speak, smell, act as well as additional aspects about them that others may not

> **The more time they spent in connection with nature, the more the characteristics and qualities of nature began to reveal themselves.**

see or notice when they have little exposure to that person."

It would take me several years to truly understand what he meant when I was in the Himalayas for three weeks. Here I would need to survive and figure out how to get shelter, water, and food as I was not allowed to bring anything but a knife. Over the next three weeks, I became very connected to my surroundings. I eventually could smell or feel the pressure change in the air as a storm approached. I did become aware of my ability to smell water even when I could not see it. The experience was powerful. It was an awakening for me to realize a new ability. An ability that was introduced to me many years before by my teacher but was then being taught to me by nature. This is one example in my life that highlights how there are signs that will be present while in a survival situation that can help you find what you need, but you have to be calm, focused, and observant.

DANGERS IN THE WATER

Once you have a good idea of where water is or when you have found it, you have to be cautious in your approach to consuming that water. In the wild, there are two major threats to your safety in regard to water. The first is what I call a visible threat and the other is a non-visible threat.

Although I name the first one a visible threat, in truth it could be hidden or hard to see. A visible threat would be a predator or creature that could be dangerous to you if it sees you as prey or a threat. Predators need water to, so they will go to water sources to drink. If you stumble across them they may see you as a target of opportunity for food. However, instinctively knowing animals will go to water, predators will often lurk and hide near it, waiting for unsuspecting or desperate prey to come for a drink. In this case, they will camouflage or hide and wait for a proper time to ambush their targets. Animals such as:

- Snakes.
- Bears.
- Crocodiles.
- Elk.
- Wild boar.
- Wolves.
- Lions.

These are a few of the common threats to be cautious of. It is easy to understand that predators may be an issue, but in truth, all animals could be a problem as some may see you as a threat or competition for resources. Therefore, even in the event that you may be dealing with what seems to be harmless animals, you should still be mindful and cautious around them.

Always approach water with caution and pay close attention to the surroundings. Carry a sharpened stick even if you have a knife as this will allow you to break the surface of the water to ensure nothing is lurking underneath. This will allow you to defend yourself and keep predators or aggressive animals further away from you if they attack. Also, make sure to consistently recheck your surroundings if you are gathering water, as there is a tendency to become engrossed in the thought of reaching and drinking it, especially if you are dehydrated. This tunnel vision will make you very susceptible to an ambush by a stalking predator. Always look up, look around, and check below the surface of the water by probing with your spear.

> **Make sure to consistently recheck your surroundings if you are gathering water, as there is a tendency to become engrossed in the thought of reaching and drinking it, especially if you are dehydrated.**

Animals also create another issue as they often bathe, urine, and defecate near or in the water. This is why, even if water is flowing and looks fresh, you should still at minimum boil it before drinking because you never know what animals or humans are depositing waste up-stream leading to unseen bacteria or parasites flowing down-stream. These dangers that exist in water are what I refer to as non-visible threats, also called microscopic dangers.

MICROSCOPIC DANGERS

Water that looks clean and clear will seem like a miracle in a survival situation. However, the truth is that no matter how good water looks it cannot be trusted. Water can be host to a plethora of invisible dangers. These are simply bacteria, parasites, and viruses that cannot be seen but will be felt if they find their way into your body. The only way to get rid of these contaminants is to boil the water you collect. Even when gathering water from leaves and crevasses,

you should understand that birds, lizards, and other small critters could have contaminated the surface of the leaf or they could have contaminated it directly. Therefore, you should express caution when drinking this water as well.

There are many contaminants that can be found in water but there are some that are more common than others. These contaminants cause illnesses that are referred to as waterborne illnesses/diseases. Waterborne disease is an illness caused by microscopic organisms that enter the body through the use or drinking of contaminated water. Some of the more common waterborne illnesses are:

- **Cholera** – A bacterial infectious disease caused by drinking contaminated water. It can cause diarrhea, vomiting, and dehydration, which if left untreated can kill in a matter of days.

- **Cryptosporidiosis** – A diarrheal disease caused by a parasitic infection. The parasites are microscopic and live in the intestines. It is passed to water through the stool of a contaminated person or animal. It is found in every region of the United States, and it can cause diarrhea, vomiting, and dehydration.

- **Giardia** – A parasitic intestinal infection that is one of the most common waterborne diseases. Common symptoms of a giardia infection are stomach cramp, bloating, gas, and dehydration.

- **Salmonella** – A bacterial infection often received from food but can also spread through drinking contaminated water. It can also be contracted through the handling of creatures such as reptiles, turtles, frogs and other animals that have been contaminated. The technical infection caused by Salmonella is Salmonellosis. Salmonella causes headaches, diarrhea, fever and vomiting that can last up to 7 days. It is rare, but Salmonella can spread from the intestines to the bloodstream, which if left untreated can cause death.

- **Shigellosis (Dysentery)** – A bacterial infection, sometimes thought of as food poisoning, is often spread through food, water, or person to person contact. Lasting 1-7 days, shigellosis can cause nausea, fever, and bloody diarrhea.

Waterborne micro-organisms are not the only invisible threats in the water. There is also the issue of unnatural pollutants such as a chemical. Chemicals from near-by facilities, crops, or vehicles can all render water toxic. In most cases, if you are attentive, take your time to observe, and know what to look for you should be able to identify signs that the water may be polluted. This is easier said than done when you are dehydrated and the joy of finding water overwhelms you. In some instances, you may even recognize some of the signs, but subconsciously ignore them. Besides the very real issue of overlooking the obvious due to desperation, if you can keep yourself composed and focused, there are five ways you can determine if water is capable of drinking, which are:

1. **Signs of Life** – Do you see life in the water. Are there living bugs, fish, and birds around it. Do you see animal tracks leading up to it?

2. **Movement** – Is the water alive? Is it moving or is it stagnate? Stagnate water may not always be completely unsafe to drink, but over time it could have become contaminated by polluted runoff or just intentional toxic waste dumped in the water.

3. **Nasty Look** – Does it look discolored with an unnatural tint?

4. **Nasty Smell** – Does it smell foul, and is the smell very unnatural?)

5. **Is it Foamy** – Foam is not always a sign of bad water. Often it is a natural occurrence that happens in an area where water is consistently agitated, like at the base of waterfalls. However, sometimes it can be a sign of heavy amounts of phosphorous from chemicals or manure.

Because water can travel far distances both on top of the earth and below it, it is important to make sure that you understand how to identify any hidden chemical dangers that may be present in a water supply. Toxic chemicals can wreak havoc on the body, sometimes much more than bacteria and parasites which your body could fight against. Taking your time when you find water and analyzing it for potential risks that may be present can be as much of a lifesaver as consuming the water itself.

In regards to chemicals, water is a lot harder to clean especially when you are not sure what chemicals may be present. Because bacteria, parasites, and viruses are all living organisms, they can be killed with extreme heat, but chemicals are entirely different. Some chemicals can be removed through air ration, and some through the more refined process of distillation.

If you know you are not dealing with a chemical and you are severely dehydrated with no means of purifying water, you will have a tough choice to make. One of the most debated survival choices is whether to drink possibly contaminated water or wait and try to find a means to boil it. Let us start by acknowledging that being sick, lost, and possibly injured is considerably worse than being one or the other. In my opinion, each situation is different, and each person must make that call on their own based on the knowledge they have and the facts that exist in their particular circumstance. In most missing person cases, most people are found within 24 to 48 hours. About 5% are missing for longer than 24 hours. As discussed earlier, the average person can survive without water for 3 days, however, when you add that most Americans do not get enough water or drink a lot of caffeinated drinks (diuretics), then most of us are clearly behind the curve. Add into this equation the stress of being lost, injured, or both, exposed to the elements, and lost water during activity and that 3 days may look a little generous. Even with the thought that a person may have less than 3 days of hydration, they still have a strong chance of survival if they just wait for rescue. The issue comes when a person has to survive for more than 2 days and they have found water but they do not have a way to clean it. Should they drink it? Armed with statistics, it is a good chance that the person, if not found in the first 48 hours, will likely be found in the next 48. It takes waterborne diseases 1-2 days to develop and sometimes people can recover on their own if they have hydration or can get basic medical assistance. Therefore, if you drank bad water on the second day of a survival situation, you may give yourself at least an extra day of survival. The issue is that after the 1-2 day gestation period of the bacteria or parasites, you then will have added another complication to an already bad situation, and it is important

> It takes waterborne diseases 1-2 days to develop and sometimes people can recover on their own if they have hydration or can get basic medical assistance. Therefore, if you drank bad water on the second day of a survival situation, you may give yourself at least an extra day of survival.

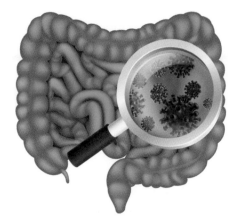

to note that there are situations where people have been lost for more than 7-40 days. Once the symptoms of a waterborne illness develop, then you will begin to dehydrate faster through vomiting and diarrhea. During this type of illness you will often lose faster than you replace which will ultimately lead to death. As I said earlier, this is a choice each individual has to make on their own based on their understanding. However, please note the clear standard is that all water should be filtered, then boiled before drinking or, at minimum, filtered. In most wilderness situations there will be an easy way to accomplish at least one or both tasks. This will give you the best odds of survival.

Now that we understand how to find water, and we know the dangers in and around it, we can focus on how to properly procure water. There are 4 specific phases to water procurement. When followed properly they will give you a great foundation of how to provide this essential component of survival.

4 STAGES OF SURVIVAL WATER PROCUREMENT

To ensure things stay simple, it is important to break water procurement down into easy to follow stages that can be remembered during a high stress life-threatening scenario. I speak about this often in my classes as a way to impress upon people the intensity of how overwhelming survival truly is. The Ninja had 4 primary stages to procuring water, which are:

> If Ninja had the acronym K.I.S.S. (keep it simple stupid) it would have meant Keep It Simple for Survival.

- Sourcing.
- Collecting.
- Filtering.
- Purifying.

Each of these stages has various methods of how they can be completed. Many of the modern methods taught require that you have the proper equipment and sometimes that equipment has a learning curve. The highlight of thinking like a Ninja and using Ninja methods is that learning how to do more with less is a primary mode of education, and then there's the idea of also being prepared with the latest easy to use, low energy, and space consuming gadget. If Ninja had the acronym K.I.S.S. (keep it simple stupid) it would have meant Keep It Simple for Survival. Breaking it down the 4 Stages of Survival Water Procurement, Ninja style is as simple as they can be, requiring little to no equipment, just a working knowledge of the proper process of what makes water safe to drink.

Sourcing – *Mizu o mitsukeru*

Sourcing is the first step to getting water. It refers to finding water in an unfamiliar area. There are two phases of sourcing water which are finding it and assessing it.

Finding it – Look for it downhill, follow animal trails, watch for birds congregating over one area, pay attention to the fly and mosquito numbers, look for transitions from sparse vegetation to thick vegetation.

Assessing it – Look for life in the water, look for signs of life moving to and from the water, assess the smell and look of the water, note the rate of flow. Is it moving fast, slow, or is it stagnate?

In a calm state, these processes are simple to do. However, in a frantic or frightened state, these observations and actions are sometimes hard to accomplish. Beyond the fear associated with being lost and injured, there is also the very real debilitating fear of making the wrong choice. In an earlier chapter, we discussed the fight, flight, or freeze concept. Freezing and not responding can happen when a person feels that making the wrong choice could make their situation worse. The best way to deal with this is through confidence, which comes with preparation. When I say preparation, I do not mean as in having a plethora of gear, I mean actual training to overcome obstacles that you could face. Having enough understanding that you can confidently think through and creatively find a solution to a problem is paramount. This would be the perfect use of the Void (Ku) element of the Ninja method of using the Go-Dai. Sourcing is not just finding what you need,

Freezing and not responding can happen when a person feels that making the wrong choice could make their situation worse. The best way to deal with this is through confidence, which comes with preparation.

it is understanding how to find the drive and answers to accomplish the tasks at hand.

Collecting – *Mizu Atsume*

Sourcing water in an area that you are unfamiliar with and dealing with a possible injury is a task. With both issues combined, every step can be a painful stab to your physical and mental moral. Once you find a water source, you may be overwhelmed with emotion and want to drink right away, but this is not safe and can lead to more extreme issues. Therefore, you will need to filter and purify it, unless you can only do one based on the materials you can find. Regardless of what you choose to do, you will need a way to gather the water. This is called the Collection Stage (Mizu Atsume), and I break it down into 2 aspects which are ***gathering and the containing***. The gathering aspect of water collection is how you retrieve the water for drinking, filtering, or purifying. The containing aspect of water collection is how you can contain the water for filtration, purification, and transport. There is a distinction between the 2 because they are not always the same. You could gather water with an article of clothing like a rain jacket or with vegetation like a leaf, however, you cannot purify it with boiling in these materials, nor can you adequately transport it long distances. You may be able to collect and boil water in a rock depression, but you will not be able to transport it to another location. Containing holds the water in place, whereas gathering is how you get the water. In survival, containing also refers to something you will have that can allow for filtering, boiling, and transporting. In the previous example, a cotton shirt could allow for gathering and filtration, while the rock depression could allow for containing and boiling. These are just two of the examples that explain why it is important to highlight the difference between these 2 aspects.

Gathering Water

Let us look at methods of how to accomplish both in a survival situation. The first is improvised gathering methods, which are creative ways to gather water. Four improvised gathering methods for water are:

- Morning dew soaked up with cloths – Asa Tsuyu.

- Tie rag to a tree – Ki ni shibaru tsukau boro

- Use clothing or a rag to absorb from a river – Kawa kara mizu o kyūshū suru nuno mochiiru

- Rainfall collection, use a waterproof jacket, bark, bamboo or a leaf – Ame.

Morning dew soaked up with cloths

Tie rag to a tree

 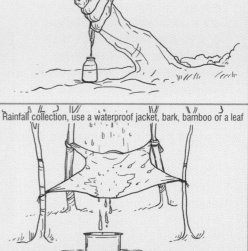

Use clothing or a rag to absorb from a river

Rainfall collection, use a waterproof jacket, bark, bamboo or a leaf

Using clothing and rags to absorb the water also serves the purpose of filtering. Although the quality of filtration provided by a shirt dipped in contaminated water or rubbed on dirty surfaces (trees and leaves) to collect dew is minimal, it still offers some benefits as it can filter out bigger particles of debris.

There are certain plants and vines that contain potable water, however, since this book is a general guide for people with little knowledge and there is no telling where readers live or what areas they could travel to where a survival situation could occur, it is in my opinion that teaching methods based on a vast majority of wilderness environments and that do not require specific identification skills as more important.

Containing Water

Containing water is a little trickier than gathering. There are 3 ways I teach that I refer to as **The Core 3 Methods of Containment**. As a part of explaining these methods, it is also important to acknowledge that in most survival scenarios just containing the water is not enough. Often a container will need to serve one or all purposes for improving your ability to stay hydrated. They will have to allow for filtration, boiling, or transporting water in them. Not all containers are created equally, so understanding how and what you are able to do with what you have, find, or make is important. The Core 3 Methods of Containment refer to 3 ways to provide adequate containment of water for 1 of the 3 purposes. These 3 methods are to carry or have a container with you, find a container in the area you are lost, or to make a container out of things you find in the environment. A further breakdown is as follows:

Carry it – Yoki o hakobu

- Have a metal canteen or water bottle.
- Have a plastic bottle, food container, or bag.

Find it – Yoki o sagasu

- Find natural depressions in rock that holds water.
- Find items like glass, plastic bottles, or pieces of metal you could make into a container make sure that the container was not used to transport chemicals by looking at it and smelling it.
- Use turtle shells or hallow skulls of animals. Be sure to clean before use.

Make it – Yoki o tsukuru

- Use a green (living) bamboo stalk.
- Improvise using a piece of clothing like waterproof sleeves.
- Burn a bowl in a thick tree branch.
- Remove a piece of bark from a tree.

Rock depression   *Glass bottle*

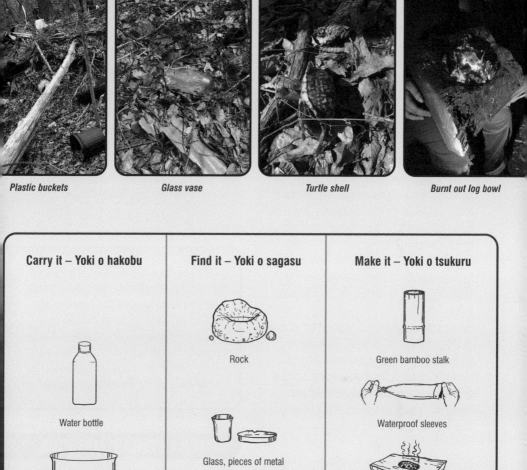

Plastic buckets   Glass vase   Turtle shell   Burnt out log bowl

Carry it – Yoki o hakobu

Water bottle

Food container

Find it – Yoki o sagasu

Rock

Glass, pieces of metal

Turtle shell

Make it – Yoki o tsukuru

Green bamboo stalk

Waterproof sleeves

Burn a bowl in a thick tree branch

Bark from a tree

There are a number of ways that a lost person can gather and contain water, but these are a few of the simplest that I have found using both methods from the past and methods of the present.

Filtering – *Rokka*

As we discussed in the previously filtering is not the same as purifying. Although it offers some protection if you have a water source that is mildly contaminated with bacteria and parasites, the chances are that even with filtering you could still get sick. This is why it is important to always look for means to boil your water. Even before boiling, the process of filtering your water can offer additional safety. Debris or smaller bugs that are present in water could find their way into your container. I can tell you from experience having a tiny stick find its way down your throat is no fun, especially if it scratches it on the way down. Using a filter can help remove big and small debris as well as aerate the water. Adding charcoal to the filter process can aid in removing some impurities and bad taste.

When a filter is needed, start first by looking at the clothes on your back. Clothing can be used for many things in a survival situation. For instance, it can be ripped to make improvised cordage; it can be used as a wound dressing, to make a brace or sling, and even as a stretcher. Its primary use, however, should be shelter. With the exception of extreme circumstances in a survival situation, I recommend keeping your clothes intact and used for the purpose they are designed for. However, there is one other thing you can use your clothing for which will still allow it to serve its primary function as well. The function I am referring to is aiding in water filtration. The reason for this is because, although you may filter water with an article of your clothing, you can then dry it out and use it for its intended purpose. It is recommended that if you choose to do this in a colder climate you should do so when you have a fire going so that you can maintain warmth while using the clothing and then immediately dry the article right after use. This will help alleviate the

danger of collecting the water and your hands and fingers going numb and losing range of motion while simultaneously dropping your core temperature and then having to attempt to make a fire afterward.

As we discussed in the shelter section on clothing material, cotton material loves water. Therefore, cotton is the prime candidate for an improvised filter. Other absorbing materials like wool can be used as well. In any case, using absorbing clothing to first gather the water and capture the debris and bigger particles and then turning it inside out and wringing it into a container can aid in providing minimally filtered water.

> *Just to mention, there are compact water filters on the market like the Life Straw that will filter most bacteria and parasites but will not help with chemical contaminants. However, this book is about teaching the person who is unprepared how to survive with the resources around them, because often those that are lost are not gear prepped.*

WATER FILTERING METHODS

Now that we understand the importance of a filter, let's discuss 4 filtering methods that are easy to accomplish with a combination of only the resources you would have if you were unprepared and what could be found in most wilderness environments.

Seep/Indian Well or Gypse Well

I like the method of using the Indian Well/ Gypse Well as a means to filter water because it uses the way the land naturally filters as a means to produce cleaner water for drinking in an emergency situation. I personally used a Seep to survive for 18 days in India. I had no resources and no way to boil water. Out of desperation, I found a flowing stream which I dug a Seep next to, and as the water seeped in, I gave it time to settle. I made a straw out of a leaf and drank out of the well, and then I covered it up after each use. Every 2-3 days, or when

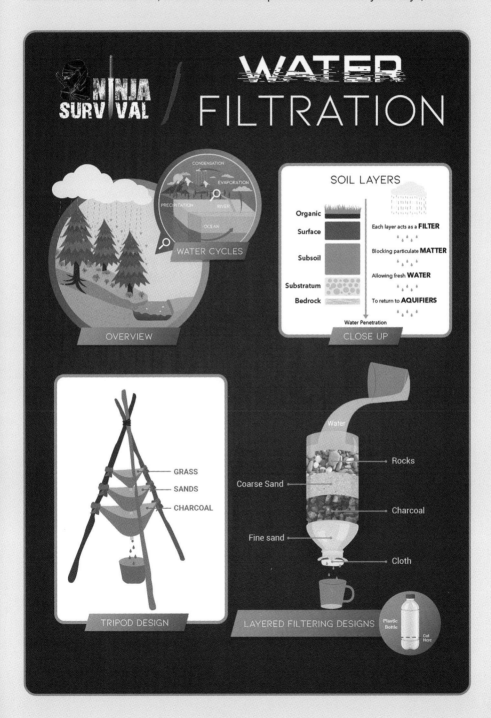

I felt the water was too exposed, I would dig a new one. I never got sick and, after returning and going to the doctor for a checkup, no parasites were discovered and I received a clean bill of health. Although I know this method works, I caution any survivor to try their best to boil all water before drinking it.

Seeps take advantage of the natural process of water filtering through the land. When water hits the surface of the earth, some of it moves along and some of it is absorbed into the land. Water permeates through gaps in soil particles. Soil that has bigger particles like gravel will allow water to pass through a lot easier than soil that have smaller particles like sand. Eventually, as water percolates into the earth through permeable layers it will reach areas that are less permeable (like clay) or non-permeable (like granite). At these areas, the water will be halted where it can either pool or move in a path where it finds the least resistance until it discovers an outlet. During this process of percolation, the bacteria and micro-organisms in the soil help break down harmful contaminants. The soil is able to cleanse water of bacteria, viruses, metals, and chemicals as a natural part of its design (vegetation also aids in this process). Springs are an example of this as they commonly are sources of pure water since it spawns naturally from an underground source. On the contrary, lakes, rivers, and streams often receive water from the surface runoff, and thus, the water passes over many impurities and not through any type of filtering before entering these waterways, therefore leaving it contaminated. A seep takes advantage of soils ability to filter out contaminants by creating a way for possible contaminated water to flow through, allowing for bigger particulates and some other contaminants to be reduced.

How to make a Seep

- Find a plot of low-lying ground that is at least 3 feet away from a waterway or body of water, even if stagnate. An area where vegetation is close is also good, as the roots of the vegetation will help with the filtering process. If there is not a body of water present but the ground is very moist, this may also be a sign of a great spot.

> The Ninja called the process of finding and digging in an area to get cleaner water *Ana Hori*.

- Sharpen a stick that is at least half the diameter of your wrist to use as a digging utensil or break and abrade the end on a rock until sharp if you do not have a knife.

- Start digging a hole 2-3 feet away from the water source that is the width and length of your forearm, from about the elbow to your fingertips, and deep enough to reach below the water table. During this process, be mindful of the energy you are expanding. Be slow and methodical as this will require less of your body's resources.

- The hole will either fill immediately or slowly. Take note of how fast the hole fills. The slower the better as this will mean the water is moving through dense soil and receiving more filtration. Also, take note of how deep the water is in the hole. You want to have at least a foot deep of water.

- Let the sediment in the water settle and then you can drink. Muddy or murky water can be consumed, but it will not taste very pleasant. However, the thing you want to avoid the most is drinking noticeable particulates in the water. Skim any of these off the top that you may see.

- When not using the well, cover it up with a leaf or grass to help keep things from falling in it. Another addition is that after you have rehydrated you might want to include rocks to sure up the sides of the well and keep sediment from falling or eroding into your well. The issue with this is that the rock may have unseen contaminates on them that you are now introducing to your well, in effect negating the filtering benefits. To fix that problem you can cook the rock in a fire first before use.

- Sometimes as you scoop the water you can disturb sediment at the bottom of the well causing a host of debris to swirl around, making it near impossible to take a drink without slurping up a small chunk of nastiness. Therefore, one trick I use is to make a straw out of a leaf, this way I can avoid the disturbance caused by the mass of my hand. Depending on the depth of the well, this can be difficult. You can also add a piece of ripped off clothing such as a cotton shirt and put it in the rolled-up leaf to create a rough filter like in a cigarette.

Find a plot of low-lying ground that is at least 3 feet away from a body of water.

3 ft.

Sharpen a stick and start digging a hole 2-3 feet away from the water source.

The hole will either fill slow or fast. Slow is better.

Let the sediment in the water settle and hen you can drink.

When not using the well, cover it up.

You can make a straw out of a leaf to avoid disturbing the water when you drink.

It is important to note that an Indian Well will not remove all contaminants from the water and is still a risk if you do not boil it. In addition, as I mentioned in my personal story, they should not be used indefinitely as it is mostly stagnant and will begin to form bacteria. It may also attract critters and animals that may investigate, drink, or contaminate it with waste. Each time you go to the seep it should be thoroughly inspected for any signs of contamination.

Improvised Layered Filters

Other than a Seep, there are 3 improvised filters that take advantage of the same style of layered filtering that the earth uses, but it is created artificially. This concept was known to Ninja as **Rokka**, and they are very easy methods and can be created with very little resources, most of which can be found in any wilderness environment in the United States. These 3 filters are the bark, sock and bottle filter. Each is created with the same layering process but they are all contained differently. The bark filter uses flexible bark from a tree as a container; a sock filter uses a sock to

I would like to highlight that I was in both the wilderness of the Himalayan mountains of India and deep in the Jungles of Columbia, and without fail I stumbled across bottles (plastic and glass), plastic bags, and pieces of ripped material. All of which can be used to create a water filter.

contain the filtration layers, and the bottle filter uses a bottle as a containment medium.

How to make a Layered Survival Water Filter

Not all these materials are needed, but if you have them all available, they can make a quality filter.

- Decide on what materials you have available to make your filter. You will need ridged or flexible containing shell such as tree bark, a sock, or plastic bottle. If you use a plastic bottle be sure to examine for the smell of possible toxins. You will need filtering materials such as gravel, sand, vegetation, cotton or tightly woven wool, and charcoal.

- Create your containing unit. You can cut a long strip of flexible sheet-like bark off of a tree and roll it up in a cone-like shape, and then tie it with a piece of material or vine, or you can use a bottle. If you use a bottle, cut at least two inches off the bottom, this will provide you with a filter and a container. Rinse both ends out. Once it is rinsed out, put the cap on the top or use a rock or vegetation to plug up the opening in both of the bark container and the bottle container.

- Start layering your filtering material. Start with vegetation, such as moss or grass, or fabric, such as a sock or a stripe from your clothing; next, add activated charcoal from your fire, if you have it, or sand; add grass or non-harmful vegetation; then add gravel.

- Place the filter over a container and fill the top with water and allow it to percolate through the filter to the container. You may want to hold the filter or use an improvised holder to keep it upright while it filters.

- At this point, the filtered water should be boiled.

If you do not have access to some of these materials, then you can improvise or minimize your diversity of layers and instead add more alternating layers of the materials you do have. The goal is that the water has to move through multiple layers over different densities to properly filter.

The water may still look murky but will contain less contaminates than when it went into the filter. It is also important to mention that in a situation where you do not have, cannot find, and cannot make a container, your best option will be to use the Seep method as the earth may do a better job filtering than you can with minimal resources.

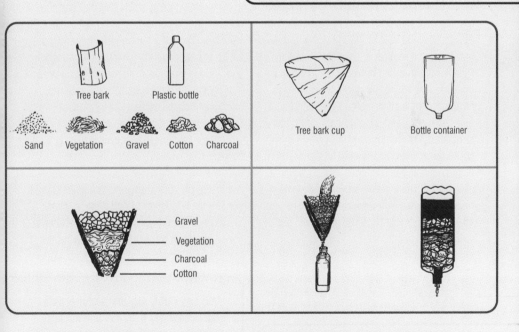

Tree bark   Plastic bottle

Sand   Vegetation   Gravel   Cotton   Charcoal

Tree bark cup   Bottle container

—— Gravel
—— Vegetation
—— Charcoal
—— Cotton

Using the methods listed here are not the only means of filtering water. However, they follow the guidelines passed down to the Ninja for generations, they are easy to make, effective, and they can be created with limited resources.

If you have the material to spare (non-essential clothing), the process of layering used in the above methods can also be used in what is called a tripod filter. When making a tripod filter, you will only need 3 layers. The bottom will be charcoal, the middle sand, and the top grass.

You can get amazing results with a primitive filter as seen here. Water on the right side of the photo is from the dirty stagnate pond shown in the collection section of this chapter. On the left side of the photo is pure bottled water. As you can see there is not much difference in the color although the pond water was not transparent when collected.

PURIFICATION – JOKA

In a survival situation, short of collecting lots of rain, the best way to get the water you need is to source it, collect it, filter it, and boil it. Rain is safe to drink, however, short of opening wide and letting the water collect in your mouth, the collection method (hand, poncho, bark, leaf, etc.) and the container could contaminate it. These contaminants could make you sick further complicating an already complicated situation. Therefore, boiling water, a process the Ninja called **Shafutsu Sakkin**, is a must if possible. A temperature between 150-180°F will kill most bacteria, parasites, and viruses in a minute or less. Water boils when its temperature reaches 212°F at sea level and 200.1°F at an altitude of 6,000 feet. This highlights that the boiling point of water becomes lower as altitude increases. Armed with this

knowledge, you can safely say that water is potable once it has begun to boil because it will have reached a temperature beyond that which is needed to kill the bacteria, parasites, and viruses that could inhabit the water when you collect it from a natural source. Some additional details are to not worry about trying to boil the water longer than a minute as you will only waste water as it evaporates. In addition to losing valuable water, the longer you burn the water the more wear and tear you will cause on your fabricated container. Unless you are lucky enough to find a glass, metal, or stone container, you will have to fashion a container out of the natural resources of the environment (wooden bowls, bamboo, bark

In a survival situation, short of collecting lots of rain, the best way to get the water you need is to source it, collect it, filter it, and boil it.

You can safely say that water is potable once it has begun to boil because it will have reached a temperature beyond that which is needed to kill the bacteria, parasites, and viruses that could inhabit the water when you collect it from a natural source.

bowls, etc.). Using natural resources means that your containers will be susceptible to damage from repeated exposure to fire. The longer you expose it to heat the sooner you will have to look for a replacement. The point to remember is that once the water begins to boil the water is safe to drink.

Understanding how water is made safe for drinking and when it is safe is only one piece of the puzzle. The next step is to understand how to actually purify water with limited to no resources. To accomplish this, you will need an effective method of boiling water that can be created with materials that can be found in the environment. I have found 3 methods that are very effective at enabling water boiling in all the wilderness environments that I have been in. These water boiling methods are:

- **Rock Boiling – Atsui ishi to no mizu o futto.**
- **Improvised Container Boiling – Sokkyo yoki to no mizu o futto.**

> *As stated earlier man-made trash can be found everywhere and with it containers for boiling and transporting water. Be sure to check for impurities and rinse before use.*

What is Rock Boiling?

Rock boiling is done by using a non-porous and heat resistant material to gather and contain water in, and then heating up non-moist rocks in a fire and placing them in the container. The heat from the rocks is transferred into the water through conduction, and it raises the temperature to a boiling point. Such containers can be living bamboo shoots,

turtle shells, and animal skulls. Immobile containers such as depressions in rocks, boulders, or cracks in granite can be used as well. Hot rocks can also be used to boil water in stone or a bark lined Seep to get filtered and purified water.

What is Improvised Container Boiling?

Improvised boiling is done by using a non-porous natural material that can absorb and pass heat without breaking down right away. Examples of natural material that can be used are shoots of living bamboo, turtle shells, and animal skulls (make sure to clean with water, ash, and heat before use). Once one of these containers is acquired, there are 2 methods of boiling:

- Rock boiling.
- Direct fire boiling.

The process of the rock boiling method is as such:

- Filtered water is put in one of the natural containers.
- Next rocks should be collected that are not near waterways as they could have moisture in them and could explode if heated rapidly, and placed in a fire.

- Once the rocks have been heated, they are carefully placed with a pair of tongs made with a living branch or a split stick with a flat surface in the container with the water.
- Repeat until the water begins to boil.
- Let the water cool, remove the rocks, and drink.

The process of the direct boiling method is the simplest and does not need a break down as it is just to gather the water and set the container over or near the fire until it boils.

These 2 methods of boiling water should not be underestimated as they are as simple as you can get when trying to find a way to purify your water. There are 2 other ways to collecting pure water that should be mentioned because although they require materials not made in nature, the material needed can often be found.

Purification Worth Mention

Transpiration or Vegetation bags and Solar Stills, known to the Ninja as **Taiyo Netsu Joryu Sochi**, are important to mention as they are easy to make and they are passive purification methods, which means you can set it up and leave it. The process will take place naturally, and thus, it requires little to no energy. Unfortunately, setting them up can be problematic as they require unnatural materials that you may not have with you, however, could be found in the environment. As I mentioned earlier, I have been to several

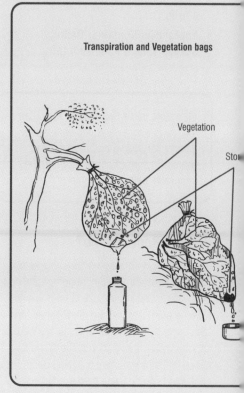

Transpiration and Vegetation bags

Vegetation

Stor

remote wilderness environments where I have managed to find plastic bags and bottles. Therefore, I think it is worth it to acknowledge that these 2 methods of gathering pure water are important. It is also important to mention 1 obvious issue that it is often times hard to know what was in or may have contaminated these materials, and therefore, trying to use these found materials could prove problematic, and they should only be used in the direst of circumstances. The exception to this is if you happen to find yourself in a survival situation with a clear plastic bag that maybe you had a sandwich in and a left-over plastic bottle from the little water you brought out on a trip.

Transpiration and Vegetation bags

These are essentially the same as they take advantage of the same process which is cap-

turing water that evaporates mainly from plant leaves. The difference is that with a transpiration bag you just place a clear bag over a branch of a tree or bush with many leaves and tie it off. With a vegetation bag you remove the branch or the vegetation from the bush or tree and place it in the bag on the ground at an angle. In both bags, a rock, button, or another tiny weighted object should be placed in the bottom to create an area where the water can settle. In both cases, the bags should be clear and located in direct sunlight. As water vapor is released by the plants, it condenses on the inside surface of the bag and begins to pool in the bottom. Even though the water that is produced from the plants is pure, if the plant material has been contaminated or if it is toxic it will taint the water. Therefore, care should be taken in the selection of tree or vegetation you use.

Solar Still

Vegetation

Stone

Solar Stills

Solar stills, like the transpiration bag, use heat from the sun to create water vapor from plants. It can also produce clean water from contaminated in a cup and water placed in a hole, covered, with a piece of clear or white plastic. The water vapor from the plants, moist soil, or container of contaminated water condenses on the plastic covering, and then follows the underside of the plastic, which is concaved to a point, where the water then falls into a collection container. The plastic can then be removed and the water in the non-contaminated container can be consumed.

It is important to remember that beyond bacteria, parasites, and viruses, there are also unnatural pollutants that can exist in water. These may not be removed during the filtering and purification process. Therefore, it is important to use the assessment we described earlier to help determine if water is contaminated.

USE THE ELEMENTS AS A GUIDE

As we discussed in earlier chapters, the elements can be used as a guide to remember the following aspects of what to do to find water. In survival, things can sometimes be overcomplicated or hard to recall. It is easy to forget to think of the elements. One example is in finding clean water using methods we discussed in this chapter but correlating them to one of the Go Dai 5 elemental manifestations.

- **Chi** – Dig a seep or well.
- **Sui** – Collect rain or water from leaves or flowers.
- **Ka** – Use heat from the sun to gather water from vegetation with a bag. This is called a transpiration or a vegetation bag.
- **Ku** – Collecting dew (condensed atmospheric moisture) from plants.
- **Fu** – Creatively using the knowledge of the process of water collection, filtration, and purification to create and acquire the water you need to survive.

Armed with these few aspects of water search, discovery, and processing will ensure someone trying to survive long enough to find rescue has a strong chance of providing the essential hydration they need to sustain the bodies functions until help arrives.

CHAPTER
7

FOOD

SHOKURYO SHUTOKU

For the average person lost in the woods, food will not be a major issue. With the proper water consumption and little work, a person can survive for up to 30 days or more without food. This, of course, is not ideal, but if you are lost for 30 days you are in the worst of worst-case scenarios. Granted, an American used to getting 3 or more meals a day totaling more than 3,200 calories going to 0 calories can easily make you feel like you are dying in the first day or 2. Tack on the stress of being lost, maybe injured, and possibly cold, and you become a calorie burning machine with no calories to replace what you are losing. This will cause major stomach cramps, headaches, and fatigue as your body lets you know that it is unhappy with the change until it transitions to getting used to not eating. The good news is that even though you may feel like you about to die, you won't. I can personally attest to this as I survived in the wild for 21 days on just over 1000 calories. I lost 40 pounds but was still capable enough to walk several miles over rugged terrain under my own will and strength. I, of course, had a lot of water that I procured from a seep well I made and plenty of rest due to a wonderful shelter I built and slept in at night. All of this gave me the ability to survive so long without proper nourishment.

In a survival situation, it is important to maintain your energy, and there are several factors that contribute to this. The main factors that are:

- **Water.**
- **Rest.**
- **Food.**

As we discussed in earlier chapters, second to exposure, lack of water is next on the list of things that would be most likely to kill you in a survival situation. Rest and recovery cannot directly kill you but could indirectly through degrading your mental and physical capabilities, which can lead to an accident. Lack of rest and recovery can also harm your ability to survive by causing physical fatigue, which will eventually decrease your ability to accomplish tasks. Last on the list is your caloric intake. Eating is obviously important to survival in general. However, unlike water and rest, you can go for a significantly long time without food. Three weeks is the standard and, as I mentioned earlier, sometimes people have been known to go longer. It is likely that in the average survival situation you will be found or find help long before the 21-day mark. However, having options in case you end up in a long-term situation is not a bad idea.

Anyone in a survival scenario should take comfort in knowing that not having food right away is not the end of the world, and their focus should be on more immediate issues like shelter and water. However, it is important to also stay broad in vision as there may be opportunities that arise where you may identify areas that you can acquire food for later consumption. Yes, I said later consumption. Sometimes eating right away is not the best option, especially if you do not have a substantial food supply. Smaller meals will actually speed up your metabolism and cause you to burn through any energy reserves you

> Anyone in a survival scenario should take comfort in knowing that not having food right away is not the end of the world, and their focus should be on more immediate issues like shelter and water.

have faster. Ask any bodybuilder about their diet, and you will find that they eat multiple smaller meals throughout the day to help them lose fat and get lean. People who have gone on this type of diet have often experienced an increase in hunger and cravings for more food until their body is used to this eating schedule. Another benefit to eating small amounts regularly is that in the course of increasing your metabolism your body will produce more heat as it goes through a process called diet-induced thermogenesis. Therefore, if you are in a cold environment, this may help you stay warm, whereas on the opposite spectrum not eating will force your body to burn through its carbohydrate reserves and impede the body's warmth. If a proper shelter is built, staying warm will be taken care of but being hungry will remain if you eat smaller meals. Imagine how stressful it would be to eat and, instead of feeling satisfied, you feel even hungrier. In my own 3-week survival situation, I decided to wait before eating due to the lack of edible resources. I would wait until I had a quality renewable food source or until I felt like I could not function properly any longer. Essentially, what I was doing was fasting. Every year, people around the world that are not in a survival situation fast and, in most cases, they receive a great benefit from this practice.

SHORT TERM FASTING VERSUS STARVATION IN SURVIVAL

Short-term fasting has been known to provide many people with positive health benefits. From weight loss to detoxification, to an increase in energy and positive mood, fasting (known to the Ninja as Danjiki) has now become something that is not primarily done for religious and spiritual reasons, but also for fitness and health reasons. Although there is a huge difference between the person living in the safety and comfort of an abundant life in the heart of modern society and that same person being lost in the woods with no food or water, there can be an overlap in benefits from fasting.

To understand why, lets first look at what happens when you fast. Glucose is what the body primarily uses for energy. Most people acquire this glucose from carbohydrates. On average, a person's body will burn through their glucose after 8-10 hours with no food. It will then tap into any extra glucose it has collected and converted into glycogen in the liver and kidney, which is called your glycogen stores. Once this has happened, the body will begin to look for other energy sources which it will find by converting fats from the body and proteins in the muscles into energy, a process called glycogenesis. These processes highlight 2 of the body's most common metabolic pathways that are the use of sugars or fats and the proteins for fuel. After about 2 days of not eating, your body will begin to feed mostly off your fats and muscles since there are no new carbohydrates coming in, and as the days go by your body will begin to cannibalize itself. However, this sounds way worse than it is. These processes are a natural course the body goes through in order to survive. Remember, early man did not have a supermarket or fast food restaurant on every corner. Sometimes they ate, and sometimes they went without eating. Therefore, the body is designed for survival during times of little to no food consumption. During a time of fasting to maximize the longevity of resources, the body will slow down a person's metabolism. It is important to note that this process can be reversed and is halted when you eat small amounts of food because the body will think

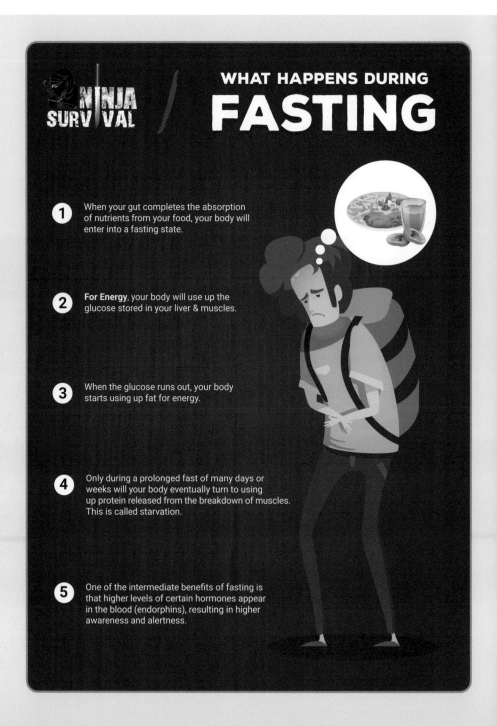

WHAT HAPPENS DURING

FASTING

1 When your gut completes the absorption of nutrients from your food, your body will enter into a fasting state.

2 **For Energy**, your body will use up the glucose stored in your liver & muscles.

3 When the glucose runs out, your body starts using up fat for energy.

4 Only during a prolonged fast of many days or weeks will your body eventually turn to using up protein released from the breakdown of muscles. This is called starvation.

5 One of the intermediate benefits of fasting is that higher levels of certain hormones appear in the blood (endorphins), resulting in higher awareness and alertness.

you have acquired a food source and can now stop its fasting process. This places your body under tremendous strain as it reverts back to using food and then back to fasting mode. This is why understanding your body is important as you may think eating a handful of berries is a good idea, especially after a day of not eating. However, although it may boost your moral, which is a benefit, it could work against you physically in a long-term situation.

Whether fasting or eating it is important to understand that you will need a lot of water as both processes require a lot of water. Fasting requires it as the body breaks down fats and proteins to produce energy whereas if you are eating the digestive system will need it to break down food. Water is the overall need regardless of what you choose, it is the primary element that needs to be present for life, period, but especially if you are without food and have to fast for a long period of time.

Although the first 2-3 days of not eating may be very unpleasant, many people who make it past this stage start to feel more focused and energized, especially after the first week. During the second week of fasting many report that they feel more refreshed, energized and clear-minded. This was a knowledge shared by the Ninja as mountain mystics shared the wisdom of fasting as a way to purify the body and to enhance the senses. This aided in their connection with nature and the ability to tap into a deep understanding of how they operated. This information was handed down through tradition as a way to give the Ninja another aspect of how to overcome the hardships of life in the wild and battle against their enemies. However, even when the Ninja were not fasting, their diets where very clean and lean. Ninja were primarily vegetarians, mostly consuming a plant-based whole food diet. Some of the common foods that they would eat were rice, yams, radish, pine fruits, millet and anything soy-based. They also would avoid foods heavy in spices that could lead to body odors as that could give away their presence if on a mission. Having a diet like this made it a lot simpler to operate covertly and maintain high energy as the wild provided a passive way to replenish food as they maneuvered through it. Since capturing and cooking food is time-consuming as well as dangerous as it could lead to their discovery. Having a body use to a lean natural diet that can be strategically harvested (acquired intently as to not leave traces by breaking branches, etc.), carried easily, and provide substantial calories to a body conditioned for lower caloric intake gave them advantage through conservation of energy, reservation of time, and proper replenishment of nutrients.

THE NINJA DIET

In addition to what a Ninja could acquire from the land while on a mission, he/she would carry rations made with ingredients that provided nutrients to aid in specific functions. These would sometimes be referred to as food pills or Ninja rations. These rations were small balls or patties made with different ingredients to promote top performance during a mission. They were in essence superfoods designed much like the modern vegan or vegetarian snack bar of today. Even our modern military have a ration called the M.R.E. or Meal Ready to Eat that they give out, however, these meals are much bigger than the Ninja food pills. The Ninja had several different types of food pills, but 3 primary ones show up in texts based on their specific focuses which center around the bodies need during long active periods with little to no resources. These 3 common food pills were:

- **Suikatsugan (Thirst Ball/Pill)** – This was made of licorice, Japanese mint, kudzu starch, dried plums, smoked plums, Poria Cocos, kasyu, and water.

- **Hyourougan** – Hyourougan is made from non-glutinous rice, fruits of the lotus, yams, fruits of the Katsura, Coix, ginseng, and crystal sugar.

- **Kikatsugan (Starving Ball/Pill)** – Kikatsugan helps a Ninja when he is in starvation. Kikatsugan is made from ginseng, buckwheat, yam, dried chickweed, adlay, glutinous rice, and sake.

These pills were said to have allowed the Ninja to accomplish incredible feats of endurance while not impeding movement by adding bulk or weight as they were carried. A review of the ingredients in several of these food rations clearly show how they could provide many of the desired benefits it boasts.

- **Porica cocos** – This is a herb that has been used for thousands of years. It aids in fluid retention and helps with fatigue, dizziness, and stomach problems. It also helps with memory loss.

- **Kudzu starch** – Is a wild vine that is considered a superfood and can be used for multiple purposes. It is used for heart and circulatory problems as well as upper respiratory problems including sinus infections. It also aids in relieving gastritis, fever, diarrhea, thirst, neck stiffness, and helps regulate glucose.

- **Smoked plums** – There are several benefits to these plums but some of the most notable for survival are intestinal health aiding with issues such as diarrhea. It helps stop vomiting, and they can also fight bacteria.

- **Dried plums** – Some of the benefits of dried plums is that they are high in fiber, potassium and vitamin A. Fiber helps you feel fuller longer, can aid in reducing inflammation, and helps improve blood sugar levels. Potassium aids in water balance, electrolytic functions as well as muscle strength. Vitamin A helps keep the eyes healthy and can improve night time vision.

- **Glutinous rice** – Also called sticky rice, is rice that only has one component of starch which is what makes it sticky. There is no gluten in the rice, but it is called glutinous because of its sticky and glue-like consistency when cooked. It takes longer to digest and, therefore, keeps a person feeling fuller longer and aids in lowering insulin levels. This rice also has some protein which aids in energy production.

- **Fruit of the Lotus/ Lotus Seed** – Is high in carbohydrates and protein as well as potassium, magnesium, and calcium. They can help stop diarrhea, boost endurance, and aid in memory functions.

- **Yams** – This food is full of complex carbohydrates, which produce longer lasting energy. They aid cognitive functions and can reduce soreness in muscles.

- **Ginseng** – This plant is a strong antioxidant and reduces inflammation. It also boosts the immune system, brain function, and energy levels.

- **Crystal sugar** – This is unrefined raw sugar and it can boost energy, help digestion, increase hemoglobin levels, and aid in reducing mental fatigue.

- **Buckwheat** – Is high in digestible plant protein and is also high in fiber so it helps in feeling full longer. It is also full of vitamins and minerals such as copper, magnesium, iron, and phosphorus that is great for the health and the growth of body tissue.

- **Adlay** – Is a grain and is also called jobs tears because of its tear-like shape. It is a quality grain that has high carbohydrates and protein content, and it is also packed with many minerals such as calcium, phosphorus, iron, niacin, and thiamin. It is known to be a good source of energy, protect against viral infection, and reduce the chances or effects of allergic reactions.

- **Chickweed** – Is a plant that is used to help with many conditions. Some of its uses include treatment for vitamin C deficiency, rabies, and muscle and joint pain. The plant is high in carbohydrates, proteins, fiber, and vitamin C.

In a review of just some of the ingredients of the Ninja pills, it becomes obvious how a Ninja could sustain a high standard of health, operation, and endurance during long active missions. These superfood rations were 1 aspect of how the Ninja could deal with hunger without having to scavenge from the landscape.

Although great to understand what the Ninja ate to maintain high functionality while existing in the wild, this does not help the modern survivor. A true survival situation is something that often hits when one least expects it and when people are least prepared. Since the focus of this book is based on someone who is not properly prepared for a survival situation, then it is important to understand methods of getting food from this perspective. This is, of course, if that person is not rescued in the likely 12-72 hour window and, even if they are not rescued in that time, if they have a sufficient water source as I highlighted earlier, a person can maintain a pretty high energy level for 7-10 days of not eating food. It is up to each individual if they want to eat sooner. If there is a plentiful food source that provides the proper nutrition, I would say go for it but if food is sparse, like it was in my 3-week survival situation, I would chose to wait and use your body's natural processes until you could find a quality food source instead of putting your body in and out of fasting or starvation mode for little to no caloric value.

FOOD IS EVERYWHERE

In the wilderness, food is often all around you. However, not all that is edible is right for you and is sufficient enough for a person trying to survive. It is important to not just understand the types of food that are common, but the advantages and disadvantages of the different foods based on the body's needs. In order to do this, first we should understand what the body needs to survive and thrive.

There are a lot of survival shows on television and it is often said that protein is the prize for the day.

> **In the wilderness, food is often all around you. However, not all that is edible is right for you and is sufficient enough for a person trying to survive.**

Proteins are indeed important for the body, but when it comes to survival, they can cause issues that need to be understood before seeking them out. In truth, the human body needs a lot of different nutrients, but there are 3 that are highly important, which are called macronutrients. These 3 macronutrients are carbohydrates, fats, and proteins. Most Americans get their energy from carbohydrates and, as we stated earlier, when this is depleted the body moves to burning fats. Once the body's fat stores are depleted, then the body will move to proteins. Proteins are indeed good and really do aid in many of the body's functions. Protein is also readily available in safe and easy to acquire forms like bugs, eggs, fish, and mammals, whereas it is tough to find strong sources of carbohydrates in the wild. An added benefit is that in many of the forms mentioned, proteins are also accompanied by fat. However, even though they are more available in a survival situation, proteins can create certain issues. One major issue is that proteins require a lot of water intake to properly breakdown; therefore, they deplete water stores in the body. During protein's metabolism, a person's metabolic rate increases which forces the body to use more energy. Do not get me wrong, if you can kill an animal or find a grub nest that provides you with a substantial amount of quality protein and fat after several days of not eating, I would say go for it. We need protein to survive, but as protein is metabolized in the body ammonia levels increase. Then it is collected by the kidney and released in the urine. Not only is your body using water for metabolizing, but it is also using water to expel the waste as urine. As stated earlier you will need a lot of water, and your body will use a lot of energy to process protein. It is also important to note that during starvation, the body will use protein for energy by breaking down your muscles, so by the time you eat you will likely be in a state where the body is primed for the process of converting protein into usable energy. Just understand that this extra work will produce more strain on an already strained system. Now that we understand if we should eat and what we need from our food, let's discuss how we get food and what we can eat. For a person not familiar with gathering food in the wild, it can be extremely difficult to make good decisions on what to eat, especially if you are stressed and possibly injured. Because this book is primarily to provide the knowledge to survive a short-term survival situation, we will focus on some of the most common and easy to acquire food sources that, with little knowledge and effort, will give a survivor the most bang for their buck in a wilderness environment.

HOW YOU GET YOUR FOOD IS IMPORTANT – SHOKURYO SHUTOKU

For a person not familiar with self-reliance wilderness skills, gathering food can be a challenge. There are 2 main ways to get food in the wild and they are **active gathering and passive gathering**, and it is important to know the difference.

Active gathering is anything that requires you to do constant work, for instance, foraging and hunting. These 2 methods of food procurement require continuous work, time and focus to accomplish. This inevitably degrades your survival situation through the usage of valuable calories.

Passive gathering is when you work a little by setting up traps, and then relaxing while the trap does the work of capturing your food. Passive gathering requires work on the front end, but normally has the potential to provide more calories than it uses. Whereas, something like hunting could require lots of calories to attempt with continued failure to succeed in replenishing those calories, if you do not succeed in killing food. In a survival situation, passive gathering is usually better because, after the small amount of work put in, the survivor can move on to other tasks while the trap retains the ability to acquire a potential food source.

FOOD SOURCES

In any wilderness environment, there will be common food sources that are easy to find. However, some will require more energy and know how to collect. These common sources of food are:

- **Insects.**
- **Plants.**
- **Fish.**
- **Reptiles.**
- **Mammals.**

Each food source has a value that encompasses the knowledge to gather it, the effort to process it and its nutritional value. Breaking down each food source is important as it will help a survivor make an informed decision that will best suit their situation.

INSECTS

In most other countries, insects are a part of the diet. However, in America, this is taboo. Insects are a good source of food because they are easy to find, gather, and process with minimal effort. The issue with insects is that most of them do not provide enough calories to be of any substantial help unless you can gather a lot of them. However, even if you

cannot find a lot of insects for consumption, you may choose to eat them as a boost in moral (for most Americans who are not use to eating bugs, this is not the case), or you can use them as bait to capture bigger calories such as fish. There are over 1,400 edible insects, but here we will discuss some of the more common quality and abundant insect food sources, which are:

- **Earthworms** – Earthworms can be found near bodies of water and in damp moist places like under rocks, rotting logs, and debris. If they are not on the surface, digging in areas that meet these criteria may lead to the discovery of earthworms. They are likely to emerge from the ground after rain as it becomes saturated with water and they move to the surface towards less saturation. Earthworms contain great nutritional value as they

Earthworm

Snails

Grub

have protein, carbohydrates, and fats. They are also high in calcium, iron, and amino acids which help repair body tissue. Worms weigh about 0.40 ounces (nearly half a gram), therefore, you will need at least 3 to make a gram. Although, earthworms are 70-80% protein, it will take quite a few of them to get a quality amount of nutrition.

• **Snails** – Land snails prefer to move at darker times in the day. Direct exposure to sunlight can dry them out, so they like to live in damp dark places such as under rocks, fallen trees, or debris. Water snails like to live at the bottom of moving bodies of clear water. Snails are low in carbohydrates but high in protein. A snail can provide almost 14 grams of protein; they are also high in potassium and magnesium. Depending on the snail, they can weigh anywhere from 1-40 grams. Therefore, a few can go a long way.

• **Grubs** – Grubs are the larvae of beetles. They can often be found in punk and rotting wood as well as under rocks and leaf litter. They are great sources of protein, and they even have some carbohydrates. Depending on the grub, they can be composed of over 40% protein. Of course, this does not mean that eating one will give you that, but it highlights that almost half of a grub's makeup is quality protein.

• **Grasshoppers and Crickets** – Although they look similar, they are different. Grasshoppers are bigger, they can fly, they have shorter antennae, and they are brighter in color (bright green). Crickets, on the other hand, are smaller,

Grasshopper

Cricket

they do not fly, they have long antennae, and they are darker in color. Grasshoppers are active during the day while crickets are active during the night. Grasshoppers can often be found in grass, and although crickets can also be found there, they prefer rocks, leaves, logs, and other debris. Both grasshoppers and crickets are high in protein and fat. 100 grams of grasshoppers can provide 25 or more grams of protein, whereas 100 grams of crickets can provide around 15 or more grams of protein, as well as 5 grams of fats and carbohydrates. A grasshopper weighs about a half of a gram so you would need at least two for every 1, so that is 200 grasshoppers for 100 grams which is a lot to gather by hand. Crickets are about 0.25 to 0.30 grams, so you would need 3 or 4 to make 1 gram. Always be sure to remove the wings and legs of these insects as they often carry parasites.

There are other insects that can be eaten safely such as beetles, termites, caterpillars, and more. However, there are others that, even though they can be eaten safely, should probably be avoided. Bugs such as spiders and ants are edible, but they can pose a potential threat as some may be venomous, fast, and can bite if threatened. Since it sometimes can be a challenge to discern from the harmful and the non-harmful, it is best to avoid these insects unless it is absolutely necessary.

As you can see by the numbers, it would take a lot of a particular insect to get the amount of nutrition you would need. This, of course, means it would take you a lot of time to collect them and, although in a lost survival scenario, you are normally in a time rich situation (meaning all your time is devoted to survival), unless you are starving (meaning you have not eaten for over a week or two) there are other things that you may want to use your time for, like gathering firewood, improving your shelter, digging another seep or prepping

a signal fire station. However, catching insects can be of benefit as they can be used to acquire bigger calories. For instance, as mentioned earlier, you can use worms or crickets to catch fish or birds. This would be a better use of your resources as one or two worms can yield a significantly greater food source.

It is important to remember that even a small amount of food can take your body out of ketosis and inadvertently cause more damage than good as your body believes that it has a consistent food source and will switch back to trying to metabolize and gain energy from food. This will cause a lot of physical and mental strain, so it is often advised to wait until it is necessary or you have a renewable food source before beginning to eat.

As a final note, if you must eat insects, there are other guidelines to adhere to when identifying for consumption. These will allow for a quick assessment that will save time and, potentially, any health issues as a result of touching or eating these bugs.

- Do not attempt to eat or touch brightly colored insects.
- Do not attempt to eat or touch hairy insects.
- Do not attempt to eat dead insects.

There is one final rule, which is probably the most important of all, and that is to always cook insects before you eat them. You never know what they have crawled over, eaten, or what parasites they may have on them or in them. Cooking will kill many of the possible dangers that could harm you, leaving you with just a valuable food resource.

PLANTS

Plants, berries, and nuts are a great source of food as they can provide good nutrients with little effort. However, they also pose a major issue for little reward as you will likely need a lot of plants for substantial caloric intake. For the average person, plants are difficult to properly identify. Therefore, they can easily become a problem as, in some cases, certain edible plants can look very

similar to other poisonous plants. If a person is not very familiar with an area, plants can be a hit or miss. In an anxious, distressed, panicked, or fatigued state of mind, a lost person can easily misread a plant species or be so desperate that they make themselves believe it is something it is not. This is why I often recommend that if you are not extremely confident you should avoid plants unless there is no other choice. However, if eating plants or berries is an absolute must for survival, there is a test that you can do to improve the chances of not eating a harmful or deadly one. The Ninja called this process **Shokumotsu tenken** which refers to a 5-step wild plant edibility test.

If after 24 hours of trying a little and then eating a bit more, you do not have any symptoms then you can add the plant to your diet.

1. Inspect the plant visually and by smell. If it is slimy or smells like peaches do not eat it.

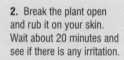

2. Break the plant open and rub it on your skin. Wait about 20 minutes and see if there is any irritation.

3. Next touch it to your lip, preferably on the side of the mouth, and wait about 20 minutes to see if there is any stinging or swelling.

4. Put a little piece in your mouth and hold it on the tongue for several minutes to see if there is an effect. If nothing, then chew the piece and hold it in your mouth without swallowing for 10 minutes.

5. If you have no negative effects such as burning, stinging, or swelling, then you can swallow and wait at least 12 hours to see if there is an adverse effect. If not, then eat more and wait another 12 hours.

It is important to remember that, for the most part, plants have little caloric value and do not offer much by way of energy unless there is a lot to collect. Nuts and berries, on the other hand, may provide more sustenance but a person will still need a lot of these to provide proper nutrition.

FISH

Most likely, if you are able to find water then you are able to find fish. Fish are a great food source that is often renewable, but they can pose a challenge to catch without the proper tools. Things such as fishing hooks, fishing line, a fishing rod, and bate are all tools that allow for ease when capturing fish. All of which can be fashioned in the wild with the right equipment. On a survival excursion in the Fujian jungle, I used an inner strain from paracord with a safety pin to catch fish. However inventive, these were items I had with me as part of knowing they could be used in a survival situation. For a person that ends up in this situation accidentally, these tools take some know how to produce from nothing, and if you are not a trained outdoor self-reliance expert, chances are you will have a hard time creating these items in the wild. For this reason, it is easier to rely on simple traps that require minimal material, little know-how, and memory to create.

Fish are full of valuable nutrients that can keep a person going for a long time. They are the staple diet of many cultures for just this reason. In the wilderness, there is little to no chance of capturing a fish that, once cooked, would pose a health risk. The exception would be a fish that is living in chemically contaminated water or one that is already dead. There is a multitude of fish that live in the bodies of water in and around wilderness environments. Some are saltwater fish living in oceans, rivers, and saltwater ponds, while others are freshwater fish that can be found in lakes, ponds, rivers, streams, and marshes. There are some fish, like salmon, that can exist in both as they start out in the ocean and move upstream to spawn. These types of transitioning fish are called euryhaline fish. Almost half of the fish in North America (41%) live in fresh water, with an additional 1% being euryhaline. Therefore, as stated earlier, any body of water found in the wild is likely to have fish in it. Some of the more common fish to find in freshwater bodies of water are trout, catfish, bass, salmon, and even eels all of which can be caught using simple methods that require little skill.

Fish traps

The traps presented in this section are easy to design in any wilderness area. They rely on natural materials that you find in the landscape near any body of water. In addition, each trap is easy to remember and requires little monitoring and little effort after building. There are 4 basic steps that will aid in choosing and constructing a successful trap. These 4 steps are:

- Know if there is a significant tide rise and fall.
- Watch the fish movement to see where they swim and congregate.
- Chose a trapping method suitable for the fish and body of water.
- Look for natural features that can be used in trap construction.

These guidelines will help in saving time and efforts when building fish traps. However, beyond observation, it is also good to know the likely places fish like to be. Such locations as behind bigger rocks near a bank, or under an undercut or overhanging brush are all places where fish will gather. Be mindful as some snakes and other harmful creatures may be in these areas for shade or looking for fish as food. Knowing all of the above information will maximize the potential of consistently finding and capturing fish in an unfamiliar environment. However, understanding these guidelines is not enough. A survivor must be able to construct a suitable means of capturing them. For the purpose of this book, we will focus on traps as a reliable means of capturing fish.

Rock or Stick Tide Trap (Pool Trap)

After observing the shift in tides and the behavior of the fish, choose a location that would be suitable for building a pool style enclosure with rocks. The way this is done is to:

1. Place a stick vertically in the creek bed ensuring that it is tall enough to show above the water during high tide.

2. Mark the stick at high-tide level. This is used as a reference when building your wall during low-tide.

3. Collect rocks near the creek and begin building a "U" or half circle style shape with the opening of the "U" facing the bank, therefore creating a completely enclosed separate pool inside the body of the creek.

4. Layer the rocks until you reach just above the height at low tide.

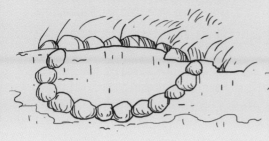

If you did the proper observation of the fish's behaviors before choosing a location, then during high tide fish will gather over the pool, and as the tide drops some will subtly find themselves trapped inside. You can then gather them by hand or use a spear/harpoon to remove them from the pool.

Natural tidal trap

Stick or Rock Fishing Weir (Non-basket Funnel Trap)

This trap relies on using the fish's natural direction of movement as a means to trap them in a place that they cannot escape from. To make this type of trap, start by identifying an area near the bank that is about 1-2 feet shallow, and then follow these steps:

1 ft.

- Gather several thumb sized sticks.

- Place them in the water creating an "M" shaped enclosure (the perspective is from the bank) that is about 3-4 feet both in length and width. The bottom of the "M" legs should be against the bank.

- Make sure the center of the "M," the part shaped like a "V," is at least the length of your forearm (about a foot long), the length from the bottom of your palm to the top of your middle finger wide at the top (about 8-9") between the shoulders of the "M," and from the last knuckle on the thumb to the tip of the pointer finger (4-6" long) open at the bottom of the "V."

- Ensure the opening is in the direction of the current.

- For an added bonus, you can add leaves and brush in the body of the enclosure to give the fish the sense that they are protected.

- Avoid building weirs and fish traps in a location where the current is so swift that it could push debris against your trap and knock several of the fence posts forming the "M" shaped enclosure out.

- Follow the same principles to make this trap with rocks, but stacking the rocks to make walls in the shape of an "M." Also, unlike the sticks that allow water to pass through easily, the gaps in the rock can get clogged up much easier, and in a place where the water is rushing to powerfully, the current could create a backfill effect and push the fish out of the trap or keep new fish from coming in.

Now that you have your trap, collecting the fish may be difficult. You will want something to catch the fish with. You could try using your hands, but the fish may be slippery which will make this problematic and energy inefficient. You can use an article of clothing, but this may be hard to control. However, one good suggestion is to make a 3 or 4-pronged fishing spear/harpoon. This will allow for an easier opportunity to catch fish as it will be akin to the proverbial shooting fish in a barrel. This is easy to make and can be used not only for fish but for lizards, rodents, and other living food sources. Just cut or break a sapling about two fingers in diameter. Use a knife or thin sharp stone to cut from the head of the stick lengthwise 3-4" in a plus like pattern. This will create 4 prongs. Place a thin living twig between the prongs down to the end of the separating cut. This will spread out the prongs so you can sharpen them. Use a vine or small strip of clothing to lash around the prongs just above the separation twigs. This will ensure they do not slide out. Begin sharpening the tips of the prongs. Now that you have 4 spread out spikes at the tip of your spear, you will have an opportunity to hit your target allowing for greater potential to maim or kill with a less accurate strike.

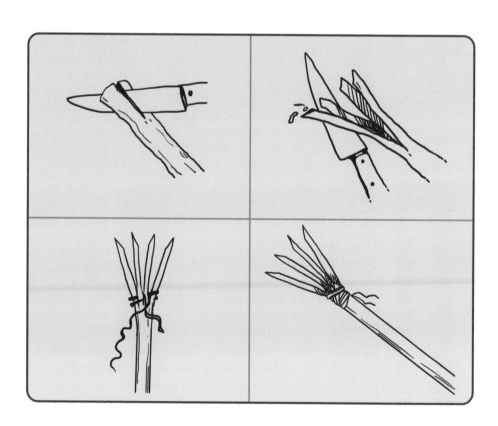

Plastic Bottle Funnel Trap

As another alternative to the standard primitive funnel trap, this same trap can be made with a plastic bottle. I add it as a possibility because as I stated in the water procurement section, discarded plastic bottles can be found in even remote locations. These materials can be used to your advantage. In this instance, the plastic bottle can be used to make a funnel trap. The disadvantage of these traps is that they limit the size of the fish you can capture. Both the size of the bottle and the opening are predetermined, and little can be done to change this. Therefore, these traps are used often to catch smaller fish such as minnows. The steps to making a plastic bottle funnel trap are:

- Remove any paper covering on the bottle
- Empty any contents and check the bottle for chemicals by visually inspecting it and smelling it.

- Once you have determined the bottle is safe, use a knife or sharp rock to cut the top half of the bottle, where the curve from the mouth meets the body, completely off.

- Turn the cone head of the bottle around and place it in the body of the bottle with the mouth side facing inward.

- Poke 3 or 4 holes at the rim where the cone and the body of the bottle meet and lash them together with small strands from your clothing, a small vine/bark, or twigs.

- Place an insect in the bottle to attract the fish. If the trap is well placed you do not need bait.

- Use living tree branches to bend over it to hold it in place while it is in the water, or you can use rocks but be sure to sit the rock in a way that will secure it without crushing it. If you have a strong enough vine you can lash the bottle to land.

As mentioned earlier, a primitive version of the funnel trap can be made from flexible sticks, vines, or bark but it takes a lot of time, effort, and only some know how to do it properly. You could also try to make a bite-activated spring trap for a fish, but this requires good strong cordage and a good fishing hook, both of which may not be available in an unplanned survival ordeal. Because I follow the "Keep It Simple Survival" method, my thoughts are to acknowledge that many people will not know or retain how to make a trap like this. However, making a rock pool, arranging sticks in an "M" shape, or cutting the top off of a bottle and putting them together is a lot simpler, less time consuming, easier to retain and of course easier to build. With the traps presented in this chapter, any person has a strong opportunity to capture fish in an unplanned, non-equipped survival scenario.

REPTILES

Spend time in the wild long enough and you are bound to come by a reptile, especially if you are near water. This means that you will be presented with another possible opportunity for food. However, depending on the reptile, this also means that you could be open to another possibility of injury.

Snakes

There are 20 species of snakes in the United States; however, members of the species can be categorized into 4 groups. These groups are:

- Cotton Mouth
  (also known as Water Moccasins).
- Rattle Snakes.
- Copper Heads.
- Coral Snakes.

Snakes are one of the more common reptiles that you will find in a wilderness environment. If at all possible, you should try to avoid them as any misstep in trying to kill one could result in a bite that you would not be able to recover from. Also, with the exception of the large boa constrictor and pythons, there are few snakes that will give you enough food to replenish what you would lose in 2 or 3 weeks without eating. Often this is a situation where the risk outweighs the reward. However, if in a circumstance where you do not think rescue is coming, you encounter a snake and decide to go for it, it would be nice to at least know if the snake is venomous or not. 3 common ways that you may be able to tell if a snake is venomous or not is:

- The head shape. If it has a big broad head and a skinny neck it could be venomous. Because non-venomous snakes do not have a venom sack, their heads are smaller.
- It makes a rattling sound. A snake rattle is a sign that you are dealing with a venomous snake from the rattlesnake group.
- Bright color patters where the colors red and yellow are touching.

Learning these signs can help in the identification of snakes but it is also important to know that they are not a full proof sign. It is also important to highlight that the condition of a person in survival mode may not allow for proper discernment of snake features.

Turtles

Turtles are a safer and easier means to get food as they are slow and cannot aggressively defend themselves against predators. This is of course with the exception of the snapping turtle, which can be dangerous. However, the snapping turtle is normally dangerous at its head, so as long as you avoid its mouth you can safely handle them. Depending on the size of the turtle they will not provide a lot of nutrients, but they are easy food in a bad situation. Another benefit is that turtles' shells are great containers to boil water in or to collect nuts and berries.

MAMMALS

Smaller rodents and non-rodents like raccoons, opossums, and rabbits are quality game in a survival situation. They can provide good nutrition, but 1 or 2 will not do much for you in the long run. You will need to kill these creatures consistently to get enough food to sustain you in a long-term survival situation. Normally, the meat in these creatures is to lean and you will need more than just this to refuel your body. It is also important to state that many small rodents and non-rodents can carry diseases that can be harmful to man even if the animal is dead. These are some other reasons that I tell people to really evaluate their need for food when in an emergency survival situation that is likely to be short term.

Capturing Small Mammals

When trying to capture small mammals with minimal resources, I often look to 2 types of traps, which are the figure 4-deadfall trap and the Paiute deadfall trap. Both traps are simple to make with limited resources, and they have been extremely effective for many years. However, out of the two, the Paiute deadfall trap is my favorite for people with little know-how even though it requires cordage, unlike the figure 4-deadfall trap which only requires sticks. The reason is that the figure 4-deadfall trap requires some skill and memory to create. Although made with only a flat rock, 3 sticks, and bait, the sticks have to be carved with certain notches and angles in certain areas to create a pressure locking figure 4 with the rock set to leaning on it. These carvings take some time to memorize and get correct, and as the size of the animal you are trying to capture increases, so do the size ratios. This changes the size of your material and where your cuts go to create the pressure locking figure 4. Getting this process wrong can easily lead to the deadfall rock falling prematurely during setup and smashing your hand or fingers. On the contrary, the Paiute deadfall trap requires less shaving and carving, some bait, and a few insignificant inches of cordage (from a shoestring, article of clothing, vine or twisted tree bark). This trap is super easy to recall, make, and set up for a novice and is a recommended go to in a pinch.

Before we learn how to make a trap, it is important to first understand the 4 basic rules of trap setting.

These rules are paramount to achieving the goal of killing small game. The 4 basic rules of trap setting are as follows:

- Size the trap for the animal.
- Place the trap where the animal is likely to go.
- Set the trap with proper bait.
- Set a clear entry point.

Making sure your trap has the proper height clearance for the animal to enter under and length clearance so the animal can move far enough under it so that it cannot get out before the deadfall can fall on it should be a strong focus. Although animals in the wild have great senses and can sniff out bait from far away, traps are more likely to be discovered, explored, and possibly set off if they are in a location that the prey has often traveled. Using bug for animals that are known to eat them and nuts or berries for animals with that diet helps ensure that the prey you are looking for takes the bait. Lastly, to ensure that there are not any accidental triggers of the trap or that the animal is able to remove the bait from a location that is less likely to set off the trap, creating a natural looking funnel that directs the prey into it adds for a greater possibility of success. Having these details, the proper way to build a **Paiute deadfall** is as follows:

Get a "Y" stick to serve as your leg or main support. This should be tall enough to keep your rock sitting at an angle and allow enough height for your target animal to walk under.	Make a lever stick that is long enough to sit a thumbs length past the "Y" stick under the rock .	Make a 1.5-2" long toggle that will connect the lever to the "Y" stick.

Make a trigger stick and sharpen it on one end for a bait skewer and so it can latch into the rough surface of the stone/deadfall.	Carve a small notch/groove around the tail end of the lever and connect your string. Do the same to your toggle.	Cut a short piece of shoestring or strip of clothing for the rope to connect the lever to the toggle stick.
	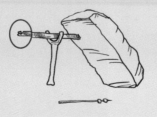	 Toggle

- Find a flat rock that is big enough to crush the animal you are trying to kill. It should be a little rough on one side.

- Get a "Y" stick to serve as your leg or main support. This should be tall enough to keep your rock sitting at an angle and allow enough height for your target animal to walk under.

- Make a lever stick that is long enough to sit a thumbs length past the "Y" stick under the rock and long enough of the tail end to slope back at a 45-degree angle to the center of the body of the "Y" stick.

- Make a 1.5-2" long toggle that will connect the lever to the "Y" stick.

- Make a trigger stick and sharpen it on one end for a bait skewer and so it can latch into the rough surface of the stone/deadfall.

- Carve a small notch/groove around the tail end of the lever and connect your string. Do the same to your toggle.

- Cut a short piece of shoestring or strip of clothing for the rope to connect the lever to the toggle stick by tying the string around the area. The rope should be long enough so that it is taught when the lever sits at about 45 degrees in the "Y" and the toggle is wrapped once around the leg/support "Y" stick.

- Shave the front end of the lever on the top to allow the rock to sit easily on the end, almost flush. Do the same to one end of the toggle.

Now set up the trap by laying the rock flat on the ground. Sitting your lever in your "Y" stick and holding it in place with your left thumb, lift the rock above the support "Y" stick and lean it in slightly so that the shaved end of the lever is just under the rock. Let the rock sit on the end and use your right hand to wrap the toggle around the supporting "Y" stick. Now you can let go of the lever and "Y" Stick with your left hand and grab the toggle. Now use your right hand to gather the trigger/bait stick and place the non-pointed end on the toggle and the pointed baited end on the rock. Once you feel the bait stick is holding in place, carefully but quickly release so that if the trap goes off your fingers are not under it. Now place debris around the outside of the trap as a means to create a funnel for where you want the prey to enter.

BE REAL! THE TRUTH ABOUT FOOD IN SURVIVAL

Knowing how to gather food in the wild is a good skill to have, however, it is not the ultimate skill for a short to an intermediate-term survival situation. There is a multitude of things that could kill you a lot sooner and that should be prioritized first. Even if at some point you do need food gathering, enough of it adds a secondary problem to the somewhat complicated task of just gathering it. It is important to view this fact truthfully. As explained, the Ninja grew up in the same wilderness that they would operate in. Living off the land was something they knew how to do well. On the contrary, the average American today does not have this experience, and thus, will find this task not as easy as the ancient Ninja. Lucky for the person that may be thrust into an unexpected survival situation, there is a high probability they will be rescued or find help long before they face the threat of starving to death.

> Knowing how to gather food in the wild is a good skill to have, however, it is not the ultimate skill for a short to an intermediate-term survival situation.

CHAPTER

8

EARTHLY FORCES
FOR NAVIGATION

CHI-MON

Ninja, like any wilderness culture, lived such natural lives that they formed a harmony with nature and seemingly became a part of it.

The things the Ninja could do were just standard capabilities of all humans but working at a level that was refined through consistent use.

The Ninja were outdoors people. They understood how to survive off the land and how to find their way in it. Their constant exposure to the harsh conditions of the wild gave them a tolerance that was unmatched by average people living in standard Japanese communities. This continued exposure to the wild gave the Ninja what seemed to be supernatural abilities to those not aware of the intricacies of the land. I remember talking to my teacher and asking him about some of the ancient reports of Ninja being able to disappear while being looked directly at; how to know when the solid ground was changing to a waterway using smell and not sight; and how Ninja could see in the dark just as well as a nocturnal animal. He smiled and told me how this was nothing supernatural, it was just extraordinarily natural. Ninja, like any wilderness culture, lived such natural lives that they formed a harmony with nature and seemingly became a part of

it. They knew the smells, the sounds, and the features of the land like that of their closest family member. The things the Ninja could do were just standard capabilities of all humans but working at a level that was refined through consistent use. Like a bodybuilder that can bench 350lbs, this is not inhuman, just a human ability that was developed over years of mindful and intensive training. To those that do not focus on the attributes needed to manipulate such weight, it seems unbelievable, but for those that exist in the world of the Gym Rat (fitness enthusiast), this is a common and obtainable feat.

In our modern day as with the standard Japanese communities in the past, the idea of knowing how to find water by smell, see in the blackest veil of night, and to navigate complex terrain without losing one's way is a difficult concept to grasp. In my own personal experience after several days of living in the wild of the Himalayan Mountains, I found myself experiencing a multitude of changes. My body became lighter and more efficient, and although not eating, I became more energized. I could hear animals and bugs moving around me even though I could not see them; I sensed changes in the air current, and could even hear and smell the slightest trickle of water a quarter of a mile away. On nights I slept without a fire, I could see clearly around me as my sight pierced deeply into the shadows. My body knew what it needed to survive, and it seemed as though it enhanced all my senses to help achieve that goal. Trees became like people with different features and characteristics that I could easily discern, rock formations were like landmarks in a neighborhood letting me know when I was close to my shelter or my favorite sunbathing spot. Even though I was on the other side of the world, in a short amount of time I became one with my environment as though it was my home. Over the next 14 days in that land, I was no longer a lost foreigner, but instead a natural part of its nature. I not only found a new me, but I could find my way around just fine as though I was born there.

SURVIVAL NAVIGATION – HOGAKU

For the modern-day outdoor enthusiast, there is a heavy reliance on technical tools to find one's way. However, as is the theme with this book, what happens when there is no modern equipment for you to use? Ancient humans navigated the world without such tools. They figured out ways of using nature to direct their path. These skills have been lost, and thus, there have been several cases where people have ventured a mile or less away from a trail and have become lost and even died. Losing your way can be frightening, and it is commonly known that in many cases, people become extremely overwhelmed with fear, and because of this they make horrible decisions that continually degrade their situation. Through understanding our ancient people, there are several easy methods that can assist in helping a lost or injured person find their way to safety. Unlike the Ninja who wanted to evade discovery of outsiders, in a modern-day survival situation where you may be lost or injured the goal is to be found. In this chapter, we will review the common mistakes people make when they are lost and the ways to avoid them. We will also review what actions should be taken in order to find your way to safety if help does not arrive.

Stay put

Thousands of people get lost every year. As discussed in earlier chapters, about 90% of those people are found within the first 12 to 24 hours. There are several things that you can do to help increase your odds of being successfully found even before you are actually lost. These steps require no technology, but instead just proper communication. Several ways to ensure help will be on the way if you get lost while out in the woods are to always tell at least two people where you are going and when you plan to be back, and let people know how you plan to travel as well as any colors or identifying marks for clothing and vehicles. When I was in the military, we had an acronym that provided a concise guideline on how to properly communicate with members of your team when you were moving through your day. This acronym was G.O.T.W.A. which stood for letting someone know:

- Where are you **GOING**.
- The **OTHER** people you are going with.
- **TIME** you are expecting to return.
- **WHAT** should be done if you do not return.
- **ALTERNATIVE** actions to take if their first responses to your absence fail.

There are many organizations that have created similar acronyms but instead of reinventing the wheel, I like to use this as a part of my modern Ninja survival teaching. Let us further examine each piece of the acronym for clarity in its use.

Going – Whenever you go anywhere you should let at least 2 people know. This method provides redundancy to a failsafe. Since many modern people are busy, it is easy for people to forget things that have been told to them. With the exception of a spouse or companion, friends and acquaintances can easily get wrapped up in their own lives and forget that you may have mentioned that you were going on a 2-day hike in the mountains. This is why it is important to tell 2 people as a redundancy. I like to call these folks detail backups or lifelines. It is unlikely that both people will forget where you said you would be. In addition to details about your trip, you should give details about your clothing, vehicles, route, and equipment. This way if you do go missing those looking know what visual color to look for, the likely areas you may be in, and how long you might be able to survive based on your equipment.

Others – Tell your 2 detail backups who you are going with and provide any contact information on that person. If the person you are going with also uses detail backups then you

will have at least 4 people aware of what is happening, raising the odds that details of your journey will not be forgotten.

Time – Give a timeframe on when people should expect you. This should include a buffer if you are going somewhere where you may think you might want to stay an extra day or two. This will help in avoiding that potential chaos that could ensue if you extend your excursion without making others aware. Time is also important because it can aid in creating a search radius based on a start location and the average rate of travel based on the terrain and mode.

What – Come up with a clear action plan that your detail backups can take if you do not return or make contact in the timeframe you said you would. This should include the numbers of law-enforcement, rangers, or other organization that is responsible for the safety of recreation in the area. This will ensure that time is not wasted on a person trying to determine what to do, who to contact, and how to contact them. Your lifelines should have a clear action plan so they can take immediate action.

Alternative – The term redundancy cannot be understated. It is always recommended that there is a backup plan for the backup plan. This will ensure that if things do not go right with the first actions taken to your absence, then there is a next step. An example may be that you are going to a place with a limited Park Ranger staff. During the time you plan to go hiking it is a working holiday or members of the staff are sick. This would hinder your detail backups ability to contact them in your absence. Alternative plans may seem ridiculous, but if your life is on the line then it is an important addition to any contingency plan.

G.O.T.W.A.

When I was in the military, we had an acronym that provided a concise guideline on how to properly communicate with members of your team when you were moving through your day. This acronym was **G.O.T.W.A.** which stood for letting someone know:

Where are you **GOING**

The **OTHER** people you are going with

TIME you are expecting to return

WHAT should be done if you don't return

ALTERNATIVE actions to take if their first responses to your absence fail

> It is important to note that continuing to walk around when lost can also be caused by the idea of HOPE. Sometimes it is not pessimism, but optimism that leads people down the wrong path to safety.

Although G.O.T.W.A. and other contingency plans like it are not new, unfortunately people do not always take the idea of getting lost or injured seriously. Therefore, people do not always plan for this eventuality, and thus, they have to hope that a rescue team is searching for them. In the interim between being lost and rescued, often there are mistakes made do to fear and panic that hinder the efforts of potential rescue. One of the first mistakes people make is that they keep walking around trying to find their way even after it is clear they are lost. Even though we highlight fear and panic, it is important to note that continuing to walk around when lost can also be caused by the idea of HOPE. Sometimes it is not pessimism, but optimism that leads people down the wrong path to safety. The denial of being lost but confidently thinking, "I am not lost; I am close to safety; I just need to go this way," is as dangerous as being lost and panicking believing "I'm lost. I do not want to get stuck here, so I think I should go this way to find help." Either way, you do not know where you are going and chances are the more you move the more

lost you get. The average person traveling on foot over flat terrain can walk a total of 3-3.5 miles in an hour. This number lessens when you add terrain features and less than optimal weather conditions. There is, however, another factor that is often not covered and that is what if the person is running. When running, the average person can cover a distance of about 1 mile every 10 minutes equaling to about 6 miles per hour. The same rules apply when it comes to terrain and weather conditions having an effect on speed and distance of movement. I'm sure you are reading this thinking, "Why would a person be running if they are lost?" Panic often induces the desire to run. If you watch videos of lost children, some will freeze, and some will run as they attempt to look for their family. This same concept goes when you are lost in the wilderness. Your heart will start to race, your adrenalin will spike, and before you know it you are off to the races. This may not sound logical but that's just it, this behavior is not manifested from logic, it is manifested from panic mode or as I heard it put before bio-logic. Panic mode reduces or completely diminishes rational thought often putting an individual on a path to self-destruction. Three to six miles is a lot of distance and that is why it is important to stop walking and stay put. Continuing to walk will make your situation worst as it will make it harder for you to be found. Do not let your mind trick you into this way of thinking.

TAKE BACK CONTROL

When a person realizes they are lost, panic will try to take over. This will cause several physiological and psychological changes that will make it hard to really assess their situation and the landscape. Stopping and using the A.D.A. portion of the A.D.A.P.T. method

we discussed earlier is the best option in this scenario. This means to Acclimate, Decide, and Act. Acclimating is a very important step as the mind will be overwhelmed during this time of high stress. On average the mind processes about 10-12 million bits of infor-

On average the mind processes about 10-12 million bits of information sent from the human body per second. This information comes from the senses as they process stimuli from the environment.

mation sent from the human body per second. This information comes from the senses as they process stimuli from the environment. Since the human brain has limited storage and processing capabilities, from the 10-12 million bits of information, only 40-50 bits can actually be processed at one time. Because of this disparity in what is taken in and what can be processed by the human mind, the brain adapts by creating shortcuts designed to help us identify what is important, what is not, and when and how to respond. This process is called **bonded rationality**, and when stress and panic are added to the equation the brains selection and rational processing of an over-abundance of information is hindered. In many ways, bounded rationality can be great but it also has faults. In some instances, the mind can receive so much information within a limited time to process that it can overlook important details as it responds with these short cuts in a sort of an auto-piloted

automatic response. These actions can often lead to a lack of mindful discernment which explains instances where people leave their homes and cannot remember if they left the iron on, or when a person is looking for something on their desk and cannot find it so they search several other places only to come back and find what they were looking for on the desk in an obvious place. This is why pausing to acclimate is important in a survival situation. While under duress in a foreign environment with an abundance of stimuli, intentionally stopping to gain your bearings is one of the most important things you can do.

While under duress in a foreign environment with an abundance of stimuli, intentionally stopping to gain your bearings is one of the most important things you can do.

In many ways, bounded rationality can be great but it also has faults. In some instances, the mind can receive so much information within a limited time to process that it can overlook important details as it responds with these short cuts in a sort of an auto-piloted automatic response. These actions can often lead to a lack of mindful discernment.

A simple method of using the acclimate principle during a survival situation is to stop all activity and sit or kneel so your body can relax. In addition to this, you can also use a technique the Ninja would utilize that taps into the earth element of the Go-Dai. To use this technique, they would simply touch or grab the dirt on the ground. This would give them a sense of grounding, pulling them from their emotions, and settling their senses back in the physical realm. To properly use this technique once a connection to the earth is made, close your eyes to avoid distraction or triggers to your mentality or emotionality through visual stimuli. This will allow you to focus on your sense of touch, enhancing the feeling of being tethered. Use your imagination to evoke a feeling of not being separate from the landscape but a part of it; think of the land as your skin and the plants as your fingers. This method of visualization represents the use of the void element (Ku). Once you feel tethered and calm, slowly start to pay attention to your other senses. First your sense of sound and then your sense of smell. After several minutes of this mindful calming and integration into your surroundings, gradually open your eyes. See the landscape as something that is part of you and not something that is your enemy. The Ninja would refer to this as a vision reset. Although your situation is the same, your goal is to see it as it was before you were lost as a calming or recreational space. This will allow you to clear-headedly handle your situation from a place of peace and not emotional pieces. The military has something very similar to this concept for snipers. There is an acronym called S.L.L.S. (pronounced SEALS) which stands for:

- **Stop.**
- **Look.**
- **Listen.**
- **Smell.**

These steps are normally done for a few minutes upon a warrior's entry into a new operational environment. This process is done to ensure each warrior can properly use his senses and decipher clearly their area of operation and the information they gather from it. The importance of doing this cannot be overstated as each one of these senses provides a plethora of information to the brain. As a general break down:

- Sight accounts for close to 10 million bit of sensory information per second.
- Sound accounts for 100,000 bits of sensory information per second.
- Smell accounts for 100,000 bits of sensory information per second.
- Skin accounts close to 1,000,000 bits of sensory information per second.

MILITARY PRINCIPLE FOR ENVIRONMENTAL

INTEGRATION METHOD

The military has something very similar to this concept for snipers. There is an acronym called S.L.L.S. *(pronounced SEALS)* which stands for:

STOP

LOOK

LISTEN

SMELL

This process is done to ensure each warrior can properly use his senses and decipher clearly their area of operation and the information they gather from it.

The importance of doing this can't be overstated as each one of these senses provides a plethora of information to the brain. As a general break down:

10 MILLION BITS OF
Sensory Information / Second

100,000 BITS OF
Sensory Information / Second

100,000 BITS OF
Sensory Information / Second

1,000,000 BITS OF
Sensory Information / Second

The sheer volume of bits of information the brain receives from each of the senses clearly shows why the stopping aspect of S.L.L.S. is an important part of the familiarization process of a new environment.

The sheer volume of bits of information the brain receives from each of the senses clearly shows why the stopping aspect of S.L.L.S. is an important part of the familiarization process of a new environment. For a sniper, taking a few moments to acclimate gives him a baseline of what is normal for that environment. For someone lost and in the grips of panic, everything can seem so foreign even if moments before that same person felt relaxed and calm. The goal is to get back to a state that aids strategic and clear thinking in an uncertain environment. The best way to do this is to go backward in the order of sensory information accumulation from the least information to the most. This means that you should stop, feel, listen, smell, and then look.

Once acclimated, the next step is to use the deciding portion of the A.D.A.P.T. method. This is when you logically and strategically think through your situation. Once the vision is reset and a clear understanding of the conditions of your situation is determined, choose what needs to be done based on the facts involved. Just to reiterate, if you are lost or injured stay put. If you gave a proper G.O.T.W.A. before you left, then you know help is on the way. This, of course, is dependent on 2 factors. The first is if you are lost or injured towards the end of your excursion putting you within the 12- 48-hour rescue window. The second is that you are near quality resources that can keep you going for the number of days that predate your set end date and the 48-hour window of rescue. This means that if you are lost or injured 4 days before anyone is expecting you, then add on a 1 to 2 days for rescue, then you are looking at staying put for an estimated 6 days. In this case, you want to set up a camp in an area with quality resources. If you are not in an area with quality resources, you will have to move to one. If you do, it is important that you leave clear signs as to the direction you are going. Clear thinking is one of the most important attributes you can have in a survival situation, so it is important to understand techniques that will aid in getting you to a point where you can do this. The goal is to strategically think through your situation and make choices from sound logic versus emotional responses.

After acclimating and deciding, the next step is to act. Taking action does not mean navigating to safety. Taking action means doing what is necessary to survive. As we discussed, often this means that you should just stay where you are and wait for rescue to come. However, there may be a point that you determine rescuers may not be able to find you, they have given up, or you can no longer sustain your life in a particular location. If this is the determination, then navigating your way to safety may be the only option.

WHERE TO START

Staying where you are and waiting for rescue cannot be overstated. Out of the over 2,000 people on average that are lost in the woods each year, almost all are found in the first 48-hours. As we stated earlier in this chapter, walking or running around looking for the path to safety will only dehydrate you faster, burn your energy, and make it more difficult for search and rescue to find you. That being said, there may be instances where moving or attempting to navigate to safety is your only option. This determination should be made cautiously and if you must, where to start your navigating may be difficult to determine.

Knowing where you came from, to know where you're going.

Of course, some of the best means of doing this are to use a GPS or to use a compass and map. But keeping with the focus of this book, what if you did not have these items? Without GPS or a compass to navigate, you will need methods of finding your bearings and selecting a route that could lead to safety. To accomplish the task of finding your location there are 2 common methods that can be used. The first method is based on the concept of "Knowing where you came from, to know where you're going." For instance, if you traveled south down a road to a hiking trail and then you started walking east before you became lost or injured, then you would know that if you could surmise your way back you would have to travel in a general north west direction. The challenge with this first step is that you would have to know your direction of origin and travel, which often is

The key here is to see as much of the landscape as possible, and often the best way to do this is not from the ground level but from above it. Even a slightly higher vantage point is better than a lower one as the canopy of a forest could make it extremely difficult to tell where you are.

not the case with modern people since most rely heavily on electronics for this. However, if you knew this information then there are easy no-tech methods to determine cardinal directions such as the shadow stick method and the crescent moon method (both of these methods will be covered in the next chapter). The second is how to gather information from your surroundings that will help you navigate to safety if you do not know which direction you came from. This method requires that you use the knowledge that you gather from observing the environment in order to deduce a navigation plan. The way humans gather the most information is through their eyes, therefore, looking around you is the best way to start your navigation planning process. However, modern humans are not as experienced with seeing the intricacy of nature like our ancestors. To most urban or suburbanites, nature seems random, but to the Ninja as well as other wilderness cultures nature has harmony and pattern to it. The Go-Dai and the Gyo-Go described in an earlier chapter aided the Ninja in his acceptance and understanding of the flow of nature. Ninja understood that certain trees like sun more than others, and thus, the limbs facing the most sun exposure would grow out while the limbs on the side getting the least amount of exposure would grow up. They also understood that animals and bugs would often place their nest on the side of trees that protected them from exposure to the prevailing winds. It was these types of signs that gave the Ninja clues to his bearings. On a similar level, a modern-day hiker or traveler that is lost can use common knowledge to help understand the landscape. The key here is to see as much of the landscape as possible, and often the best way to do this is not from the ground level but from above it. Even a slightly higher vantage point is better than a lower one as the canopy of a forest could make it extremely difficult to tell where you are. Traversing to the top of a large boulder, high hill, or ridge will aid in seeing the true features of your surroundings. This will help in getting to understand where you are,

what is around you, and the best routes to choose to navigate your way to safety. Following the S.L.L.S. or vision reset principle, once at a higher elevation, can be highly revealing. Things such as the smell of fire burning or food cooking travel easily, and its direction is more distinguishable on an unobstructed air current; this is also the same with sound. Sounds such as people talking, cars, rivers, and waterfalls will all carry far in the non-obstructed open air. When it comes to sight, it is easier to see smoke from a fire, gathering birds (which may be a sign for the location of water), and special features of the land such as ridges and valleys when at a higher elevation. All of these signs can aid in formulating a good plan for where and how you can move to safety, and often more so than being on the ground level of the wilderness.

Get to the high ground. Conduct a vision reset.	Smell, listen, and then look for signs of people.	Listen and look for signs of animals and insects that will likely be near water
Map out your route to where you believe you need to go. Stop periodically while in transit to reevaluate.	Look for signs of water or water flow movement and follow it down hill.	Move along ridges versus right along the side of rivers or streams as they will be easier to navigate.

There is one main issue when it comes to getting to a higher vantage point, and that is either being injured or the possibility of becoming injured. If you are hurt, especially in your lower extremities, trying to navigate even the slightest elevation can be problematic and dangerous.

Even if you are not injured, climbing slippery terrain or on loose gravel/dirt can also lead to injuries. If you add the idea of being tired and hungry, the risk of making a wrong move is tripled. However, if your situation is dire enough, these are all risk you may have to take.

LEARN YOUR WALK

Every person has a manner of walking which is known as their gait. A normal gait is dictated by the proper functioning of several areas of the body such as the eyes, ears, muscles, brain, and sensory nerves. There is no coincidence that these same senses and muscles aid in the S.L.L.S. process we discussed earlier as it would only make sense that that would allow us to experience the world would also aid in how we move through it. Every person has a strong side and a weak side. Because of this strong and weak side imbalance, people often will have a tendency for their gait to drift to one direction. Everyone drifts when walking if they do not have visible aids to keep them on the path. This is easy to see in our modern cities and neighborhoods as the whole construct is a series of roads, sidewalks, bridges, and paths. Everywhere you look there are a plethora of paths laid

out for movement. This is designed to keep the flow of movement steady and contained. However, without these visual cues we find that our natural tendencies to drift takeover. This understanding has become more prevalent with the introduction of the cellphone. As people started taking their eyes off the road as they text, scroll Facebook, or look at a map their car begins to veer to one side.

There are some other factors that can affect natural drift. These factors include injury, inflammation, trauma, and pain. They can change the way a person walks which is referred to as a gait abnormality. It is obvious to understand how injury to the lower extremities will affect your gait, however, less discussed is how injury to one side of the upper body can change the way you walk. As you walk, the movement engages your whole body. Whether a person is aware or not, their arms swing, torso rotates, and head bobs. These movements, no matter how small, engage a myriad of muscles in

A normal gait is dictated by the proper functioning of several areas of the body such as the eyes, ears, muscles, brain, and sensory nerves. There is no coincidence that these same senses and muscles aid in the S.L.L.S process we discussed earlier as it would only make sense that that would allow us to experience the world would also aid in how we move through it.

As you walk, the movement engages your whole body. Whether a person is aware or not, their arms swing, torso rotates, and head bobs. These movements, no matter how small, engage a myriad of muscles in the body.

the body. When a painful injury has occurred, the body will employ processes to aid in the protection of the injury such as swelling and pain. In addition, we will attempt not to move that portion of the body as to avoid the pain. While walking in pain we will have a tendency to try to compensate with the non-injured side, therefore if the injury is on our non dominated side, it will exaggerate the veering to that side while on the contrary, if it is on the dominant side then we will veer to that side. A good example for understanding this is to relate it to bench pressing a heavyweight. A person's dominate stronger side will push the bar higher while their weaker side struggles to push the weight to the same height. This causes a slight slope in the bar angled towards the weaker arm. The slope is amplified when there is a heavier weight.

In addition to gait abnormalities, weather conditions can also affect the way you walk. Heavy rain, snow, or extreme sun on one side of the body or face often causes a person to move away from the direction of exposure. Without a clear point of travel, then these environmental forces can gradually increase your drift.

Understanding drift is very important because it can cause a person to walk in circles over the course of a medium to long distance depending on their stride. There have been many cases of people lost that continually walk in circles unaware that they are doing it. This is why it is imperative to understand how to walk a straight line. To aid in properly being able to walk a straight line, first you must understand the direction that you tend to veer and how intense the drift. A simple method of doing this would be to get with a friend and go to an open flat field

that is at least 30 yards long. Somewhere in that field place a stick or landmark to walk to. The landmark should be as close to the end of the field as possible. Stand on one side of the field and have a friend blindfold you and start you off walking toward the stick placed in the ground. Count your steps as you walk and once you reach the area of the stick your friend should stop you and remove the blindfold. You can now reference how far and to which side you veered based on your relation to the stick. You will also have an idea of the amount of drift based on how far you drifted at your natural pace. This is valuable information, and you can also perform this experiment with a simulated injury. However, this is not a full proof method as in a real situation you may have uneven and obstructed terrain to traverse. Each obstacle changes your course slightly as you navigate it. This is another reason that choosing a distinguishable tree, or rock in the distance, and on course with the direction you want to move is important. As you make it to each landmark choose another and this will help alleviate drift.

DRAG YOUR FEET

If you have determined that you need to move to another location, leaving signs is going to be important. Other than leaving arrows drawn on trees with charcoal from your fire, or making them with turned up soil in a grassy field, simply dragging your feet can disturb enough of the ground to leave clear signs of your travel direction for those who search for you. The soil transference and disturbance will be very noticeable to even the least trained search and rescue man. In addition, you can break branches that are at eye level to provide a sign that you have been in that area.

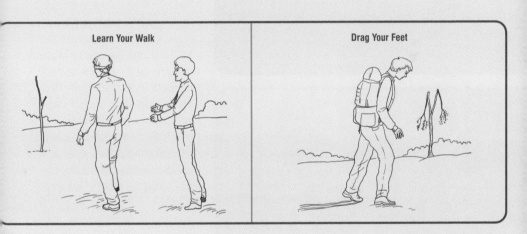

Learn Your Walk

Drag Your Feet

WHERE TO GO

Walking aimlessly when lost is sure to get you dead fast. It is beyond important to know how to identify your landscape and things in it that can give you the best chance of moving in a direction that can aid in finding

Walking aimlessly when lost is sure to get you dead fast.

safety. As mentioned earlier, getting to high ground will help you see important details in your environment. The process of seeing your area and discerning what elements exist in it is called visual mapping. Much like looking at a Google satellite view, identifying roads, neighborhoods, stores, etc. before going on a journey to a new area helps with confidence in navigating by providing some familiarity with that area. Visual mapping can be a great advantage to anyone

lost, but it holds no advantage if you do not know what you are looking at. Most people have had the experience of going to a new neighborhood and all the houses and streets looking the same. It is easy to get confused and turned around the first few times going to a new environment. Only after visiting the same area multiple times, do we start to notice differences and take note of landmarks and names of streets that help us find our way. However, part of this is visual identification and the other is recognition of landmarks for what they are. Imagine being given directions and someone says go three blocks and turn right at the corner store. If you do not know what a block or a corner store is then it will be impossible for you to distinguish it from any other area or building. The same concepts exist in the wilderness. Not only is it hard for the untrained person to recognize the differences in the environment out of lack of exposure, there is also a lack of knowledge as to the different identifying features of the environment. Most people will not spend enough time outdoors to learn how to identify all the flora, fauna, and landmarks in their region. This is not an easy task even for most outdoor enthusiast. However, there are some basic things people can do to aid in navigation without being an expert, and that is knowing how to identify the features and characteristics of the land. Just like you do not have to know every feature to identify the difference between a house and a building, you do not have to know all the features of a draw to distinguish it from a valley. However, being able to generally identify the difference between the two means that, in comparison, if you plot a course on to move to the right side of a building but you arrive at your destination and you see something other than the right side of that building, then you know you navigated to the wrong spot. Knowing terrain features is an invaluable skill that is easy to learn and retain. Therefore, it is something I believe every person going outdoors should understand.

TERRAIN FEATURES

There are 10 total terrain features that everyone spending time in the wilderness should know and understand. These terrain features can be broken down into 5 major ones, 3 minor and 2 man-made. Understanding these terrain features will help in every aspect of survival. The proper location for building a shelter, where to find water, the most efficient way to traverse the land, and the most likely area to find people can all be determined with a basic knowledge of the terrain. Of course, it helps to know how to use a compass, read a map, and find your way using the stars. However, knowing the 10 terrain features and their importance is not something you can lose or leave behind and is easier to retain.

Five major terrain features

For the 5 major terrain features, there is a common acronym that I was first introduced to in the military. The acronym is **H.V.R.S.D.** which can be phrased as Hidden Valley Ranch Salad Dressing. This acronym stands for:

1. **Hills** – An area of high ground which from its apex; the ground slopes down in all directions.
2. **Valleys** – A long stretched out groove that is usually formed by streams or rivers. Water always flows from higher ground to lower ground. Often if you are standing in a valley there will be 3 high sides and one low side.
3. **Ridges** – An area of sloping high ground that normally has steep descending slopes on 2 sides and 1 gently ascending and descending slope on another side. The gently ascending and descending sides often create a traversable path.
4. **Saddles** – An area that dips down between two higher points. This could be an area between 2 hills or a break between a ridge crest. A good way to know if you're in a saddle is if you have 2 high points on opposite sides of you and level lower ground in the remaining 2 sides of your position.
5. **Depression** – A low area that is surrounded by high ground on all sides.

Valley

Depression

For the last 5 terrain features that include both the 3 minor and the 2 man-made, I like to use the phrase "Sam draws cliffs, caves and flowers." This has helped countless of my students retain this information. The phrase breaks down as:

3 Minor Terrain Features

1. **Spur** – A line of higher ground that normally extends off of a ridge. This is often created by water erosion from parallel streams that create draws down the side of a ridge. Like a ridge, the ground slopes down in 3 directions.

2. **Draw** – Like a valley, if you are standing in a draw the ground slopes upward in 3 directions and drops down in 1 direction. Draws are created by streams in the same way as a valley, however, draws are not as refined as valleys and allow for little to no maneuverability. Lastly, draws are normally perpendicular to ridgelines while valleys tend to be parallel.

3. **Cliff** – An area of land that drops off in a near vertical decline.

CLIFF

2 Man-Made Terrain Features

1. **Cut** – An area where machines were used to cut through raised ground. This is normally done to make roads.

2. **Fill** – An area of lower ground that was filled with dirt or other material to make level ground for the forming of a road or railroad.

To aid in the recall of the 8 natural terrain features there is a simple method that I was taught in the army that I favor since the tool used is nothing more than your hand. I like this method because using your hand is something you cannot forget and something you will never be without. To use this method, make your hand into a fist. Six of the 8 natural land features can be identified by the features of your fist.

- **Hills** are the top knuckles of your fist. The 4 knuckles represent 4 hills.

- A **ridge** is a line that crosses the apex of your knuckles which extend from the outside edge of your pinky knuckle to the outside edge of your pointer finger knuckle.

- **Spurs** are represented by the tops of your fingers between the knuckles on the back of your hand and the middle knuckles before the fingers.

- **Saddles** are represented by the dips in between your top knuckles.

- **Draws** are represented by the creases in

between your fingers extending from the knuckles on the back of your hand and the middle knuckles before the fingers.

- A **cliff** is a drop off at the outside edge of your hand on both the pinky side and the pointer finger side.

The final 2 of the 8 land features which are valleys and depressions, require you to shape your hand in a cup-like shape.

- A **depression** is symbolized by the center of the cupped hand as it can hold water or sand without it falling out.

- A **valley** is represented by tilting the hand forward and lowering the fingers creating a concaved slide. If you had water in your cupped and angled hand, the water could only flow out between your pinking and pointer finger this would represent a valley.

When it comes to navigation think about what people did before the use of maps, compasses, and in our modern age, GPS (global positioning systems). People walked

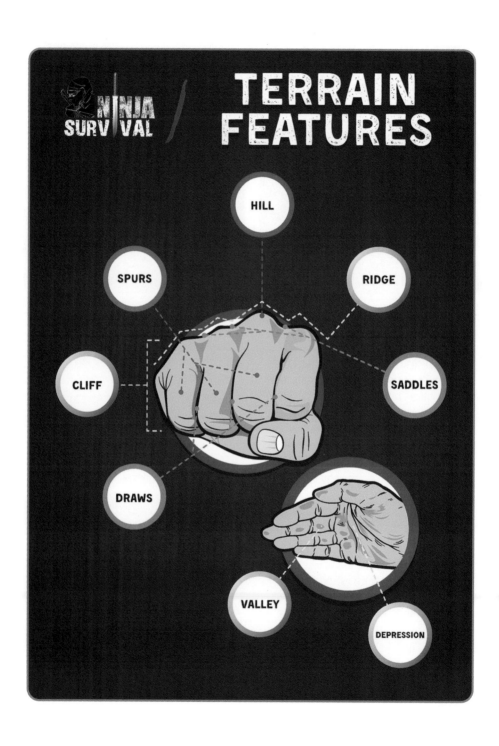

in nature with the mindful eye attentive to changes in the environment and were aware of the differences in the landscape from one area to another. The first 7 terrain features where like highway signs and city markers labeling specific areas, while rock formations and strange tree abnormalities might be seen as street signs. To the Ninja, nature was nothing short of a living being with moods and characteristics that changed as part of a process. This was similar to the growth of a male or female person that changes features, goes through puberty, and personality shifts over time. They became acquainted with

> Think about what people did before the use of maps, compasses, and in our modern age, GPS (global positioning systems). People walked in nature with the mindful eye attentive to changes in the environment and were aware of the differences in the landscape from one area to another.

these processes and changes and naturally developed an awareness and sensitivity to changes that were integrated into their way of life.

USING YOUR BASIC KNOWLEDGE

Unlike ancient man, most people do not grow up living in the wild 24/7. Furthermore, their natural senses are dulled due to their lack of use. In modern society, the reliance on innate traits that could be skills if honed are dormant as many of these skills are replaced with apps, software, and mechanical devices that accomplish these tasks for us. Fortunate for us, like the ability to run, these skills never leave. They just need to be worked and redeveloped. In the aspect of navigation, most people have a basic knowledge that has been accumulated over the course of their life that can aid in navigation. All this knowledge falls under the category of the Keep it Simple Survival philosophy and can be of great assistance in helping a lost or injured person maneuver to help or safety.

The *first step* is to follow the water. Water is held to the same law of gravity as all things on the planet, which means that it flows downward. Since all living things need water to survive, then it is likely that other humans will at some point be at a place on the path of which water flows. Surveying an area from

the high ground or low, a lost person should look to identify valleys or draws. The person can use these to navigate to a stream or river which can be followed in hopes of finding rescue. Even when dry, looking at the bed of the stream or for signs of leave and brush that has been move and pilled against rocks and trees near the edge of waterways, you can determine which way the water flowed.

Second, if the landscape is difficult to read and identify as a ridge or valley, look for signs of animal paths. As we discussed in the chapter on water, animal paths will often converge in a juncture in a "V" or arrow-like shape pointing to the water (this is referenced in the water chapter).

Third, looking or listening for flocks of birds or water favoring insects, such as mosquitos or flies, can aid in finding waterways that can then be followed in the direction of flow until you find help.

In a pinch, these 3 methods are a simple use

of common or easy to retain knowledge that will aid in navigating to safety. It is recommended that this information is locked into the memory of any outdoor enthusiast.

FINDING YOUR WAY

This chapter would not be complete without a clear guide on how to find your way to safety with no navigational tools nor complex methods of navigation that require an abundance of knowledge and recall. The goal is to give an average Joe or Jane a baseline of information that can be retained and utilized with little to no training. The simple steps that I have found to be very helpful in aiding to find safety when lost are as follows:

- Get to the high ground.

- Conduct a vision reset.

- Smell, listen, and then look for signs of people. As rescuers search for you there may be great disturbances in the woods such as animals fleeing, talking, dogs barking, and vehicles passing. You may be able to smell campfires from campers or hikers. Also, as you get use to the wild smells of nature synthetic smells of cologne, shaving cream, and food will be highly distinguishable.

- Listen and look for signs of animals and insects that will likely be near water (geese, ducks, flies, etc.).

- Listen and look for signs of water.

- Map out your route to where you believe you need to go. Stop periodically while in transit to reevaluate using the S.L.L.S./vision reset method. This will ensure that you do not become complacent or panic does not creep into your mind and hinder you from noticing a change in course or important signs that may have developed.

- If you find water, follow its flow downstream. This is not a full proof method, but it is likely that you will find some level of civilization somewhere close to the water downstream. This is the same for railroads and roads found at cuts or fills. However, it is important to understand where the general direction of civilization is, or you could travel miles in the wrong direction.

- Move along ridges versus right along the side of rivers or streams as they will be easier to navigate.

The guidelines above are simple and relatively easy. The Ninja were capable of using many more tricks such as using plant, moss, cloud movement, wind, and a whole host of other methods to understand how to determine direction and how to move in the environment. However, these methods are not full proof and can change as the environment changes. Therefore, it would take a medium to high level of skill to be competent and confident in being able to use these methods. For a person not intimately acquainted with using these methods in their area of operation, trying to use them as a way to save one's life in an extreme situation is not recommended. For the modern outdoor recreational dabbler that is not an avid traditional outdoorsman, I would recommend the list of methods above for survival purposes.

CHAPTER

9

HEAVENLY FORCES

TEN MON

> Through the task surrounding sustainment of life such as fishing, farming, and hunting, they became highly aware of the sky and celestial entities such as the sun, moon, and stars affecting the environment they operated in.

Beyond the land, there is the sky. Early man, as well as the Ninja, spent lots of time looking at the sky and learning its characteristics. This was especially true for the night sky as they had very few distractions and no city lights to pollute the sky. They became fascinated with their relationship to the stars, both in relation to physical location and spiritual connection. With no television or cellphones, ancient people watched the world around them. Through the task surrounding sustainment of life such as fishing, farming, and hunting, they became highly aware of the sky and celestial entities such as the sun, moon, and stars affecting the environment they operated in. In addition, Ninja also formed an understanding of how these forces affected human emotions and spirits. This knowledge would, to others, become mystical, but for the Ninja, it was all natural. To them, there was a connection between all the forces at play in the universe, and so the Ninja sought further knowledge in how this connection could be understood and used to enhance their lives. For people whose livelihood relied on living in the wild and off the land, it's not difficult to imagine the value and power of such knowledge as knowing how to predict changes in the weather, seasons, shifts in wind patterns, and how the phases of the moon were crucial. For a tactician, it is also understandable how such knowledge can aid the completion of clandestine intelligence gathering and success in guerilla warfare.

With none of the modern-day gadgets to aid in finding your way, the most natural ways to navigate besides looking at the land is to use the sky. The Ninja referred to this as Ten Mon, the use of heavenly forces. However, this is not knowledge that is specific to the Ninja alone as people all over the world have used the sky to navigate for thousands of years. Unfortunately, because of the earth's movement in relation to stars and planets, as well as a person's location, some of the techniques for understanding how to navigate using the sky can be a daunting task. For the outdoor expert or survival enthusiast, these skills are learned, practiced, and perfected for fun or interest. On the contrary, for most people, there is not enough curiosity or training to become proficient at retaining and recalling these skills. Therefore, for the inexperienced recreational adventurer, methods of navigation which are easy to retain and recall that requires little experience to accomplish, are paramount. There are 3 main methods that fit these requirements and they are:

- **Shadow Stick Method.**
- **Crescent Moon Method.**
- **L.U.R.D. Method.**

It is important to note that these 3 methods are not 100% accurate, but they are close enough to give you a general sense of one or more of the cardinal directions.

> For the inexperienced recreational adventurer, methods of navigation which are easy to retain and recall that requires little experience to accomplish, are paramount.

SHADOW STICK METHOD

The first of the 3 methods known as the Shadow Stick Method is one I consider the best for wilderness survival because all of the material can be found easily, also once performed, it allows you to travel in the determined direction you need to go immediately. The only issue is that it requires open land that will not have any impending shadows cast by nearby trees or rock formations. This type of clearing can be difficult to find in a heavily wooded forest. The Shadow Stick Method takes advantage of the travel of the sun. In the northern hemisphere, the sun rises in the east and sets in the west. As the sun travels through the sky, it casts a moving shadow as its light rays hit an object from different angles. Using the shadow cast, a person can determine the directions of west and east by which you can then deduce north and south. The way to set up the Shadow Stick Method of navigation is as follows:

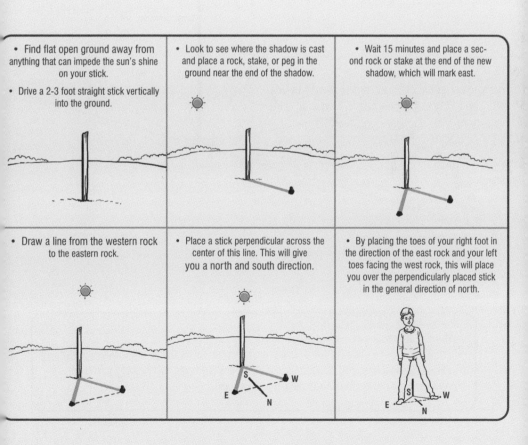

- Find flat open ground away from anything that can impede the sun's shine on your stick.
- Drive a 2-3 foot straight stick vertically into the ground.

- Look to see where the shadow is cast and place a rock, stake, or peg in the ground near the end of the shadow.

- Wait 15 minutes and place a second rock or stake at the end of the new shadow, which will mark east.

- Draw a line from the western rock to the eastern rock.

- Place a stick perpendicular across the center of this line. This will give you a north and south direction.

- By placing the toes of your right foot in the direction of the east rock and your left toes facing the west rock, this will place you over the perpendicularly placed stick in the general direction of north.

To improve the accuracy of this method as we discussed in the shelter building chapter in the section on time, if you use the information gained by the Shadow Stick Method and build upon it to complete a sundial then you will be able to get a more accurate sense of the cardinal directions. This works because, after creating a sundial, you will end up with an arc with the center of the arc closest to the vertical shadow casting stick. Because

at mid-day, the sun is at its highest peak in the southern portion of the sky in the northern hemisphere which will cause the stick to cast a short shadow in the northern direction. This shadow will represent true north. If you draw a line, or place a stick on the ground, on the other side of the stick at mid-day you will have the southern direction. Using these 2 directions a person can easily determine east and west.

Survival Sundial – Telling Time with the Sun

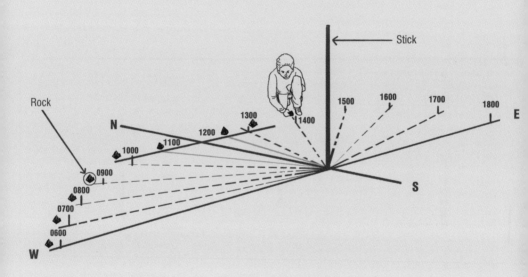

With the proper amount of moonlight to replace the sunlight, this technique can also be done at night if you can get a clearly defined shadow on the ground. Although not something I would use to navigate at night in the wilderness, this method could be good for night navigation and movement in a desert.

DIRECTION USING THE MOON AND STARS

The next 2 methods of natural navigation are done during the night. These methods are the Crescent Moon Method and the L.U.R.D. Method. Although both are simple, they are only a way to aid in getting a general sense of direction. It is highly recommended for safety that information gathered using these techniques shouldn't be used until daylight. In my small opinion in a big world, navigating at night during a survival situation is over-rated. The reason I say this is because as I have already established in earlier sections of this book that night movement in a wilderness environment, when you are already lost or injured, is not recommended. It is very easy to get off track or to injure yourself further when you cannot see where you're going and where you're stepping. I learned this first hand during several of the night land navigation courses I took in the army. During every exercise, several of the teams or individuals went out healthy and strong, but when we came back several of us were battered or bruised and, in some cases, severely injured from getting a branch to the face, tripping over a

> I suggest no movement at night in the wilderness, but instead one should use the night to rest and plan. During your reflection and strategic planning (which is part of the acclimate and trim aspect of our A.D.A.P.T. principle), you can look up at the stars and reaffirm your location and direction, and more importantly rest your mind and body for the day's trek.

root or log, or falling in a hole or down a hill. Never was there a night navigation training exercise where someone didn't get injured. In a survival situation, this is more likely to hurt your situation then help it. Outside of the wilderness setting, there might be some instances where this is recommended such as in the desert. Moving around in the hot desert sun may be more detrimental than moving at night. Therefore, in this situation, it is often recommended to move during the night. Also, there are fewer obstacles in the desert that can harm you while maneuvering in the dark, unlike the trees, branches, roots, and rocks that make up the wilderness landscape. For the interest of safety, I suggest no movement at night in the wilderness, but instead one should use the night to rest and plan. During your reflection and strategic planning (which is part of the acclimate and trim aspect of our A.D.A.P.T. principle), you can look up at the stars and reaffirm your location and direction, and more importantly rest your mind and body for the day's trek. The first of the 2 methods for identifying the direction at night is the **Crescent Moon Method**, which is done by using the 2 horns of the crescent moon. Simply look up at the moon and draw an imaginary line from the top horn to the bottom, then continue down to the horizon. In the northern hemisphere, this will give the general direction of south. This method works because the moon only shines because it reflects the sun. Since the sun moves on an east to west plane, while the moon is reflecting the suns light either on its right or left side, it is reflecting the sun from the east and west. Therefore, in the Crescent Moon Method, a line is drawn angularly through the endpoints (horns) of the lit side down to the horizon which will provide the general direction of south or north based on where you are in the world. In the northern hemisphere, this will point south.

Crescent Moon Method

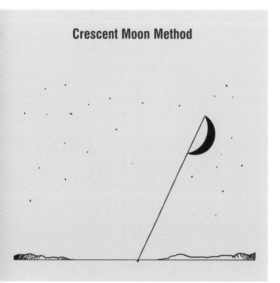

The second method of using the heavens to navigate is a star navigational technique known as the *L.U.R.D. Method*. Often when people think of using the stars, they think of using one of the constellations such as the Southern Cross or the Big Dipper. Some believe that, even easier than the constellations, is to find the North Star (Polaris) since it is positioned approximately above the North Pole, and therefore, it can serve as a good reference for north. However, these constellations and stars are often very difficult for the average person to find. In addition, when adding stress and environmental factors such as visual obstruction due to the forest canopy, clouds, or weather conditions, the task of identifying a single star or a constellation for navigational purposes becomes even more difficult. This is why knowing the L.U.R.D. Method is important. Using this method only requires the use of a single star (other than

the North Star) that is clearly visible and near the horizon. Since the night sky is full of stars, it is likely that a person will be able to get a clear line of sight on at least one. The way this breaks down is that L.U.R.D. stands for the relative directions of Left; Up; Right; and Down, which in order, represents the cardinal directions of north; east; south; and west. It is easier to understand when seen side by side as:

- **Left = North.**
- **Up = East.**
- **Right = South.**
- **Down = West.**

The way this acronym is used to find direction is to get 2 sticks, one at least 5 feet and the other about 3 feet. Next, choose a star that can be seen clearly that is near the horizon. Next, jam or hammer the 5-foot stick in the ground where the top of the stick lines up with the star when sighting over it. The second stick should be lined up with the first and placed in the ground about 4 or 5 feet away. The 2 sticks simulate the front and rear sight of a pistol or rifle giving you a fixed point to monitor the position of the star. From a kneeling position, you should now be able to peer over the top of the 2 sticks and see the star. Watch the star from this position for about 20 minutes and note the movement of the star. It is important that you are comfortable so that you do not have to fidget or move during this time as to not change your perspective. Lastly, cross reference the directional movement of the star with the acronym to determine the direction you are facing. For example, if the star moves left then you are facing north, and if it moves up know you are facing east, etc.

L.U.R.D Method

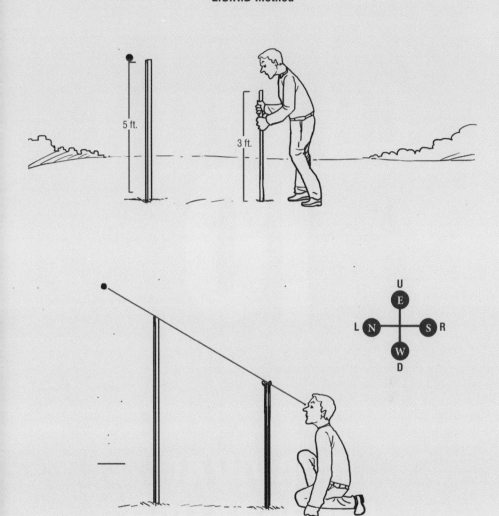

When it comes to natural navigation there are a host of things that can pollute the process or make it difficult to determine an exact coordinate. Therefore, determining direction is like understanding body language. With body language, there is not one expression or gesture that clearly exposes a person's intent. Instead, it is a series of expressions and gestures that create a clear picture. This is the same with natural navigation using a culmination of the methods presented here will be the best option for properly determining where and how to move to give you the best option for finding rescue.

CHAPTER
10

SURVIVAL
PREPARATION

PREPARATION IS THE KEY

SEIZON JUNBI

> **More often than not, people who are rescued from the wilderness after they have become lost or injured are normally found without survival gear and use the knowledge that they have learned from reading, television, or word of mouth to help them survive.**

Preparation is key, but as I stated in Chapter 3 on shelter, it is impossible to prepare for any and every eventuality. However, it is possible to gather knowledge and train ahead of time-based on the types of environments you are normally in or may find yourself in. In the spirit of the Ninja, the goal of this book is to give an average Joe or Jane some simple steps that will help them survive in a wilderness environment with little to no equipment. In addition, this is based on the reality that most people will not be consistent in training for a survival scenario, and those same people are highly unlikely to prepare by buying gear and equipment, and then keeping that equipment with them at all times. More often than not, people who are rescued from the wilderness after they have become lost or injured are normally found without survival gear and use the knowledge that they have learned from reading, television, or word of mouth to help them survive. After over 18 years of teaching people self-defense and several years of teaching survival skills, I will tell you there is a small percentage of people who will leave a class and continue training. Minimally, each student may walk away retaining 10-20% of what they were taught. On multiple occasions I have taught a skill, then had students practice it and, after maybe doing it once or twice, they start talking or asking what's next. This is usually followed by the statement "I have that down, what's next?" I hear this almost every class, and every time I am slightly stunned to hear it. I normally add a pressure drill, having students perform under stress, to prove to them they need more practice. However, since their life is never really on the line, there is still a disparity in taking it seriously. The point of this story is that it highlights that most people will not leave masters of what they were taught or even with the drive to become proficient. Therefore, if I am being realistic, I want to give them enough knowledge that is presented in such a simple way that it can be retained and recalled easily. This will give them a greater potential of being able to create what they need when in need since they will likely not be expecting an emergency and, therefore, will be unprepared. Knowledge does not trump experience, but when the experience is lacking, knowledge is the most important asset you can have.

> **Knowledge does not trump experience, but when the experience is lacking, knowledge is the most important asset you can have.**

HOMO SAPIENS, THE ORIGINAL MACGYVERS

As we mentioned earlier, having the right tools can always help you when it comes to preparation. If someone were to ask me what they should always have with them, I would say:

- 3 layers of clothing, 1 wicking, another heat retaining, and another environmental.
- A good life-straw or water filter, and way to collect and boil water.
- 2 types of fire starters, at least 2 lighters or a faro-rod.
- A first aid kit.
- A multipurpose knife.

Having the right items can make your job so much easier, however, if you do not know how to use them you will always fall short. Remember my quote, "Knowledge is King, Application is Queen and together they rule." Therefore, the best thing anyone can do for survival preparation is to understand these 5 aspects:

- Know who they are and how they will respond mentally.
- Know how they react to certain stressors emotionally.
- Know how to heal themselves.
- Know what they need physically.
- Know how to be creative.

If you think about our ancestors, they did not have any of the gadgets and comforts we have today. With nothing but their mind and hands they were able to sustain life, grow a community, and survive for generations. They spent a lot of time cold, hot, hungry, and sick, while also exposed to predators. They learned through experience how they responded to different stressors, and by necessity, they learned how to deal with and overcome such obstacles. In our modern society, it is easy for us to avoid discomfort, and therefore, never truly know how we will respond to it. This often does not give us the tools to overcome such discomforts when we are not in control. That is why true preparation starts with the question of who you are and how you think, not what you have.

> **With nothing but their mind and hands, our ancestors were able to sustain life, grow a community, and survive for generations.**

3 LESSONS OF PREPARATION

In my Ninjutsu training with Stephen K. Hayes, we focused on 3 primary lessons for survival which are the foundation of my teachings today. His teaching focused on what I came to call the 3 Keys of Ninja Survival. These keys are:

First: Work at setting up your life in such a manner that the possibility of chaos and catastrophe does not strike. The best way to deal with danger is to not be where danger is or to prevent it from materializing by setting yourself up to recognize the potential signs of danger in yourself and the world around you. This by no means is saying random things will not happen. It is just saying be mindful of what you can do to minimize these types of challenges.

Second: Become skilled in controlling your emotions and overcoming the instant responses that can cause the wrong actions to be taken. Understand the importance of taking a deep breath, reacquiring your focus, and seeing the truth of matters. This can be achieved through mindfulness training such as meditation.

Third: Train and grow in your physical abilities to be resilient and capable in various scenarios. Learn your body; understand its natural and unique responses to danger. Know how to control instinctual responses, direct focus, and which physical limits you can break through and how to do it when needed.

3 Lessons of PREPARATION

"Knowledge is King, Application is Queen and together they rule"

SETTING UP YOUR LIFE

First: Work at setting up your life in such a manner that the possibility of chaos and catastrophe doesn't strike.

CONTROL YOUR EMOTIONS

Second: Become skilled in controlling your emotions and overcoming the instant responses that can cause the wrong actions to be taken.

BE RESILIENT AND CAPABLE

Third: Train and grow in your physical and mental abilities. Focus on becoming resilient and capable in various scenarios.

These 3 keys of survival are the foundation of what made Ninja one of the most revered and successful warriors of ancient Japan. The lessons of the Ninja stem from life and are about ensuring it, therefore, they are timeless in their application. Today, we as Americans do not live in small mountain villages, trying to exist outside of the aristocratic culture of the land, while surviving off of it and striving to understand the deeper secrets of the scheme of totality. However, we are trying to survive.

Life in its very essence is survival, therefore, survival is fundamentally about living.

CHAPTER

CONCLUSION

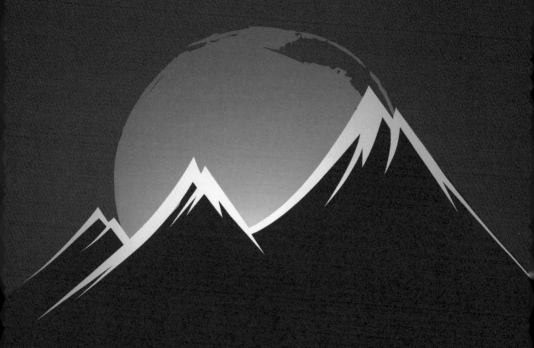

EARTH   WATER   FIRE   WIND   VOID

My teacher told me once that "Ninjutsu is life." Needless to say, that as a master Ninja, he did not break this down for me at that moment because he knew I needed to learn the truth of this statement on my own. Over the 20 years that I have trained in this martial art, I have come to understand what I believe this means. The word Ninjutsu is actually made of two words which are "Nin" and "Jutsu." The word Nin translates into perseverance, endurance, and stealth, while Jutsu translates to "the art or method of." Together the word Ninjutsu can translate to the Art of Endurance or Perseverance. So of course, the question arises, "The endurance of what?" To me, this is a broad statement because people and their lives are broad. No two people will live the same life and have the same experiences but even if they do, they will not experience them the same. Therefore, for each person, the hardships and triumphs they experience will be different. That is why every person will have or perceive different challenges to endure and persevere beyond. Ninjutsu does not mean to specifically persevere over racism, physical disability, depression, financial hardship, physical attacks, etc., it simply means to endure and overcome. Each person will have to overcome their own personal challenges even if some of those challenges are shared with others.

For every person in the world, since birth, life has been about survival. In the beginning, the baby learns to cry as a means to get what it needs to survive, and eventually, that baby grows to a child and begins to learn how to provide some of those basic needs. Later, that child grows into a teenager and starts to take more responsibility for overcoming and solving problems that enter his/her life until, eventually as an adult, the needs of survival are the full responsibility of that person. Yes, we go to work, pay for cable and new clothes, however, at the core, every day we are trying to meet the basic needs of survival. Every day we are enduring

Ninjutsu does not mean to specifically persevere over racism, physical disability, depression, financial hardship, physical attacks, etc.; it simply means to endure and overcome. Each person will have to overcome their own personal challenges even if some of those challenges are shared with others.

hardships and trying to overcome challenges. We are constantly looking or working toward solutions for potential problems. Our living spaces have become storage boxes of gadgets that help us deal with what we perceive as obstacles or problems. However, no matter what the problem or the solution everything stems from the individual. Each individual is striving to endure and to persevere every day. The Ninja believed this and developed ways to understand and strengthen the common mechanisms that all humans have for dealing with this, which are the mind, body, and spirit. Life is a series of challenges that need to be endured and overcome. Some

harder than others but all still requiring understanding and action. The Ninja saw nothing as separate from this principle as it was the fundamental truth they weaved into everything they understood about the world, so much so that it would become the name of their way of surviving, and that it would become their name since the word Ninja translates to "One who endures; one who perseveres." The Ninja way is a series of principles and guidelines for overcoming the hardships of life that arise as one strives for survival. The bases of their method are simple, if you truly want to understand survival, you must understand yourself, understand your world, understand how they relate, and apply what you know as a means to work in harmony with it to gain what you need to survive!

if you truly want to understand survival, you must understand yourself, understand your world, understand how they relate, and apply what you know as a means to work in harmony with it to gain what you need to survive!

Special Thanks

If I am anything, I am a collection of the kindness and love that has been poured into my life from my family, mentors and friends. I would like to give thanks to the many who have helped grow my life to what it is today.

Special contributors

Stephen K. Hayes	Wes Massey	Chris Lenyk
Aaron Phillips	Robert Ashton	Lyndon Johnson
Brian Adams	Sarah Bartell	Raul Rubier

Published by Tuttle Publishing, an imprint of Periplus Editions (HK) Ltd.

www.tuttlepublishing.com

Copyright © 2021 Periplus Editions (HK) Ltd.

Library of Congress Control Number in process.

ISBN 978-0-8048-5408-5

Distributed by:

North America, Latin America & Europe
Tuttle Publishing
364 Innovation Drive, North Clarendon
VT 05759 9436, USA
Tel: 1(802) 773 8930; Fax: 1(802) 773 6993
info@tuttlepublishing.com
www.tuttlepublishing.com

Japan
Tuttle Publishing
Yaekari Building, 3rd Floor
5-4-12 Osaki Shinagawa-ku
Tokyo 141 0032 Japan
Tel: 81 (3) 5437 0171; Fax: 81 (3) 5437 0755
sales@tuttle.co.jp
www.tuttle.co.jp

"Books to Span the East and West"

Tuttle Publishing was founded in 1832 in the small New England town of Rutland, Vermont [USA]. Our core values remain as strong today as they were then—to publish best-in-class books which bring people together one page at a time. In 1948, we established a publishing office in Japan—and Tuttle is now a leader in publishing English-language books about the arts, languages and cultures of Asia. The world has become a much smaller place today and Asia's economic and cultural influence has grown. Yet the need for meaningful dialogue and information about this diverse region has never been greater. Over the past seven decades, Tuttle has published thousands of books on subjects ranging from martial arts and paper crafts to language learning and literature—and our talented authors, illustrators, designers and photographers have won many prestigious awards. We welcome you to explore the wealth of information available on Asia at **www.tuttlepublishing.com**.

Asia Pacific
Berkeley Books Pte Ltd
3 Kallang Sector #04-01, Singapore 349278
Tel: (65) 6741-2178; Fax: (65) 6741-2179
inquiries@periplus.com.sg
www.tuttlepublishing.com

24 23 22 21   5 4 3 2 1   2101TP
Printed in Singapore